Ethics of Scientific Research

ISSUES IN ACADEMIC ETHICS

General Editor: Steven M. Cahn

Campus Rules and Moral Community: In Place of *In Loco Parentis*
by David A. Hoekema, Calvin College

University-Business Partnerships: An Assessment
by Norman E. Bowie, University of Minnesota, Twin Cities

A Professor's Duties: Ethical Issues in College Teaching
by Peter J. Markie, University of Missouri–Columbia

Neutrality and the Academic Ethic
by Robert L. Simon, Hamilton College

Ethics of Scientific Research
by Kristin Shrader-Frechette, University of South Florida

Ethics of Scientific Research

Kristin Shrader-Frechette

Distinguished Research Professor
Environmental Sciences and Policy Program
and
Department of Philosophy
University of South Florida
Tampa, FL 33620-5550

ROWMAN & LITTLEFIELD PUBLISHERS, INC.

ROWMAN & LITTLEFIELD PUBLISHERS, INC.

Published in the United States of America
by Rowman & Littlefield Publishers, Inc.
4720 Boston Way, Lanham, Maryland 20706
3 Henrietta Street, London WC2E 8LU, England

British Cataloging in Publication Information Available

Library of Congress Cataloging-in-Publication Data

Shrader-Frechette, K.S.
Ethics of scientific research / Kristin Shrader-Frechette.
p.   cm.
Includes index.
1. Research ethics.   2. Scientists—Professional ethics.
I. Title.
Q180.55.M67S48   1994   174'.95—dc20   94–19148 CIP

ISBN 0–8476–7981–0 (cloth : alk. paper)
ISBN 0–8476–7940–3 (pbk. : alk. paper)

Printed in the United States of America

∞™ The paper used in this publication meets the minimum requirements of
American National Standard for Information Sciences—Permanence of
Paper for Printed Library Materials, ANSI Z39.48–1984.

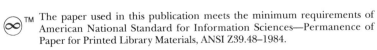

Acknowledgments

Just before he died in 1936, Soviet physiologist and Nobel Prize winner Ivan Petrovich Pavlov warned young persons that science demands undivided allegiance and passion from its followers. In this volume I argue that part of this passion ought to be directed at the ethics of scientific research.

Much of the work in this book stems from original research (1984–1987), supported in part by the National Science Foundation, Ethics and Values Studies, under grant ISP-82-09517, "Ethical and Value Issues in Siting Radioactive Waste Facilities," and grant BBS-86-159533, "Normative Concepts in Ecology and their Consequences for Policy." This volume also arose as a result of evaluations of the research of others (1991–1993), supported in part by the U.S. Department of Energy and the state of Nevada under grant 685873,9.3.7, 4-C, "Expert Judgment in Assessing Radwaste Risks." Any opinions expressed in this book, however, are mine and do not necessarily reflect the views of the National Science Foundation, the Department of Energy, or the Nevada Waste Project Office.

This volume is better than it might have been thanks to the constructive criticisms of Michael Davis, Robert Fullinwider, Paul Gomberg, and Earl McCoy. Their responses have been invaluable in improving what is written here. Any errors that remain are my responsibility.

Helen Longino, Carl Mitcham, and Carl Cranor deserve special thanks for their scholarly contributions to the book. Daniel Wigley and Sharon Ostermann also have done superb jobs, as research and editorial assistants. My greatest debt is to my family and especially our children, the research scientists of tomorrow. They can make a difference.

University of South Florida   K.S.-F.
Tampa, Florida

Contents

Chapter 3

Basic Principles of Research Ethics: Objectivity   45

Chapter 4

Basic Principles: Promoting the Public Good   63

Chapter 5

Handling Conflicts Through Stage-Two Ethical Analysis: Giving Priority to the Common Good   81

Chapter 6

Research and Uncertainty   **101**

Chapter 7

A Case Study in Conservation Research: Uncertain Science in Controversial and Litigious Times   **119**

Chapter 8

Gender and Racial Biases in Scientific Research (Helen Longino)   **139**

Chapter 9

Engineering Design Research and Social Responsibility (Carl Mitcham)   **153**

Chapter 10

Public Health Research and Uncertainty (Carl Cranor)   **169**

1

The Importance of Research Ethics: History and Introduction

In May 1953, the U.S. government conducted two atomic bomb tests in Nevada. Fallout rained on ten herds of sheep grazing nearby. Although 4,500 sheep died, and many ranchers went out of business, researchers employed by the U.S. Atomic Energy Commission (AEC) argued that the two weapons tests had not caused the livestock deaths. As a result, federal courts dismissed ranchers' claims for compensation. Years later, both the scientists and the AEC were implicated for perpetrating a fraud upon the court. Their deception came to light in 1980 after the governor of Utah obtained the release of previously classified federal documents concerning the sheep deaths. The documents showed that the AEC researchers and officials—including Bernard Trum, a scientist who later became director of a primate research laboratory at Harvard University—had induced the original scientists to deny their conclusions that radiation had indeed caused the fallout deaths.[1] Researchers' fraud in the weapons testing case, however, has harmed more than sheep. Between 1951 and 1963, the United States conducted more than one hundred above-ground tests of atomic bombs in Nevada. Despite the tests' scientific, military, and national-security benefits, a 1991 study by physicians concluded that an additional 2.4 million cancer deaths, worldwide, will have been caused by these twelve years of U.S. weapons testing.[2] In 1990 the U.S. Congress decided to compensate many of the citizens who could prove that they or their family members were harmed by fallout.[3]

As the weapons tests illustrate, along with the monumental intellectual advances and the economic technocopia scientific experimentation creates, research in scientific and engineering disciplines has raised serious ethical questions, some of which concern risks to thousands of people. In 1986, for example, Soviet scientists and technicians were performing an unauthorized experiment at the Chernobyl nuclear power station. They accidentally cut off the water supply, triggering a massive reactor meltdown, explosion, and fire that spewed radioactive materials into the atmosphere. Some experts predict that these materials, circulated around the globe, will cause up to 475,500 additional cancer deaths, worldwide, over the next several decades.[4]

What is Research Ethics?

Despite the enormous benefits and the potentially serious consequences associated with research science, even members of national commissions dealing with research ethics find it difficult to define "research."[5] One way to understand the term is to distinguish it from "practice." For the most part, "research" refers to an activity enabling us to test some hypothesis or to draw conclusions and contribute to knowledge. In the case of nuclear weapons tests in the United States, for example, one hypothesis tested was that adding deuterium and tritium gas to an atomic bomb's fissile core would boost the efficiency, and therefore the yield, of the weapon.[6] Professionals' practice, however, unlike their research, does not test some hypothesis but rather enhances the welfare of clients through an action already expected to be successful, an action not taken merely as a hypothesis.[7] Although both professionals' research and practice are governed by ethics, the "ethics" of research ethics refers to individual and communal codes of behavior based on a set of principles for conducting research.[8] "Research ethics" thus specifies the way researchers ought to conduct themselves when they investigate fields such as astronomy and zoology. In this volume we are concerned with the conduct of all scientific researchers.

Scholars have been interested for some time in the norms appropriate to *science*, as evidenced by books such as Charles Babbage's *Reflections on the Decline of Science in England* (1830). Likewise, although doctors in the 1800s were punished for experimenting on their patients without those patients' consent, only recently has anyone begun to discuss the norms of research in general. Few wrote about research ethics until a series of scandals, involving fabricated experiments and deception of research subjects, occurred in the 1960s and 1970s. In 1974 the U.S. Congress required institutions receiving federal research grants to have research ethics committees—institutional review boards. By 1983, major research universities, such as Harvard, Yale, and Stanford, had guidelines for dealing with misconduct in research, in part because of a report of the Association of American Universities (AAU) calling for clarification of research policies. By the mid-1980s most hospitals and research institutions throughout western Europe and the United States had research committees. The governments of Sweden, the Netherlands, and the United States require that an independent research review committee approve research protocols, especially in the biomedical sciences. For example, all federally funded research in the United States involving human and animal subjects must be reviewed for both scientific design and ethical adequacy. Researchers seeking funding from U.S. government agencies now must explicitly address questions of research ethics such as whether humans or other animals will be research subjects and whether an institutional review board has evaluated the research protocols or procedures.

In 1982 the Swedish Council for Research in the Humanities and Social Sciences published four research ethics principles:

• Experimental subjects ought to give free informed consent to the research.
• They have the right to decide the conditions under which they will participate.
• No unauthorized persons will have access to research data.
• The data cannot be used outside the research project for commercial or nonscientific purposes.

Despite such widespread and recent progress in research ethics, however, there are at least two fundamental problems. Most countries do not have government-mandated regulation of research; even where such regulation exists, often it covers only drug experimentation. A second difficulty is that even if a nation has research ethics committees, many times they are associated only with a particular institution and typically they cover only cases involving human and animal subjects of medical or scientific experimentation.[9]

To remedy some of the incompleteness in the discussion of ethical issues, in 1975 the U.S. National Science Foundation began funding studies of ethics and values in scientific and technological research. This program has continued to the present under the direction of Dr. Rachelle Hollander.[10] The U.S. National Academy of Science (NAS), National Academy of Engineering (NAE), and Institute of Medicine (IM) also have attempted to direct more attention to the ethics of the research process. In 1992 and 1993 the joint NAS/NAE/IM Panel on Scientific Responsibility and the Conduct of Research published a two-volume landmark study, *Responsible Science*, which describes the contemporary research environment and suggests methods for encouraging responsible research and for dealing with misconduct.[11]

Two broad categories of ethical problems arise in connection with scientific research: those related to *processes* and those related to *products*.[12] Research processes may harm people, for example, if subjects do not give free informed consent to the procedures they undergo or if they are recruited by deceptive means. They also may be harmed by the products of research, as were the "downwinders" in Nevada, Utah, Arizona, and California, victims of radioactive fallout produced by above-ground nuclear-weapons testing.[13] Radioactive products of U.S. nuclear weapons testing have caused epidemics of leukemia and other cancers throughout the areas receiving the heaviest fallout. For example, the movie *The Conqueror* (1954) was filmed in a windy, dusty canyon near St. George, Utah. No testing took place in this canyon, but the location was downwind from the Nevada test site. When actors such as Pedro Almendariz, Dick Powell, Jeanne Gerson, Susan Hayward, and John Wayne succumbed to cancer, Agnes Moorehead remarked: "Everybody in that picture [*The Conqueror*] has gotten cancer and died."[14]

Scientific Research, Harm, and Free Informed Consent

Just as research *products* may hurt selected groups of persons—such as the cast of *The Conqueror*—so also research *processes* tend to harm those already socially disadvantaged. Typically, experimental subjects for research are in positions of relative disadvantage, both within the larger social system and within the research situation itself.[15] As the example of Nevada victims of nuclear-weapons tests showed, research can threaten the welfare of thousands of people who may have no idea that their lives are at risk. Moreover, the number of people put at risk by research may be greater than we think, because research misconduct is probably underreported. Less than half of all burglaries in the United States are mentioned to the police, and most embezzlements are never reported.[16] If misconduct in research—such as unauthorized experimentation or testing—is as underreported as embezzlement, then serious ethical problems exist. For example, when the Bureau of Drugs of the U.S. Food and Drug Administration (FDA) recently carried out 496 inspections of clinical studies, it found numerous problems with research processes and practices. These problems included lack of patient consent, inadequate drug accountability, protocol nonadherence, record inaccuracy, and record nonavailability; since 1962 FDA investigations undertaken in response to reports of suspected research misconduct have resulted in the disqualification of one in every four investigated researchers.[17]

If the FDA's statistics are typical, then unethical research practices, processes, and consequences cause more serious and more widespread harm than is immediately evident. A 1986 General Accounting Office (GAO) report revealed that 90 percent of the Department of Energy's 127 nuclear facilities—many of which conduct research—had contaminated groundwater that exceeded regulatory standards by a factor of up to 1,000. The report also revealed that environmental violations at U.S. Department of Energy and Department of Defense installations will cost $300 billion to clean up.[18] Typically, however, the public does not know of the dangers posed by government facilities. The deaths resulting from the Chernobyl experiments are known only because the magnitude of the disaster was unavoidably public. The "statistical casualties" would have been easier to cover up if one could not attribute the increases in cancer deaths to a known event or if one could not trace the causal chain of harm.[19] Such tracing is difficult because the dangerous effects of experimental research often occur after the end of the project, are never studied, or are misattributed to other causes.[20] For instance, when the government engaged in above-ground testing of atomic bombs in the western United States, officials adamantly denied that the tests caused any negative consequences on "downwinders." Epidemiological studies, performed years later, finally exposed the connection between government testing and health effects.[21] Hence, in research ethics as elsewhere in life, what the people don't know *can* hurt them. Yet, if people have basic human rights to bodily security and rights to life, then they also have rights to information necessary to safeguard those basic rights.

Because scientific and technological research involves potential risks as well as benefits, people should have the right to exercise free informed consent regarding such research and technical activities. After all, consent (either implicit or explicit) is a precondition of most just laws and policies and indeed a general precondition of governmental power over citizens. One may thus argue that researchers have the duty to secure public consent to the imposition of research-related risks, just as doctors must obtain patients' consent before performing risky medical procedures.[22]

Investigating research ethics is important not only because the failure to do so could lead to public harm but also because individual research subjects are frequently threatened. Obviously most people would not knowingly put themselves at grave risk, especially if they stood to gain no significant benefits. Hence the main reason that research subjects are often at risk is that they have not been informed and have not consented to the risk. Most of the "Instructions to Contributors" in journals that publish research on human beings do not mention informed consent, and most journal editors do not require guarantees that authors have met standards of free informed consent in their work.[23] Consequently, consent-related violations of research ethics may occur frequently. In one recent experiment at Stanford University, psychologists had to terminate prematurely (after a week) a role-playing situation because the research subjects had not given free informed consent to the harmful consequences of the research. The researchers assigned volunteer subjects roles as either "prisoners" or "guards," and allowed the guards to brutalize and degrade the prisoners. The guards themselves were harmed (in less obvious ways) by learning that they enjoyed being powerful and using their power to make others suffer.[24]

Like S. Milgram's experiment on obedience to authority (in which subjects followed directives to torture other persons),[25] the Stanford experiment harmed subjects physically as well as psychologically. Both experiments also jeopardized subjects' value systems by inducing some of them to do what they believed was wrong. By encouraging subjects to behave unethically, the studies illustrated the fragility of an individual's ethical strength and independence. The research also showed that when we study human behavior in an experimental situation, we can put subjects at risk in a variety of ways: through coercion, deception, violations of privacy, breaches of confidentiality, stress, social injury, failure to obtain free informed consent, or threatening their values.[26] Because this volume does not deal primarily with biomedical ethics, we do not discuss in great detail threats to experimental subjects. Instead our emphasis is on scientific research generally. Nevertheless, many of the most significant harms to research subjects come from experimenters' failures to obtain subjects' free informed consent. Analogously, many of the significant public harms arising from scientific research generally come from scientists' failures to obtain the public's free informed consent.

According to most authorities, "free informed consent" includes four analytical components: disclosure, understanding, voluntariness, and competence. These components require that the researcher provide full information about possible research hazards; that the subject understand and assent to the research; and that the subject be emotionally, mentally, and physically competent to give consent.[27] Because researchers have a built-in conflict of interest—they need subjects in order to obtain information—they must also be careful to protect subjects' well-being. External controls, such as research-ethics committees, are often necessary to guarantee experimental subjects' rights to free informed consent.[28] In many situations, however, free informed consent may be difficult, even impossible, to achieve. Florence Kluckhohn's covert research or participant observation of Navajo Indians and Laud Humphreys's study of male homosexual activities in public toilets were both possible because the researchers deceived the subjects they were studying.[29] Certainly researchers could not have obtained accurate data on phenomena such as trustworthiness and obedience without some level of deception. Likewise, documenting sexist behavior would probably require observance of social interactions in situations in which the subjects remain unaware that they are being monitored with respect to sexism. More generally, to the degree that researchers feel pressure to violate ethical norms regarding deception in order to obtain reliable results, it might be difficult for them to satisfy standards of research ethics.[30] Max Weber suggested that living an ethically blameless life was impossible for a politician; it might be as difficult for certain types of researchers. Some researchers thus may face the classical political problem of ''dirty hands,'' of being unable to function both effectively and innocently, of being unable to do accurate research while remaining respectful of the rights of subjects and the public.[31]

Recognizing the frequently incompatible requirements of free informed consent and socially beneficial research necessitating some level of deception, moral theorists have devised a number of modified forms of consent that aim to satisfy both requirements. These include *ex post facto* consent (getting approval of research subjects retroactively), proxy or presumptive consent (getting approval from mock subjects), and prior general consent (getting general approval for deceptive procedures before the experiment).[32] Although many researchers have rejected the idea of deceptive research and have cited the abuses that can occur when experimenters do not obtain *direct* informed consent, there is still debate concerning alternative forms of consent that might justify deceptive research procedures. Regardless of their positions on the defensibility of deception and modified forms of consent in research situations, virtually no moral theorists justify deception in cases in which it seriously jeopardizes the welfare of research subjects. Experts also agree that although deception for the purpose of ensuring spontaneous reactions may be justified, deception for the purpose of avoiding refusals to participate is never justified.[33] Because deception deprives research subjects of the respect to which they are entitled, and because it undermines trust between researchers and subjects and perhaps within society at large, it is very difficult to justify deception in research. Research ethics analyzes experimental situations, aiming to minimize deception, to evaluate the importance of deceptive research, and to ensure adequate ''debriefing'' procedures after the research is finished.[34] We shall not discuss these themes in detail, in part because there are numerous excellent volumes that deal with biomedical ethics,[35] and there is no need to repeat their insights here. Rather than focusing on duties to research subjects, the primary emphasis of our discussion of the ethics of scientific research is on objectivity, on ways of dealing with uncertainty, and on duties to second and third parties.

For scientists engaged in university-based research, students may be some of the second or third parties to whom researchers owe duties. For one thing, university scientists face a conflict of commitment between teaching and research that may cause them to shortchange their students because of the time scientific investigations require. Ignoring student needs is particularly likely in universities that base salary increments primarily on research productivity.[36] A scientist's over-commitment to scholarly activity may harm graduate research assistants if the researcher spends inadequate time helping them with their own work or channels graduate research and course content along lines profitable to the professor rather than along avenues basic or useful to the student. When scientists derive profit from outside consulting or grants, or when they begin their own companies, they are especially likely either to ignore student needs or to direct their own teaching, student research, and subject interests along the lines of their own profits. In such a situation, a researcher may use graduate students to further outside economic commitments. Moreover, because university scientists typically wield power over students' grades and recommendations, their emphasis on their own research and profits creates a situation of student dependency from which it is difficult to escape.[37] In joint projects among professors and students or in graduate-student research, professors may also cause harm by failing to give students' research adequate recognition or by stealing student work and publishing it as their own.[38]

Scientific Research, Conflicts of Interest, and Intellectual Property Rights

Research ethics is important not only because it helps students, the public, and experimental subjects avoid research-related harm, but also because it provides a framework for examining the ends and goals that research serves. Because taxpayers ultimately fund much university-based scientific work (especially at public institutions), academic researchers have a special duty to ensure that their work serves socially desirable ends and goals, such as democratic freedom, societal welfare, equity, and growth in knowledge. Indeed, as we shall argue in chapter two, under the ''trusteeship model'' for research professionals, *all scientists* have a duty—to varying degrees—to ensure that their work serves socially desirable ends. Without ethical scrutiny, however, scientists could too easily lose sight of their societal responsibilities and duties to taxpayers. Instead, they might choose work with narrow industrial, economic, or military ends, rather than projects that benefit the public at large. For example, although there are numerous benefits from cooperation between university researchers and industry,[39] including development of relevant knowledge and applications, funding to purchase expensive scientific equipment, and helping students obtain future employment, sometimes this cooperation can result in threats to public values, freedom, equity, and authentic growth in knowledge. In 1981, for instance, the West German pharmaceutical company Hoechst gave $70 million to Harvard's Department of Molecular Biology in exchange for rights to market all research discoveries made in the department and to exclude all funding and research that interfered with Hoechst's proprietary position. As one observer put it, ''Hoechst . . . purchased . . . control of an entire university department. . . . [E]veryone in that lab is an indentured servant to Hoechst.''[40] In the past, Harvard's patent policy required that all health-related discoveries made in its labs be dedicated to the public. In the last decade, because of deals with companies like Hoechst and Monsanto, Harvard has assigned patent rights—intellectual property rights—in exchange for financial support.[41] During the same year as the Harvard deal with Hoechst, Massachusetts Institute of Technology (MIT) signed a contract with entrepreneur Jack Whitehead to establish a biomedical research center. Whitehead gave MIT $125 million in exchange for MIT's relinquishing patent rights and control over finances, hiring, and choice of research. The agreement gave Whitehead's children the majority of positions on the financial committee of the institute's board.[42]

Research being diverted from public to private ends—serving special rather than societal interests—is not just a problem in the West.[43] Several corporations and countries, interested in African mineral resources, have literally "bought" entire universities in Nigeria, Zaire, and Ethiopia by virtue of paying scientists to do corporate research. At some African institutions, as many as 80 percent of the professors have been supported by a single corporation.[44] Industrial influence over university research also continues to be very great in Japan, where the government recently awarded more than $100 million in taxpayer monies to fund university–industry research cooperation so as to ensure that Japanese companies dominate the international biotechnology market.[45] Whether such a situation is ethically desirable, as we shall see in later chapters, partially depends on who benefits from such an arrangement and what the relevant duties and consequences are.

Profits and financial investments interfere with research not only in cases where outside interests "buy" researchers, but also in situations where scientists are not as objective as possible because of their personal investments of time and money in a particular area of research. Michael Gold's *Conspiracy of Cells* tells the story of how researchers ignored warnings that a particular cell line was contaminated and would give erroneous results if used in culture experiments. Researchers who had spent money, time, and careers on this contaminated line ignored the warnings published in both *Nature* and *Science*.[46] If such examples are typical, then some researchers may be selling their integrity in much the same way as the medieval Church sold pardons and indulgences.[47] If university scientists move from being public servants to entrepreneurs,[48] then they may lose some of their accountability to the public. They may help to blur the lines between disinterested scholarship and personal profit.[49] Nobel Laureate and MIT faculty member David Baltimore owns more than one million dollars in shares in a biotechnology company designed to commercialize his inventions. Other university scientists have similar conflicts of interest, such as owning shares of more than $10 million each, because of businesses supported by their research.[50]

Investigating questions of research ethics in this context is important because academic researchers may be more loyal to their businesses than to their universities. Also, they may divert university resources in order to support their personal consulting. Their interests may lie more with profits than with scientific research, which suggests a third problem: secrecy. Because of some funders' proprietary privileges, scientific colleagues may no longer be free to exchange information, for fear that a rival commercial interest might obtain it.[51] For some scientific researchers, knowledge has become intellectual property. For example, all U.S. Department of Defense (DOD) contracts include pre-publication review or license to censor.[52] This secrecy may be an enormous problem because more than 50 percent of all American scientists and engineers have defense contracts, and more than 65 percent of all U.S. federal research money pours into defense-related projects. The DOD and the National Aeronautics and Space Administration (NASA) together account for more than 70 percent of all federal research and development dollars.[53] These statistics suggest that research secrecy and fear of industrial espionage limit societal benefits and growth in knowledge. Also, a few scientific researchers, able to monopolize a certain area of work due to funders' secrecy requirements, have an unfair advantage over their colleagues. In several countries, some areas of university research likewise may run the risk of becoming conduits for the military–industrial complex.

Despite its practical benefits, scientific research in some cases may be jeopardizing both progress in basic science and important democratic values.[54] If military spending and economic growth have an inverse relationship,[55] and if secrecy and censorship can stifle scientific progress, then military spending at research universities may lead to massive cultural and intellectual distortions.[56] Researchers who depend on industry or military monies to supply their labs or to pay their graduate students are unlikely to bite the hand that feeds them. They may perform their research and interpret their results in a way favorable to their funders, rather than remain as objective as possible. Moreover, because industry and the military control so much university research funding, they already may have succeeded not only in shaping basic, long-term research along the lines of short-term tasks[57] (thus threatening academic freedom) but also in redefining research.[58] Science and research may have become limited to projects that receive outside funding and profit the university, rather than what is judged important by one's peers.[59] Scientific researchers' becoming more interested in profit, patents, and intellectual property rights—rather than in knowledge—may also cause graduate students, eager for financial support, to be channeled not into basic research or areas of greatest academic or societal merit, but into projects having limited intellectual importance but great commercial potential.[60] Research scientists must ask themselves: ''What would have happened to Einstein and the general theory of relativity if a businessman had come up to him when he was 20 and said, 'Don't bother with relativity—it'll never make any money. Why don't you work with my company on something profitable instead?' ''[61]

If business, rather than academic peers, defines "quality research," scholars who have not been "bought by industry" may be placed at a disadvantage. Abundant evidence shows that professors have been discriminated against because of lack of favor by corporate sponsors.[62] At many major universities, the departments that are expanding are those with industrial funding. Departments suffering the most cuts are those "unprofitable" areas that do not interest the business world.[63] Although much can be said for commercial relevance, university researchers also ought to consider the words of noted Harvard biologist Richard Lewontin. As Lewontin put it, when he heard about the Harvard arrangement with Hoechst: "What about the rest of us who are so foolish as to study unprofitable things like poetry, Sanskrit philology, evolutionary biology, and the history of the Chansons? Will . . . [the dean] have time to hear our pleas for space, colleagues, funds, and students between meetings with the University's business partners?"[64]

Many private research laboratories likewise have complained that university scientists, subsidized in a variety of ways by taxpayers, have unfair competitive advantages.[65] Antitrust legislation prevents collaboration among corporations desiring to apply new discoveries, yet collaboration between university researchers and industry presents some of the same ethical difficulties. Moreover, because university research dollars in the United States result in two to four times as many patent applications as do research dollars from all other sources, including businesses' own corporate laboratories,[66] any company working alone is likely to be disadvantaged. This disadvantage thus propels an even greater push for corporations to "buy" certain departments in an effort to monopolize researchers' knowledge, the intellectual capital of the future.[67] In situations where scientific research is often a commodity, raising numerous questions of research ethics—especially questions about who profits from the research and whether public research resources have been converted to private gain—is essential not only to justice but also to the health of research, society, and democracy. In order to balance researchers' institutional and private duties, scholars have suggested developing conflict-of-interest guidelines for university scientists who work on projects having commercial value.[68]

Scientific Research and the Environment

Research ethics is important not merely to help prevent harm to the public, to research subjects, and to democratic institutions, but also to help protect the environment. Practicing questionable research ethics can threaten the environment in at least three ways:

- Choosing research (or agreeing to do paid research) on unsustainable products and processes may indirectly harm the environment and decrease the probability that sustainable products and processes will be available. (Sustainable products and processes satisfy economic needs without jeopardizing the prospects of future generations.)[69]
- Certain types of research may be direct causes of environmental pollution and degradation, as in the case of space exploration and experimentation littering low-earth orbits (120–250 nautical miles above the earth) with numerous projectiles from previous launches and spacecraft.
- Some research methods, especially in economics, indirectly cause environmentally suspect decisionmaking.

The previous section of this chapter illustrated how private interests sometimes have threatened the public birthright of university research. (Subsequent chapters define and defend this "public birthright" in more detail.) These same private interests, frequently concerned with maximizing short-term gain, also may direct and pay researchers for work on processes and products that bring profit despite their environmental unsustainability. Hence, the choice of problematic research topics and practices is a concern of research ethics. Some areas of biotechnology provide a good example of how scientists work in environmentally questionable areas. For instance, U.S. researchers are purposefully modifying at least 30 crop and forest tree species to withstand lethal doses of herbicides. Such research goals raise the ethical question of whether we should use biotechnology to further pest-management strategies that rely on greater doses of toxic chemicals. These chemicals are extremely hazardous to humans and to other members of the biosphere (who have not been genetically engineered to withstand them). Apart from the 27 corporations—mainly chemical companies such as Dow, Monsanto, and Dupont—that have initiated herbicide-tolerant plant research on most agricultural crops, more than $10.5 million of taxpayer money has been used to fund state and federal genetics research on herbicide-resistant crops.[70] Because of their threat to humans, wildlife, and ecological welfare, use of hazardous chemical pesticides may not contribute to sustainable agriculture. By doing genetic-engineering research on herbicide-tolerant crops, researchers thus may help to perpetuate the high chemical dependence of conventional farming, a dependence that does not always reflect a correct understanding of the basic biological systems that make agriculture possible. Researchers also may help promote a temporary approach to weed control, as opposed to an ecological approach to weed management. Moreover, by using monies to create herbicide-resistant crops, researchers do not have those funds available to develop weed-management strategies that contribute to long-term sustainability and conservation of natural resources.[71] Scientists ought to assess carefully their research on herbicide-tolerant crops and determine whether such research is an ethically desirable use of biotechnological skills. From a purely human point of view, research on herbicide-tolerant crops may be analogous, in part, to research on how to kill the canaries in coal mines. Knowing that canaries succumb to methane poisoning before humans do, miners use canaries as "early warning" signals of dangerous levels of gas. If researchers make crops genetically resistant to herbicides, those plants may be unable to function as early warning signals for dangerous levels of chemicals in our food.

A second environmentally problematic effect of some research is pollution. One of the most well-known cases of how researchers may have failed to practice research ethics and may have caused environmental degradation has occurred in the Antarctic. Science reigns supreme in Antarctica. Research has ruled the ice since the mid-1950s, and the U.S. National Science Foundation (NSF) alone currently spends $221 million annually on Antarctic research.[72] Established in 1955, McMurdo Station is the largest U.S. base for scientific research in Antarctica. For decades, however, U.S. research teams have bulldozed garbage, old machinery, and drums of toxic waste over the hill and into nearby Winter Quarters Bay, the anchorage used by Robert F. Scott in his first expedition in 1902. Although McMurdo sits on a continent largely untouched by humans, it is one of the world's most polluted spots. In 1990, the NSF embarked on a $30 million program to clean up McMurdo, and in 1991 the 26 nations active in the Antarctic ratified a treaty to protect the continent's fragile ecosystems. The 1991 protocol refers to the continent as "dedicated to peace and science."[73] Despite the researchers' shift toward environmental responsibility, the past practices of scientists working for the NSF suggest that research-induced environmental damage should remain a concern of those interested in research ethics. In 1991 the Environmental Defense Fund sued the NSF to try to stop it from incinerating waste in Antarctica prior to completing an environmental impact assessment. (Other nations doing research in the Antarctic routinely remove their waste by ship.) If the most educated scientists from the wealthiest nations can perform research activities in ways that have contaminated Antarctica with PCBs, hydrocarbons, and sewage, then such problems of research ethics seem likely to occur again.[74]

Scientific researchers also may contribute to environmental problems by using research methodologies biased against environmental protection. Much of contemporary economics, for example, especially if practiced in particular ways, leads to policy conclusions that appear to be biased against accounting for environmental costs and benefits of societal policies. Several years ago, for example, U.S. government economists did important research on the relative costs of coal- versus nuclear-generated electricity. Following the standard benefit–cost practice of including only market-based parameters in their study, the researchers ignored the millions of taxpayer dollars spent annually on U.S. nuclear waste storage because these dollars represented a government subsidy, not a market-based cost. After ignoring one of the major costs of nuclear generation of electricity, the researchers concluded that a 1000-Mwe coal plant was $200,000 cheaper per year than a 1000-Mwe nuclear plant, when both produced the same amount of electricity.[75] However, if one takes into account the cost of waste storage, one can show that the coal plants are $2 million cheaper per year than the nuclear plants when both generate the same amount of electricity.[76] As this example indicates, researchers who employ questionable economic techniques and assumptions encourage problematic policy decisions.

Smoking provides another excellent example of how researchers' questionable economic methods may encourage environmental and human threats. Tobacco causes more death and suffering among adults than any other toxic material in the environment; tobacco addiction accounts for 2.5 million deaths annually. Yet global tobacco use has grown by 75 percent during the last two decades. In the United States, nearly one-fifth of all deaths are attributable to cigarette smoke. Although the health consequences of tobacco use are well known, policies to avoid them lag behind, in part because economic methods of computing the costs and benefits of tobacco use do not take account of externalities, nonmarket costs and benefits. Even if one does not cost the suffering tobacco victims and their families bear, but instead measures the economic benefits of the jobs and incomes the tobacco industry creates against the economic costs of increased health care and lost workdays of smokers, tobacco's economic costs alone would exceed its benefits by two to one. Researchers do not always point up this fact because most of these economic costs are external to the current methods of economic accounting. If all the ''external'' costs of smoking—such as increased health care—were included, they would amount to between $1.25 and $3.15 per pack. If researchers paid more attention to the unbiased presentation of all the data on smoking, and if they noted the real costs of tobacco, then government policy regarding smoking might change. Moreover, with heavy taxing of tobacco, government could cover more health costs associated with its use and also prevent the needless loss of lives and environmental pollution smoking causes. In short, if scientists (economists, for instance) accepted responsibility for the policy decisions (regarding taxing tobacco, for example) following indirectly from their research methods, then their research might not contribute to so much (tobacco-induced) human and environmental misery.[77]

Our existing accounting system makes it almost impossible for researchers to assess the effects of externalities on the economy. These effects include, for example, polluting the air with tobacco smoke or exceeding the carrying capacity of the earth. Because researchers who employ traditional techniques—associated with determining benefit–cost ratios and the GNP—ignore these effects, they cannot measure accurately economic progress or decline. In some cases, however, ethics seems to require researchers to admit the questionable assumptions in their economic and other methods and to help prevent the environmental damages caused by uncritical use of such research methods. The energy assessment of Herbert Inhaber is a famous example of a research report that employed highly evaluative, ethically questionable assumptions that led to environmentally damaging policy conclusions. Commissioned by the Canadian Atomic Energy Control Board and summarized in *Science*, Inhaber's research estimated the dangers from alternative energy technologies. He concluded that the risk from conventional energy systems, like nuclear or coal power, is less than that from nonconventional systems, like solar or wind energy, and that non-catastrophic risks (like those from solar) are greater than catastrophic (like those from nuclear power).[78]

How did Inhaber arrive at his surprising conclusions? He made some suspect evaluative assumptions. For instance, in *estimating* the risk posed by particular energy technologies, he assumed that all electricity was of utility-grid quality, i.e., able to be fed into a power grid.[79] This means that he ignored the low-risk benefits of solar space heating and hot-water heating, neither of which can be fed into a power grid. Indeed he ignored the wide variety of low-temperature forms of solar energy which could supply *40 percent of all U.S. energy needs*, at competitive prices and at little risk.[80] Another highly evaluative assumption central to Inhaber's risk estimates is that all nonconventional energy technologies have coal backups.[81] This means, in the case of solar thermal electric, he attributed 89 percent of the risk to solar effects (especially construction of components) even though the coal backup caused them. Moreover, Inhaber assumes that nuclear fission requires no backup,[82] even though these plants have a down time of 33 percent per year for check-ups, refueling, and repairs.

In the area of *risk evaluation*, Inhaber's assumptions are just as unreliable. When he aggregates and compares all lost work days, for all energy technologies, he ignores the fact that lost work days are more or less severe, depending on the nature of the accident causing them and whether or not they are sequential. On Inhaber's scheme, a lost work day due to cancer or acute effects of radiation sickness is no different than a lost work day from a sprained ankle.[83] Yet obviously the cancer could result in premature death, and the radiation exposure could result in mutagenic effects on one's children. Neither is comparable to a sprained ankle. Inhaber made a similar questionable assumption in his research evaluating the severity of risks. Unlike other hazard assessors, he totally ignored the distinction between catastrophic and non-catastrophic risks; he assumed that 1,000 construction workers, each falling off a roof and dying, in separate accidents, was no different than 1,000 worker fatalities because of a catastrophic accident in a nuclear fuel-fabrication plant.[84] Numerous risk assessors, however, typically distinguish between catastrophic and non-catastrophic accidents. They suggest that because of increased societal disruption, n lives lost in a single catastrophic accident should be assessed as a loss of n^2 lives.[85] Regardless of whether or not this n^2 interpretation is a reasonable one, the point is that Inhaber made numerous subjective judgments, such as assuming that the distinction between catastrophic and non-catastrophic accidents could be ignored. In so doing, he passed off his results as purely objective science. Instead, tracing Inhaber's methods, step by step, shows that virtually every assumption he made in estimating and evaluating alternative risks increased his alleged nonconventional risks (associated with more environmentally sustainable technologies) and decreased his alleged conventional risks (associated with more environmentally degrading technologies). The Inhaber work illustrates clearly that attention to objectivity (see chapter three) and to research ethics may help to prevent both environmentally questionable research and problematic environmental policies.

Scientific Research and Biases Such as
Sexism and Racism

Research ethics not only attempts to prevent harm to the public, to research subjects, to democratic institutions, and to the environment, but also encourages more objective practices, procedures, and methods in obtaining knowledge. In other words, research ethics strives to prevent bias. Despite its drawbacks[86]—such as increasing bureaucratic control over scholarship—research ethics is important because reducing bias enhances virtually all social and intellectual values. If one reduces bias in research, thanks to careful attention to ethics, then one serves the intellectual value of objectivity and the social value of having accurate information on which to base policy decisions.

Bias will likely arise when researchers do not see their methods and practices as subject to ethical constraints. Sometimes this bias takes the form of social and political prejudices that infect work in the humanities and social sciences.[87] In the natural sciences, such bias often takes the form of interpreting research results in ways consistent with the philosophies of particular funding groups. For example, 25 different scientists, all employed by Exxon Company USA, argued at an April 1993 meeting of the American Society for Testing and Materials that Alaska's Prince William Sound has almost fully recovered from the 1989 *Exxon Valdez* oil spill. Other scientists at the meeting argued that the Exxon scientists were able to draw such a conclusion because of the way they interpreted their data on oil contamination. Exxon researchers likely ascribed to other sources a portion of the oil that actually came from the *Exxon Valdez* spill, according to other scientists. They also accused the Exxon researchers of ignoring findings that conflicted with their biased conclusions, findings based on much longer observations and on larger sample sizes. One scientist compared Exxon's efforts to "looking at one tree" and then generalizing that conclusions drawn from it could "represent the whole forest."[88] To the extent that the Exxon researchers or any of the other scientists have interpreted the oil-spill data in biased ways, their interpretations and conclusions are open to ethical question. As the controversy over the oil-spill research illustrates, research ethics requires investigators to look at the ethical constraints on their selection, use, and interpretation of data.

As the discussion (in chapter two) of the famous Tuskegee syphilis experiment illustrates, racist bias also can infect both the procedures and the products of research, in part because experimental subjects are so vulnerable. Moreover, socially disenfranchised groups—such as women and blacks—are more likely to be harmed by questionable research practices and products, even after researchers become aware of their racist or sexist bias. For example, in 1986 the U.S. government issued a policy requiring biomedical researchers to ensure that their study populations did not underrepresent women, African-Americans, Latins, and other racial and ethnic groups. Despite this explicit directive, in June 1990 U.S. congressional investigators issued a startling report that confirmed continuing bias against using women and members of various racial and ethnic groups as research subjects. The General Accounting Office issued a report showing that the failure to have representative research populations is widespread and continuing. For instance, the National Institute of Health (NIH) sponsored a study showing that heart attacks were reduced by taking an aspirin a day. The research subjects were all men. Other studies showing the relationship between cholesterol and cardiovascular disease have been conducted almost exclusively on men, even though heart disease is the leading cause of death among women. Such exclusionary research practices lead to damaging consequences; for example, male-only studies of heart disease led the American Heart Association to recommend a diet that could actually increase the risk of heart disease for women. Likewise, another study found that due to physiological differences, African-Americans given the "normal" dose of lithium (established by research only on white males) frequently had toxic reactions and a higher risk of renal failure.[89]

Charles Babbage, professor of mathematics at Cambridge University, was very concerned with avoiding bias in research. In 1830 he described various forms of scientific bias and dishonesty, among them "trimming," "cooking," and "forging."[90] Trimming consists of smoothing irregularities in the data to make them look accurate and precise. Cooking occurs when one discards some data and retains only evidence that fits the theory. Forging is inventing some or all of the research data reported. However, not all data gathered in a study can be used, and most researchers must simplify their problems and their data—studying only white men, for example—in order to make the studies tractable. Hence, one scientist's "cooking" may be another researcher's simplifying the data for managability. The existence of problems like cooking and trimming, and the flare of controversies like those over choosing research subjects or interpreting the *Exxon Valdez* data, argue for analysis of the ethical issues inherent in the practice of research. Without such analysis, we open the way not only for widespread anti-science sentiment, but also for policy based on bad research and for countless harms to humans and the environment. Without the analysis that characterizes research ethics, we open the way for devaluing the truth, the foundation upon which all human effort rests. Without this foundation, we shall lose our way in the very world that science seeks to understand.

Overview

How can research ethics help us find our way in the world of research science? For one thing, it points out what can go wrong[91] if one does not pay attention to the constraints on experimental practice, its products, and its goals. But how does one practice research in an ethical way? Perhaps first of all, those trained and paid to research ought actually to do it. One of the first tenets of research ethics, as we explain in chapter two, is that certain scientists have a duty to do research. They also have duties not to do specific kinds of research. Chapters three and four focus on the basic principles that govern how to perform research in an ethically acceptable way. This performance is constrained primarily by the demands of professional ethics, that is, by duties to the profession, to society, and to clients/employers. In chapters three and four, we develop three main principles of research ethics and show that they focus either on epistemological requirements of *objectivity* (the subject of chapter three) or on the ethical requirements of avoiding harm in the use, interpretation, and dissemination of research and thereby *promoting societal welfare* (chapter four).

Because objectivity is a major goal of research ethics, in chapter three we discuss what it means to do objective research and how the unavoidable value judgments necessary to all research hinder objectivity even in the purest areas of science. We also discuss the "ethics of belief" and whether it is reasonable to hold scientists ethically responsible for their research conclusions. In chapter four we investigate the ethical basis for the principle that scientists have a duty not to jeopardize societal welfare in their research. Maintaining objectivity and avoiding harm to public welfare would be relatively easy if we always understood research situations clearly. But because research is, by definition, at the frontiers of knowledge, the subjects under investigation and the consequences of scientific research are never completely foreseeable. Indeed, much decisionmaking about how to practice research focuses on how to behave ethically in situations of factual uncertainty. As a result, one of the main ethical problems of researchers—a problem that we emphasize—is developing guidelines for how to behave in such situations of conflict and uncertainty. We do not spend much time discussing clearly reprehensible behavior because it is obviously wrong. We all know, for example, that falsifying data is wrong. It is much less clear what behavior is ethically justified in a situation of uncertainty. In chapter five, we attempt to develop guidelines for researchers' behavior under uncertainty. We evaluate the duties and consequences associated with each of the three basic principles of research ethics outlined in chapters three and four. We argue that, in most cases of conflict in research ethics, our first priority should be to protect public welfare; duties to clients or employers and to the profession are secondary. We also explain that duties to objectivity need not conflict with duties to protect the common good, and that researchers have the responsibility to adhere to principles of "ethical objectivity" as well as "epistemic objectivity." In chapter six we continue to discuss ethical conflicts in research, and we attempt to develop additional principles to deal with uncertain situations such as incomplete research data or underdeveloped theories. We argue that different norms govern applied research as opposed to pure research. In particular, we argue that in cases of applied research under uncertainty, in which both types of errors cannot be avoided, we ought to minimize type-II errors (false negatives) rather than type-I (false positives).

To illustrate our discussion of duties to the public and duties to minimize type-II statistical errors, in chapter seven we provide a case study in research ethics, a conflict over how to interpret data on species extinction. We show how the principles for which we have argued in earlier chapters provide a framework for solving this conflict. Chapters eight, nine, and ten present case studies authored, respectively, by Helen Longino of Rice, Carl Mitcham of Penn State, and Carl Cranor of the University of California, Riverside. These case studies illustrate how to resolve and analyze ethical problems associated, respectively, with sexist bias, engineering design, and methods of assessing risks from toxics. Together these chapters should provide the reader with a beginning understanding of what might go wrong in scientific research and how ethical analysis can help to prevent it.

2

Professional Codes and the Duty to Do Scientific Research

Burdened with the duty to avenge the death of his father, Hamlet swears in the first act of Shakespeare's play:

> The time is out of joint. Oh, cursed spite
> That ever I was born to set it right.[1]

As the previous chapter suggested, the current times are frequently "out of joint" in the sense that some scientists fail to take account of research ethics and, as a consequence, endanger the health and welfare of the public, research subjects, and the environment. We also argued that flawed research may push society "out of joint" by creating biased studies, by helping to justify questionable policy decisions, and by emphasizing profit rather than justice in the quest for knowledge. Like Hamlet, scientists have the duty to "set things right" in their research. They have the duty to perform research in ethical ways and, more fundamentally, they have the duty to do research. This chapter examines the origins of these duties and the justification for them. We also attempt to clarify the conditions under which one has a duty to perform or not to perform certain types of research.

Research-Related Duties and the Public Good

Because knowledge itself is valuable, there is a prima facie justification for research. Nobel Prize winner Eugene Wigner speaks eloquently of this justification when he shows the ways in which scientific research

23

and the pursuit of knowledge contribute both to our spiritual welfare and to our pleasure while diverting us from the "rampant quest for power."[2] He also notes that Einstein's example shows that one does not have to be a full-time scholar to make an important discovery. Einstein worked at the Swiss patent office while he created the special theory of relativity. Following Einstein's example, many people might be able either to engage in valuable research or at least to do some kind of scholarship that develops their own abilities. The most serious duty to engage in research in a particular area, however, falls on members of a specific profession. Because researchers are professionals who have received training, education, and benefits from society, they have an implicit contract with society. Hence researchers arguably have the traditional trustee's responsibility to preserve, develop, and extend the intellectual assets that they have received (in part) from the public and that they hold in trust for that society. According to the trustee model of the professions, there is some historical moment at which each profession took over a specific class of intellectual assets from amateurs in the public. They took over these assets with the understanding that they would manage and expand this societal asset—particular types of knowledge and research methods—through time. Moreover, although not every professional has the duty to do innovative and important research, nevertheless scientific professionals collectively have the duty to perform research, to manage and expand the knowledge system over which they are trustees for the public.[3] Because not all professionals are able to make revolutionary breakthroughs, however, the duty to perform scientific research is proportional to our ability to do so. Steven Cahn's injunction from an ancient Hebrew sage is appropriate here: "It is not your duty to complete the task, but you are not free to desist from it."[4]

In addition to research duties that exist by virtue of professionals' roles as trustees of knowledge for the public, scientists trained to do research often have a duty to perform such work because of their contractual obligations to their employer. College, university, laboratory, or industry employers often require scientists to do research. Those highly trained in a particular area likewise have a duty to do research because, as members of specific professions that contain almost all of the available expertise in a certain area, they have a near monopoly over information about, and implementation of, certain socially relevant policies. Because society has helped scientific researchers, in part, to gain this monopoly, these scientists have a duty to make good on the societal investment in them. Because others have not received such an investment, because it gives scientific researchers the benefits of a monopoly, and because researchers exhaust most expertise in a certain area, they have a duty to engage in research and to publicize their findings. Along with specialized knowledge, power, and benefits, however, come special responsibilities. Scientists' responsibilities for research in their respective fields arise largely because they are the only people qualified to perform it. Hence, they have a responsibility because of their trustee status, their ability, their near monopoly over advances in certain areas, their training, and their knowledge.[5]

Scientists also have a duty to do some research because most research funding comes from society, with the government as the major source.[6] Insofar as the public supports research, scientific professionals have a responsibility not to waste resources and to perform the research agreed on. Even when industry funds research, members of the public at large ultimately pay for the work, in part because they buy the products and thus generate research monies. Because society (through university accreditation, taxes, and so on) often pays for research products or oversees the training and competence of research professionals, individuals who seek advice or counsel from scientific professionals have a right to expect accurate information. Moreover, to the degree that professionals need to engage in research to remain knowledgeable, they have a duty to do that research. Likewise, students and employers have the right to expect that their professors and employees remain knowledgeable and up-to-date in their professions. Professors at four-year colleges and universities are expected, by virtue of their contracts, to contribute to knowledge in their fields and to work with students of almost any level and ability. To do so, they must perform research. Without doing such research and thereby exposing their ideas and experiments to scrutiny and criticism through publication, professors cannot as easily have their work evaluated. Researchers' submitting their work for publication is thus comparable to pilots' undergoing periodic testing. Both procedures enable professionals to keep their skills at a level necessary to fulfill their duties.[7]

The Duty Not to Do Certain Scientific Research

We have argued that professionals' trustee responsibilities, their abilities, their monopolies over advances in certain areas, and society's investment in them obligate them to do research. One may ask, however, whether professionals also have a duty to do certain types of scientific research and not others. If our arguments in the previous chapter are correct, then although scientists have duties to do research, not all types of research are ethically justifiable. Indeed, given the research abuses surveyed in chapter one, it is already obvious that scientists have at least five general rules of thumb to guide them in avoiding certain research:

1. Scientists ought not do research that causes unjustified risks to people.
2. Scientists ought not do research that violates norms of free informed consent.
3. Scientists ought not do research that unjustly converts public resources to private profits.
4. Scientists ought not do research that seriously jeopardizes environmental welfare.
5. Scientists ought not do biased research.

In subsequent chapters we shall examine in more detail a number of other rules and principles to guide scientists in performing their research. Let us examine more closely each of the five general rules listed above.

Scientists Ought Not Do Research That Causes Unjustified Risks to People

The first general rule—against performing research that poses unjustified risks to people—warns against doing research that, without adequate justification, causes either serious threats to people or grossly inequitable distributions of those hazards. In 1993 the U.S. National Research Council (NRC) emphasized this point about risk distribution in its evaluation of research methods for assessing pesticide toxicity. The NRC noted that researchers typically collect few data regarding pesticide exposures for infants and children. Laboratory tests, the NRC contends, do not adequately account for the vulnerabilities of children largely because research methods for measuring pesticide residues focus on foods eaten by the average adult. To remedy scientists' inadequate attention to children's chemical exposures, the NRC report recommended research methods that divide the safe reference dose of the chemicals by a factor of up to 10.[8] The NRC report shows that research can be ethically questionable if it encourages policymaking that causes unequal treatment of a segment of the population, even though the overall harm is small.

In some areas of research, unequal treatment of research subjects is deliberate. As Herbert Kelman notes,[9] counter insurgency activities provide a clear "illustration of the use of social research by the powerful for the direct manipulation of the powerless." For example, during the Nixon era, government researchers accumulated private information about people whose only "crimes" were opposition to Nixon-administration programs and policies. Although the products of politically motivated research typically are used only against a minority of people, they pose severe risks to civil liberties, free speech, and equal treatment. Currently in Nevada, sophisticated social-science researchers are using millions of dollars of utility-industry monies, collected from ratepayers all over the United States, to manipulate the opinions of Nevadans, 80 percent of whom oppose having the world's first permanent geological repository (for high-level nuclear wastes and spent reactor fuel) in Nevada.[10] Both the acquisition and the application of this social-science knowledge is questionable, in part because the Nevadans fear the facility. It will be hazardous forever, and we know little about the geological and hydrological stability necessary, in perpetuity, to keep the wastes from killing millions of people, contaminating the water supply, jeopardizing economic growth in the area, and so on. Allen Keesler, President of Florida Power and chair of the utility industry's American Committee on Radwaste Disposal, began a 1991 "advertising blitz," funded by ratepayers, to "re-educate" the people of Nevada along the lines that social-science researchers said were most likely to be successful.[11]

Scientists Ought Not Do Research That Violates Informed Consent

As the Nevada case suggests and as chapter one already illustrated, researchers also ought to follow the second rule, prohibiting research that violates norms of free informed consent. For example, scientists are not justified in putting subjects or members of the public at grave risk, without their consent, as scientists working for the AEC did when they conducted more than 100 above-ground tests of nuclear weapons in the western United States. The most egregious examples of coercive research include Nazi experimentation on inmates of prison camps, Japanese experimentation on prisoners of war, and U.S. experimentation on criminals. All such research has violated basic human rights to life, to equal treatment, and to fairness. Nazi scientists and doctors shot inmates to study wounds; starved prisoners to study nutrition; placed humans at 70,000 feet, unprotected, to see what would happen; surgically grafted people to each other; and burned Polish nuns with exposure to radiation.[12] Japanese experimenters engaged in similar activities during the war, except that many of their deeds did not become public. The U.S. government protected Japanese scientists in exchange for learning the results of their research. The experiments and the U.S. protection remained secret until 1981.[13] Such experimentation is not only heinously harmful and unnecessary, but its coerciveness makes it ethically unjustifiable. Because experimentation on prisoners is conducted in an atmosphere in which valid consent is unlikely, many experts have condemned such research.[14]

Similarly, given the vulnerability of many aging people and their often hampered ability to express free informed consent, other scholars have challenged research on the elderly, notably institutionalized elderly,[15] and on children.[16] Especially questionable are experiments on children who are unlikely to benefit from the research in which they are involved. A classic case of questionable research on a child occurred in 1984, when researchers transplanted a baboon heart into a dying infant, "Baby Fae," even though the heart had no chance of helping her live beyond several days.[17] Likewise, because of embryos' vulnerability and their obvious inability to give free informed consent, scholars have questioned using them as research subjects. *In vitro* fertilization and using embryos in research, however, differs from using older children or the elderly as experimental subjects. The seriousness of the harm done to embryos depends in large part on one's position on the defensibility of abortion.[18] Although scholars are divided on the acceptability of embryo research and its societal consequences, most countries do not allow embryo experimentation beyond a few weeks after fertilization. Nevertheless, embryos may represent a vulnerable class of research subjects often in need of protection. Indeed, to the degree that any research subjects are unable to give genuine free informed consent, their participation is questionable.[19]

Black people have been especially vulnerable as research subjects because of the tendencies of experimenters to treat them in prejudiced ways and to ignore their rights to free informed consent. One of the most famous instances of research-related racism occurred in the Tuskegee syphilis study that took place from 1932 until 1972. In order to determine the natural course of untreated, latent syphilis in black males, the U.S. Public Health Service studied 400 syphilitic black men. Owing in part to the prejudices that widespread syphilis occurred "naturally" among blacks, that blacks would not seek treatment for known disease, and that they did not deserve the same consideration as whites, members of the Health Service lied to the syphilitics who believed they were being treated for their disease. As a consequence, many of the men died prematurely and spread the disease more rapidly than would have occurred if they had been given treatment. Even when penicillin became widely available in the early fifties, the subjects never received it and continued to be deceived by the "researchers" who claimed to treat them.[20]

Nonhuman animals also are especially vulnerable as research subjects, and many spokespersons for animal rights have described cruel, unnecessary, and unethical treatment of animals used in experiments.[21] One of the most infamous series of animal experiments was conducted in Philadelphia by Dr. Thomas Gennarelli. Between 1969 and 1984 he caused numerous monkeys and baboons to have head injuries, even though he had no particular research hypotheses.[22] His studies are questionable because, in the absence of specific hypotheses and particular tests of them, the research probably accomplished far less than it might have and the primates suffered unnecessary pain and injury. Like the question of embryo experimentation, one's position on the issue of animal experimentation rests in part on whether one believes that animals have any rights or whether humans have duties to them. Typically those who oppose use of nonhuman animals, especially higher animals, as research subjects claim either that the animals have rights, that the harm created by animal experimentation outweighs the benefits, or that alternatives (to animal experimentation) exist.[23] Those who support use of animals in research tend to argue that animals have no rights, that speciesism is an inadequate rationale for prohibiting animal experimentation, or that animal experimentation serves a greater good.[24] Regardless of whether scientists argue for or against use of animals in experiments, however, scholars generally agree that researchers must justify the expected benefits of their studies and that they ought not use animal tests when alternatives exist.[25] Most people generally agree that animals represent a vulnerable class of research subjects deserving protection.

Certain types of research pose more risk to subjects than others. There is a great difference, for example, between biomedical versus deviance research (on crime or mental illness, for instance). In biomedical research, experimenters presuppose the larger normative framework of society. In deviance research, they cannot presuppose these norms because to do so would be to make an implicit judgment on the reasonableness or rightness of the deviance. As Jeffrey Reiman points out, because deviance researchers are forced to call into question societal norms, in at least some senses, as a rule they seem more likely (than biomedical researchers) to violate ethical norms regarding treatment of research subjects. The Tuskegee syphilis study, however, is an obvious exception to this rule (that deviance research poses a greater ethical threat than medical research). Probably the Tuskegee researchers erred because they did not follow societal norms of combatting racism or because they themselves reflected the racial biases of society. If biomedical researchers follow correct societal norms, however, then their work will likely involve fewer threats to research subjects than experiments related to deviance.[26] Raising questions of research ethics thus appears to be most needed in investigations of the norms of societal behavior.

Scientists Ought Not Convert Public Resources to Private Profits

Scientific research can harm not merely members of the public or research subjects but also society as a whole. The third general rule dictates that to the degree research poses an unjustified risk to societal welfare, it ought not be done. Failure to pay attention to research ethics—especially to the societal goals that scientific research, especially in public universities, ought to serve—could damage not only the democratic freedom of society but also its educational missions. In universities dominated by industrial support, for example, the curriculum may be more narrowly focused, more devoted to applied research, and less supportive of ''unproductive'' scholarly activities. As Nobelist Isidore Rabi warned, this narrowness could pave the way for a repetition of what happened in Germany during the 1930s. The rise of militaristic nationalism, fueled by the dominance of narrow technical and professional training, eroded ethical values and liberal university education and lay the foundation for Hitler. Given such a restrictive conception of the university and scholarship, it was no accident that in 1937 the Prussian Academy of Sciences condemned Einstein because he criticized the violations of civil liberties in the Nazi regime.[27] Once an Einstein, or any other disinterested researcher, is condemned for speaking about the public interest, then the narrowing of the ivory tower can strangle democracy as well. No country can survive the theft of its universities' researchers or their capacity to criticize. Democratic institutions require the free flow of information and criticism, and both government and the public need universities and researchers to provide this independent perspective. Otherwise government must blindly choose the answers offered by various private groups—such as corporations—who are by nature self-interested. Because they are *self-interested*, they cannot be trusted to judge what is in the *common interest*. Democracy needs the Socratic gadfly, the detached observer, the unbiased scientist, and the social critic. Although a healthy economy and progressive society need university and industry cooperation, neither society nor the university nor science itself can afford for researchers either to become "hired guns" for special-interest groups or to threaten academic integrity.[28]

For a taxpayer-supported university to allow unregulated industry or private individuals to reap what the taxpayer has sown, especially in a scientific situation involving secrecy,[29] may encourage taxation without full representation of the people. Such underrepresentation may allow universities to sell to private interests something that is, in part, a public birthright: research partially funded and encouraged by society. Of course one can argue that most corporate and military research serves public interests. The ethical objection arises to the degree that such research does not serve genuinely public interests. The celebrated case of George and Gladys Dick, the two University of Chicago scientists who discovered how to mass produce an antitoxin used in immunization against scarlet fever, illustrates the dubiousness of private interests' controlling discoveries, including patents and intellectual property rights, made in part through public funding. These two researchers were nominated for the Nobel Prize in medicine in 1925 but did not receive it. Despite the importance of their discoveries, the Nobel Committee apparently did not agree with their patenting, therefore exercising control over, a substance having significant public health consequences.[30] Such situations suggest that, at some point, researchers at a university (like Carnegie Mellon, with 60 percent of its research funds from the Department of Defense) may become no longer members of an academic institution, but employees of the Air Force, Monsanto, or Hoechst.[31] In such cases, the academic freedom of scientists may become nothing more than the right to be bought by the highest bidder. Such funding patterns, especially in the area of classified scientific research,[32] decrease both researchers' and university autonomy as well as the free informed consent of the public. To believe otherwise is naive. As we already have suggested, such funding patterns are open to question, in part because of researchers' contractual and trustee responsibilities to society. As Harvard Professor of Zoology Richard Lewontin retorted: "The prospect of the university [in its personnel and promotion actions] treating with an even hand and without the slightest prejudice a researcher/professor in whom it has already invested $200,000 in a joint financial venture [with industry] is ludicrous.''[33] Profit-making ventures among scientists in taxpayer-supported universities, especially ventures with large corporations, are questionable because they could violate justice, autonomy, consent, fair play, and ordinary prohibitions against monopolies. For example, in the United States, of all corporate monies given to universities, one-third was provided by only ten corporations, and one-fifth of all industry funds, millions of dollars, came from only two corporations.[34]

Such business–industry connections with academia are not questionable in themselves, of course, because the connections often serve a number of goods, such as increasing the relevance or applicability of scientific research or helping to provide jobs for students or research assistants. Nevertheless, the connections present problems to the degree that they threaten autonomy, freedom of research, and the public interest in research. Michael Davis argues forcefully that the problems associated with business–university connections have been overestimated. He suggests three ways that university–business links can threaten learning: attracting scientists who want to get rich rather than to teach and learn, profit motives' clouding researchers' judgments, and funders' control of university-produced information.[35] Whether Davis is correct about the overestimation of the problem, clearly a potential problem exists; otherwise there would be no university regulations governing outside funding. To the degree that researchers' connections with private interests seriously threaten societal welfare, it is important to question whether the research ought to be performed, or at least performed in particular ways.

Scientists Ought Not Seriously Jeopardize Environmental Welfare

Scientific research dominated by monopolistic control or conflicts of interest can threaten not only public but environmental welfare. As chapter one and the fourth general rule (against performing certain types of research) suggest, numerous examples exist of ethically questionable research that leads to environmentally unsustainable development. For instance, research on how to mine fossil aquifers, underground aquifers that hold water hundreds of thousands of years old, is questionable because the aquifers receive little replenishment from rainfall today. Depending on these aquifers is like depending on an oil well that will eventually run dry. Groundwater depletion is sure to cause serious environmental and economic depletion in the future, as in Saudi Arabia where 75 percent of water needs are met by fossil groundwater.[36] Researchers who encourage such practices may bear some of the responsibility for subsequent environmental problems. Similar ethical responsibilities face researchers who spend public monies and their time on projects that divert society from environmentally and ecologically sustainable products and processes. Research on commercial nuclear fission, for example, may not be sustainable because of its dependence on uranium, its ethically questionable distribution of energy risks and costs (including liability costs), and its inability to guarantee that the radioactive waste can be isolated from the biosphere.[37] An important environmental question for research scientists might be whether the research contributes to an efficient, sustainable, solar-hydrogen energy economy or whether it merely follows the direction of those more interested in the status quo or in short-term profits.[38]

Sometimes scientists ought not perform research if it must be done in ways that are biased against environmental welfare. Classical economic methods like benefit-cost analysis are biased, for instance, because they do not include the costs of natural resources and "free" goods, such as air and water, or the costs of "public" goods, such as defense. Likewise, typical economic methods often ignore the fact that market prices diverge in a number of systematic ways from authentic values, especially environmental values. Such methods ignore the distorting effects of monopolies and speculative instabilities in the market. As the example of nuclear subsidies (mentioned in chapter one) shows, market analyses ignore all externalities, all costs and benefits not traded on a market. Because so many environmental goods are either part of a commons or not traded on a market, classical ecomomic methods ignore them.[39] This suggests that, to the degree that researchers uncritically employ such economic methods, they may bear partial responsibility for misguided policy decisions or harmful environmental consequences that arise from use of questionable economic techniques.

One of the most problematic techniques typically used by economic researchers is "discounting future costs." This discounting results in an undervaluation of future environmental costs and deaths caused by present activity, and it encourages policymakers to maximize short-term gain, much of which has disastrous long-term consequences. For example, if a toxic waste dump kills one person this year and the researcher counts the present value of that person's life as worth more than $64,000 in a benefit-cost analysis, then at a 6-percent discount rate, one death caused by the dump 20 years later will be counted now as $20,000 because $20,000 is the amount which, if invested now at a 6-percent rate, will yield approximately $64,000 in 20 years. If economic researchers use a 6-percent discount rate to evaluate present and future costs and benefits, after 300 years a human life would be counted as worth less than one-millionth of what it is worth now. Likewise, if we cause some pollution or resource depletion to occur in 300 years and if economists discount these future costs at a 6-percent rate, the costs would be counted (in our present benefit-cost analysis) as worth less than one-millionth of what the same costs are worth now. Yet if moral philosophers like Derek Parfit are correct, there is little ethical justification for discounting in such situations. Parfit argues that, although reasons, such as technological progress, exist for economic discounting of future costs, one cannot justify their temporal discounting. The *moral* importance of future events does not decline at some *n* percent per year.[40] Because of the ethically and environmentally problematic character of researchers' using discount rates, scientists need to examine whether they ought to perform research that depends on such problematic techniques.

Researchers' and policymakers' employment of the gross national product (GNP) also may contribute to environmental degradation. According to this internationally accepted system of economic accounting, a researcher subtracts depreciation of a plant and its equipment from its overall output of goods and services, but the GNP takes no account of the depreciation of "natural capital" such as the loss of topsoil or the destruction of forests. Hence the GNP-based accounting system used throughout the world may overestimate economic progress and underestimate the economic costs of environmental degradation, thereby helping to generate environmentally destructive economic policies. In the language of economics, firms are allowed to internalize profits but to externalize many costs (such as environmental degradation or pollution-induced health expenses). Because the GNP represents an incomplete accounting system, researchers who use it uncritically may fail to assess the real costs of societal activities. As a consequence, they may help to devalue and therefore undermine the human and natural-resource support systems for the economy. This undermining takes place because researchers who uncritically use the GNP and its associated techniques are sanctioning the environmental equivalent of "deficit financing." One of the most visible examples of such environmental deficits is deforestation. If tropical forests are clear cut or burned, the land rapidly loses its fertility because most nutrients are stored in vegetation. After several years of farming, the land becomes waste, even though the economic system takes no account of the consequent costs associated with tropical deforestation.[41] Thus, to the degree that a scientific method generates conclusions that lead to such faulty policy consequences, scientists ought to question whether they should engage in the research.

Scientists Ought Not Do Biased Research

In general, deliberately and seriously biased research probably ought not be done, as we argue in chapter one and suggest in the fifth general rule against certain types of research. Such bias not only thwarts the purpose of research but also can lead to questionable policy consequences. For example, scientists obviously cannot contribute to the solution of societal problems like ill health if the research data they generate concern mainly the male half of the population or primarily the white segments of society. With respect to both racism and sexism, researchers sometimes show at least four types of biases in their choice and definition of problems for research:

- Even though diseases have different frequencies (e.g., lupus), symptoms (e.g., depression, gonorrhea), or complications (e.g., AIDS) in the two sexes, researchers typically ignore gender differences in forming their hypotheses.
- Although some diseases lead the list of causes of death for women (e.g., heart trouble), they are defined as male diseases, and scientists perform research mainly on predisposing factors among males.
- Research on conditions specific to women (e.g., dysmenorrhea) receives low funding, prestige, and priority among researchers.
- Scientists often attribute data based on personal experiences of women to psychological or social factors, even when there are physio-chemical bases for the data (e.g., prostaglandins' relationship to dysmenorrhea).[42]

Race and gender bias has led to almost unbelievable studies, the most amazing of which was a project—studying the impact of obesity on breast and uterine cancer—conducted only on men.[43] Other federal researchers have studied aging for 20 years and included only male research subjects, even though two-thirds of those defined as elderly are women.[44]

The two main alleged justifications for white-male-only studies are that including women would "complicate" some research because of hormone changes in the menstrual cycle or could damage children conceived while their mothers were research subjects. Both rationales fail, however, because male hormones also "complicate" some research and because not all potential female research subjects are sexually active. Moreover, protecting potential children of research subjects is a questionable rationale for excluding women because some experiments also damage sperm in ways that could cause birth defects. Finally, excluding women from experiments does not actually protect them or their children. It likely increases the liability of both health and drug professionals. Exclusion of women merely moves the source of liability claims from experimental subjects and their children to more hidden victims, to damaged future children and injured women patients who receive treatments and drugs that have been tested only on men.[45]

Research Scientists Ought to Evaluate Consequences

Given the potential of research (like that exhibiting sexist bias) to contribute to public harm, many scholars believe that in research ethics "the major moral standard" is "the ability to foresee direct and global consequences of one's technical work so as not to harm human beings or the environment."[46] Because some harm is often unavoidable, however, dangerous consequences of research usually require assessment in the light of relevant duties and the benefits associated with the research. Also, although scientific research may threaten public welfare, as in the case of testing commercial nuclear reactors or attempting to measure alleged race- or sex-related differences in intelligence,[47] not doing certain research also poses public risk. Not doing research into energy technologies, for example, might result in higher utility costs and greater burdens on the poor, both indirectly causing greater fatalities among people whose incomes are most sensitive to the price of energy. In other words, the economic costs of regulating research induce mortality risks, and sometimes these risks may exceed those caused by the failure to regulate.[48] Given these two types of risks, one cannot condemn all dangerous research, because prohibiting research may also cause risks. For example, if we stopped all recombinant DNA research, we might be ethically remiss in failing to benefit those—perhaps with genetic diseases—who might be helped by the research.[49] Correctly answering questions regarding research ethics thus requires a balancing of the benefits and harms likely to arise both from research and from the failure to do the research. It also presupposes a balancing between the rights of scientists to pursue their work wherever it may lead—using whatever methods seem most likely to lead to success—and the rights of society to regulate research whenever it affects public welfare.[50] In later chapters we give some examples of how to balance these conflicting, research-related rights and duties and how to balance research-related harms and benefits.

Just as scientists have a duty to do research but to avoid ethically questionable research, so also they have a responsibility not to become so ethically scrupulous about their work that they threaten the societal ends research should serve. For example, on grounds of ensuring objective test results, proponents of research ethics might argue that medical experimenters should always use placebo controls, so as to confirm the efficacy of the particular tested drug. Such a narrow interpretation of objective (and therefore ethical) research methodology, however, fails to take account of behavior that might better serve the interests of both the public and experimental subjects. Suppose that the medical experimentation involved trials of a new therapy for a lethal disease (such as AIDS) and that the victims/research subjects were near death and had exhausted all other possibilities for saving their lives. In such a situation, if the subjects gave free informed consent, it might be reasonable to avoid placebos and instead to use new therapies having even a small chance of helping them. The rules of research ethics must remain flexible enough to allow for special cases. Rather than merely applying general rules concerning the ethics of scientific research, we should use such rules as guides but also employ ethical analysis in a case-by-case manner. Later chapters illustrate how to perform these analyses.

The rules of research ethics ought not be so controlled by institutional review boards—research ethics committees—that the committees, rather than individual scientists, assume responsibility for behavior and for analyzing particular research situations.[51] In joint efforts among scholars in developed and developing nations, research ethics committees have often imposed stringent rules on experimentation based on experiences in highly industrialized countries. Scholars in less developed nations, however, sometimes criticize these rules as ethnocentric, as failing to take account of the contexts in which the joint research takes place, as inapplicable, and as examples of the ''intellectual imperialism of western research ethics.''[52] Other scholars have criticized some rules of research ethics as too rigid. For example, they claim that, although U.S. researchers have been at the forefront of the pharmaceutical innovation process, this trend is not likely to continue. They cite the growing number of regulations on pharmaceutical experimentation, which cause the research and development process to become longer and costlier, while the product life cycles become shorter. Research committees within the drug regulatory process have driven the average regulatory approval time to about 30 months, increasing the difficulty for scientists and their employers to recognize a profit on pharmaceutical inventions. If research ethics committees are too rigid in regulating the processes and products of research, they become a disincentive rather than "a stimulus to further innovation." Less innovative drug research, in turn, ultimately hurts the very people whom research ought to benefit. Hence, although scientists have a duty to do research, they also have both a duty to avoid certain ethically questionable types of research and a duty to help avoid over-regulation of their research in ways that do not benefit society.[53]

In stressing that researchers have a duty to avoid both some types of investigations and over-regulation, we implicitly assert that scientists need to examine the *consequences* of their actions and omissions regarding research as well as their professional *duties*, in order to evaluate the ethical acceptability of their work. But if scientists have the duty to examine the consequences of their actions and omissions, although (by definition) not all consequences can be known ahead of time, then many "hard cases" in research ethics involve situations of uncertainty regarding consequences. (Chapters five through ten give some examples of how to analyze the consequences associated with particular cases of decisionmaking in research ethics.) Indeed, the more practical and innovative scientific research is, the more difficult it is to evaluate its consequences.[54]

In some cases it is possible to use consequences to evaluate the acceptability of research. In 1967, many members of the medical community questioned the ethics of Christiaan Barnard's performing the first heart transplant because experimenters knew, ahead of time, that there was no way to prevent subject death through infection and rejection of the transplanted heart. In other words, because these negative consequences of performing transplants were unavoidable in 1967, Barnard's transplant experiment raised many ethical questions. Also troubling were Barnard's failing to obtain free informed consent from the subject, Louis Washkansky, Barnard's failure to tell Washkansky's wife that her husband was dying, Barnard's telling Washkansky he might be able to return to a normal life, and Barnard's taking money from American journalists in exchange for giving them access to him and to Washkansky.[55] Likewise, the expected negative consequences of Dr. Denton Cooley's implanting an artificial heart in Barney Clark argue that this heart experiment may have been unethical. Doctors knew ahead of time that the implant would not be very successful, given that Clark smoked two packs a day and had heart and lung disease. Moreover, Cooley neither gained the approval of his institutional review board, nor did he obtain permission of the family to continue his research on Clark after his condition had deteriorated.[56]

Because of the centrality of evaluating potentially serious consequences of research, the code of research ethics adopted recently at the universities of Göteborg and Uppsala requires scholars to interrupt the work if they "foresee bad consequences in the application of it."[57] But given the uncertainties regarding the results of research such as experimentation on embryonic stem cells or on differences among races,[58] it is often difficult to assess the variety and magnitude of consequences associated with particular research. In chapters eight, nine, and ten, Helen Longino, Carl Mitcham, and Carl Cranor, respectively, outline some of the ways that biased research can lead to harmful consequences that include racism, sexism, threats to public safety, and risks to human health. If the consequences of research are unclear, and if the proposed research appears to present neither violations of subjects' free informed consent nor serious threats to their welfare, however, then how scientists ought to behave is less clear. One solution to assessing uncertain consequences might be to admit the relevant uncertainties and to be explicit about the value judgments that guide the decision either to perform or to refrain from certain research. For example, a number of reports published by the U.S. National Research Council/National Academy of Sciences have explicitly endorsed agricultural research and experimentation dedicated to the values of multidisciplinary work, incorporating indigenous knowledge, and promoting environmental sustainability.[59] Despite uncertainties regarding the consequences of such work, scientists can decide whether to engage in or avoid the research in part on the basis of the implicit or explicit value judgments central to the research. Hence, scholars must be clear about implicit or explicit value judgments underlying their work. Scientific researchers might determine, for example, whether they can justify their military biological research by adopting the value judgment that development of *defensive* military materials is ethically acceptable whereas development of *offensive* materials is not.[60] Or, scientific researchers might investigate why they hesitate to engage in experiments on agricultural mechanization on the grounds that mechanization displaces farm workers. Likewise they might investigate whether they are ethically justified in doing mechanization research on the grounds that mechanization has kept the U.S. tomato processing industry from moving to Mexico.[61] Despite the uncertain consequences of scientific research, such examples illustrate that researchers' putting their values ''up front'' increases the probability that the work will undergo explicit ethical scrutiny. Scientists' being explicit about their ethical and value judgments also enables others to assess more clearly the ethical defensibility of their work, the justifiability of their problem choices, and the desirability of their specific research ends or goals. Obviously in a finite world of finite funds and a finite number of researchers, not all scientific work can be done. That is why questions of what research we ought to perform, and why we ought to perform it, should be subject to ethical scrutiny.[62]

Scientific Research and Professional Codes of Ethics

If the duties of scientists to perform or to avoid particular research derive in large part from their professional responsibilities, one may ask whether professional codes of ethics can provide guidance regarding the nature of the duty to do research. After all, most professionals' codes of ethics recognize a responsibility for the public good, and doing research promotes the public good.[63] Analyzing professional codes of ethics thus becomes an important way to clarify researchers' obligations. In chapter nine, Carl Mitcham provides some examples of how codes of engineering ethics have influenced perceived obligations of engineering researchers.

If scientists interpret their codes of ethics merely as sets of uncontroversial maxims, however, then the codes may have some limitations. As the American Association for the Advancement of Science (AAAS) notes, sets of *general* principles do not always provide insight into *specific* cases of decisionmaking, in part because they are ''dependent on the basic integrity and wisdom of the persons using them.''[64] Although general principles ''do not determine the solution to moral problems,'' nevertheless, ''they indicate what needs to be justified, where the onus of justification lies, and what counts as justification.''[65] John Ladd especially criticizes the value of *general* principles of ethics: ''the whole notion of an organized professional ethics is an absurdity—intellectual and moral.''[66] He reasons that authentic ethical principles are established only by case-by-case argumentation, not ahead of time by fiat.[67] Ladd admits that codes of ethics may be useful to inspire individuals, to sensitize them to certain problems, to enforce rules of the professional, to offer moral advice in instances of perplexity, or to alert prospective clients as to what they might expect from professionals.[68] Nevertheless he believes that codes also generate a number of problems. Because codes of ethics can enhance the image of the profession, serve as status symbols, and protect the monopoly of the profession in question, they can also lead to "mischievous side effects," says Ladd, citing complacency and a shift of attention from societal to more individual problems. He believes that codes of ethics sometimes come to represent the "tyranny of the majority" and serve to suppress the dissenter, the innovator, and the critic.[69] Hence, for Ladd, the attempt to impose professional codes of ethics runs contrary to the notion that "persons are autonomous moral agents."[70]

As Michael Davis argues, however, Ladd's criticisms of professional codes of ethics are overly severe. Davis notes that, for most norms discussed in such codes, "the present standard, whatever its faults, is better than none at all."[71] One reason to prefer a standard code over none at all is that, despite the fact that codes rarely determine behavior, nevertheless they restrict it.[72] The *Code of Ethics* of the Institute of Electrical and Electronic Engineers, for example, tells engineers they ought to "avoid real or perceived conflicts of interest wherever possible, and to disclose them to affected parties when they do exist."[73] The code obliges engineers to disclose conflicts of interest, rather than keep silent and claim that the conflicts do not affect their behavior. Hence codes of professional ethics often provide specific useful restrictions on behavior. Codes that are too vague, of course, may need amendment.[74] Several years ago, the AAAS Committee on Professional Ethics proposed that scientific and engineering societies clarify the basic rules reflecting the moral consensus among professionals.[75] The committee also urged the societies to determine the degree of individual independence necessary to maintain a respect for personal autonomy and individual choice.[76] Nevertheless, as representatives of Sigma Xi, the Scientific Research Society, point out, such autonomy must not allow researchers to ignore the codes in practice and rationalize their own actions as "justifiable exceptions" to the rules.[77] Like all rules, however, those in professional codes of ethics will never specify how to apply them in all situations. Thus, professional codes of ethics often provide no clear way to distinguish priorities among conflicting obligations (e.g., to employers versus the public), even though they proscribe certain behavior. Indeed, the AAAS committee noted that scientists' codes of ethics are typically general and abstract and that "very few of the societies' statements provided a clear basis for establishing priorities between two or more rules which . . . may present the scientists . . . with conflicting obligations."[78]

Codes and Conflicts Among Research-Related Principles

The codes of ethics of the American Fisheries Society, the Society for Range Management, the Ecological Society of America, the National Association of Environmental Professionals, and the Registered Professional Entomologists provide examples of the failure to establish priority among conflicting ethical obligations.[79] Consider, for instance, two potential conflicts exhibited in the code of the Ecological Society of America. Tenet 22 asserts that members "shall be obligated, when they have substantial evidence of a breach of this Code by another member to bring such conduct to the attention of the offender and to the Council."[80] Yet tenet 23 of the code says that members ought not "attempt to injure the reputation or opportunities for employment of another ecologist or scientists in a related profession by false, biased, or undocumented claims or accusations."[81] Because what constitutes biased or undocumented research is in part a matter of interpretation, it is easy to see how a conflict between loyalty to the profession and to one's ecological colleagues could exist, especially if the colleagues' research were controversial and perhaps arguably misrepresented the profession. Moreover, because the code provides no clear method to resolve such conflicts, the general and vague principles governing researchers' behavior could result in a new "McCarthy era" during which one group of scientists was asked to inform on another.[82]

Tenet 14 of the same code also presents the potential for harm because it takes a neutral stance toward whistleblowers and stops short of insisting on a duty to make the truth public. This tenet enjoins ecologists to "respect any request for confidence expressed by their employers or clients, provided that such confidence will not contribute to unnecessary or significant degradation of the environment and does not jeopardize the health, safety, or welfare of the public."[83] Nevertheless tenet 20 of the code charges ecologists "not to associate with, or allow the use of their names, reports, maps, or other technical materials by any enterprise known to be illegal . . . or contrary to the welfare of the public or the environment."[84] Obviously, a conflict might arise between these two tenets of the code and between duties to one's employer and to the public.

Similar potential conflicts appear in the code of Registered Professional Entomologists of the Entomological Society of America. Tenet 3.2 of this code, for example, enjoins the entomologist to "cooperate in upbuilding the profession by exchanging information . . . where disclosure of such information does not conflict with the interests of clients and employers."[85] Tenet 4.1 likewise requires entomologists merely to avoid illegal activities themselves, not to report them when they threaten the public: "The professional entomologist will act as a faithful agent or trustee for each employer or client, and will not knowingly engage in illegal work or cooperate with any person so engaged."[86] On the other hand, tenet 2.1 of the code requires entomologists to "have proper regard for the safety, health and welfare of the public in the performance of professional duties."[87] It is easy to see how tenet 2.1, according to which an entomologist might blow the whistle on misleading research regarding a dangerous but legal pesticide, conflicts with tenets 4.1 and 3.2, which require entomologists to act in the interests of their employers. Moreover, it is unclear how an entomologist could follow tenet 2.1, thereby protecting public welfare, and at the same time follow tenet 4.6: "The professional entomologist will not disclose information concerning the business affairs or technical processes of present or former employers or clients without their consent."[88] If the employer-directed research activities were dangerous or illegal, the entomologist probably could not obtain consent to reveal them. Hence the conflict.

The code of ethics of the American Fisheries Society reveals similar potential problems. It recognizes no rights of the public to accurate research information and no obligation of environmental professionals to engage in whistleblowing. Nevertheless, section I of the code asserts: "The member will not knowingly permit the publication of his reports, or parts of them, in a manner calculated to mislead."[89] This tenet might conflict with a principle specified in section III of the code: "He will not disclose any information concerning the business affairs or the technical processes of clients or employers without their consent."[90] A conflict might also arise between preventing the publication of misleading statements (section I) and avoiding criticizing another professional's work (section IV): "he will refrain from criticizing another professional's work in public, recognizing that the Fisheries Society and the Fisheries Press provide the proper forum for technical discussions and criticisms."[91]

Not surprisingly, the code of ethics of the Society for Range Management exhibits the same sorts of conflicts. The first tenet requires members to "be interested in the public welfare and recognize in all actions that the land upon which we depend for livelihood must support generations yet unborn."[92] Yet the eighth and last tenet requires members to "recognize the Society for Range Management, its meetings and publications as the primary forum for technical discussion." Many respond, however, that when professionals have engaged in technical decisionmaking, they have not prevented environmental destruction, e.g., of Yellowstone. For this reason, a number of writers argue that public-interest decisionmaking should take place initially in the public arena rather than in professional research journals or meetings.[93] Despite such arguments, the Range Management's code of ethics provides no clear basis for deciding whether the public interest requires that range managers use a private or a public forum for whistleblowing. The code of ethics of the National Association of Environmental Professionals reveals a similar problem. It enjoins members to "encourage public participation [in environmental policymaking] at the earliest feasible time," yet does not specify what time is "feasible." It urges members to help maintain "the integrity and competence" of the profession but offers no guidelines regarding criticizing the research of a fellow professional who may jeopardize public interest because of dishonesty or incompetence.

Conclusion

As the potential conflicts within these professional codes of ethics reveal, "any set of general principles . . . cannot provide precise answers for every difficult case" of research ethics,[94] even though the principles help us by setting limits on behavior. This means that, although there is a duty to do research, we often require additional help in settling conflicts in research ethics. In addition to professional codes of ethics, we need guidance regarding analysis of various cases involving research ethics. In the next chapter we begin such an analysis.

3

Basic Principles of Research Ethics: Objectivity

In September 1978, Janet Parker, a photographer for the Department of Medical Microbiology at Birmingham (England) University, died of smallpox. She succumbed one month after being stricken, after the World Health Organization (WHO) had announced the success of its worldwide program to eradicate smallpox. The virus existed only in designated laboratories that allegedly met WHO biological safety standards. No attempt was made to enforce these standards at the laboratory through which Parker was infected, however, and researchers ignored elementary safety precautions under the pressure to complete the smallpox research by the WHO-imposed deadline. Henry Bedson, head of the Birmingham Department and a distinguished virologist, committed suicide shortly after he confirmed that Parker had been infected.[1]

The tragic case of Parker's death illustrates several clear violations of research ethics. Bedson likely erred in risking the health of his staff in order to increase the probability of research success. A number of groups within the university, government, and WHO also erred in failing to enforce safety standards at the laboratory even though they were charged with doing so. Thus, in several ways, the appropriate behavior regarding research ethics in the Birmingham smallpox case is uncontroversial. The researchers violated safety standards required by law. However, the requirements for ethically correct actions in most situations of research ethics, especially situations involving uncertainty about data or conclusions, are much less clear than in the Birmingham case. As the last chapter illustrated, although many professionals have a duty to engage in research and to perform it in unbiased ways, to discover ethically correct behavior, we often need not only codes of ethics but also analysis of particular situations. This chapter is a first step in presenting some of the analysis essential to ethical thinking about scientific research. We argue that research ethics requires us to examine both *general principles* of ethical behavior—like those found in professional codes—as well as to evaluate the *duties* and *particular consequences* associated with a given situation. This chapter outlines a two-step approach to analyzing questions of research ethics.

Two Stages of Ethical Analysis

In analyzing problems, most moral philosophers employ one of two main theoretical approaches, deontological/contractarian ethics or utilitarian ethics. Philosophers such as Locke, Rousseau, Kant, and Rawls represent the deontological or contractarian (social-contract) position. Prominent utilitarians include Adam Smith, Bentham, Mill, and Harsanyi. Deontologists or contractarians base their accounts of ethics on general principles related to *duty* or *obligation*, apart from whether following such principles actually leads to desirable consequences. Utilitarians base their accounts of ethics on actions or rules that lead to desirable *consequences*. Thus, although deontologists and utilitarians sometimes might recommend the same ethical behavior, their reasons for doing so differ. A deontologist might argue, for example, that researchers have a *duty* always to avoid any sort of deliberate misrepresentation of data in their work. A utilitarian, however, might argue that researchers ought to avoid any deliberate misrepresentation of their data because doing so would lead to more desirable *consequences* than not doing so. Or, a utilitarian might argue that, in a particular case, researchers *may* deliberately misrepresent research data so as to bring about a desirable consequence—protecting persons from harm, for example.[2]

Deontologists/contractarians and utilitarians each contribute important insights to ethical analysis. In fact, a number of thinkers note that complete ethical analysis requires both types of theory.[3] In order to provide as complete a discussion of research ethics as possible, we include both deontological/contractarian and utilitarian methods of analysis. Thus, we develop a two-step method of investigating research ethics. First we use deontological analysis to develop some general ethical obligations or principles applicable to research behavior. Next we employ both deontological and utilitarian analyses to investigate a particular priority ranking of the general principles. By employing both types of theories, we avoid begging questions about the primacy of deontological versus utilitarian accounts of ethical decisionmaking. We also attempt to perform as inclusive an ethical analysis as possible, illustrating reasoning used by each of the two main camps of ethical theorists.[4]

We base our discussion of research ethics on the view that one ought to engage in ethical analysis at two different levels or stages. In the first stage, one attempts to sort out all the reasons that might justify alternative positions on a question involving ethical behavior or conflict. At this level of analysis, one follows the sort of ethical reasoning deontological/contractarian thinkers espouse.[5] The philosopher at this stage attempts to arrive at some very general prescriptions or rules of thumb to aid in decisionmaking. These are "prima facie principles." In using the label "prima facie," we follow Hare,[6] Ross,[7] and Rawls[8] and refer to principles that are presumed to be correct, unless they have been rebutted. Of course, we often encounter considerations that argue against following a prima facie principle or duty in a particular case. For example, one has a prima facie obligation to do what one has promised to do, such as meet someone at a particular time. But if an emergency occurs, if the individual with the obligation can save another person's life by not meeting someone else as promised, then this prima facie obligation can be overridden by "other things," e.g., the importance of trying to save another's life. Hence, in specifying prima facie principles, one specifies duties that appear, for the most part, to be true. We can determine actual required behavior only by subjecting the prima facie principles to further analysis, to decide whether they are binding in the face of a variety of potentially rebutting considerations. In using deontological methods to discover researchers' general ethical obligations, for example, at least two prima facie principles come to mind. These principles, discovered at the first stage of analysis, provide the general rules of thumb upon which reasonable and unbiased persons typically agree. One such principle might be (x), "always report research results with as much objectivity as possible and with no deliberate bias or interpretation." Another such principle might be (y), "always present research results in such a way as to avoid their possible misuse and misapplication." Once people arrive at a set of general intuitive principles (such as [x] and [y]) to guide research behavior, they may move to the second, or critical, stage of ethical analysis.

At the second level of ethical analysis, one investigates the prima facie principles developed at the earlier stage and uses deontological and utilitarian analyses in an attempt to decide which principles ought to override the others. For example, we might argue that the two prima facie principles just mentioned, (x) and (y), conflict. Suppose a psychologist found, after doing research on IQ, that for some reason blacks' scores appeared to be lower than whites', even when tests were allegedly unbiased. Should the researcher follow principle (x) and report these results as objectively as possible? Or should the researcher follow principle (y) and interpret the results in a particular way, so as to avoid their being misused by racists? At the second or critical stage the analyst examines all relevant obligations and all relevant consequences of the conflicting principles in the particular situation, so as to determine which principle ought to receive preference.[9] A number of moral philosophers recognize universalizability (universal applicability) as one of the main constraints on one's choice between principles such as (x) and (y). Universalizability requires that if one makes a moral judgment about a particular situation, then one must be prepared to make the same decision about any other precisely similar situation. In other words, one must be consistent.

Principles of Research Ethics: The First Stage of Analysis

To discover and justify prima facie principles to guide us in determining answers to specific questions of research ethics, we use rational contractor theory. According to this theory, especially as articulated by John Rawls, valid ethical principles are those that rational people would unanimously advocate, if they behaved in a fair and just manner. Often people do not behave in a fair and just manner, he notes, because they give special consideration to their own particular circumstances, such as being wealthier or healthier or more intelligent than others. To avoid people's choosing ethical principles on the basis of their own particular biases or circumstances, Rawls proposes a thought experiment. He asks us to suppose that individuals (choosing valid ethical principles) are placed behind a "veil of ignorance," such that they remain unaware of any kind of advantages or disadvantages that they or others possess. The prima facie moral rules or principles they select while behind the veil of ignorance should then be those that a rational, disinterested person would select.[10] Determining the behavior and rules that best benefit the public interest hinges on this Rawlsian theory about what prima facie ethical rules would be chosen by rational, disinterested people. Walter Lippmann has argued that what serves the public interest is what people would choose "if they saw clearly, thought rationally, and acted disinterestedly and benevolently."[11]

When rational and disinterested people choose prima facie ethical principles to govern their behavior, such principles—although reasonable and defensible—cannot be empirically confirmed, because no amount of data about what people *actually* do constitutes evidence for what they *ought* to do. If 95 percent of people were racists, for example, their behavior would not constitute evidence that racism ought to be ethically acceptable. Or, as philosophers say, " 'is' does not entail 'ought'." To believe (erroneously) that factual data support or confirm ethical claims or principles is, according to many philosophers, to commit the "naturalistic fallacy,"[12] the fallacy of reducing ethical reasoning to purely factual reasoning. Instead, we support ethical principles by giving valid arguments that the principles are fair, consistent, or treat persons as they deserve.

If we move behind the "veil of ignorance," as Rawls outlines, we can discover a number of prima facie ethical principles governing research ethics. These prima facie principles fall into one of three categories, based on the three major areas of ethical responsibilities of the professional (responsibilities to the employer or client, to third parties, and to other professionals/the profession).[13] For many scientific researchers, the employer or client is likely a university or a government agency (representing the public) sponsoring the research. Third parties usually are members of the public, all people affected by the behavior and decisions of the researcher. Professionals are other research scientists with similar training, knowledge, and interests. Because taxpayers ultimately fund most research, as mentioned in chapter one, very likely the ultimate client for much scientific research is the public. If so, the ultimate client is probably the same group as third parties. On Michael Bayles's scheme, professionals such as research scientists have at least six responsibilities to the employer or *client*: honesty, candor, competence, diligence, loyalty, and discretion.[14] He believes they have at least three responsibilities to *third parties*, to people who are not their clients: truthfulness, nonmaleficence, and fairness.[15] With respect to the *profession*, researchers have responsibilities to do candid and independent research, to reform the profession (so that their research serves the public good), and to promote respect for the profession so that it can contribute to the public good.[16] All three types of ethical norms are justified, in large part, by their promoting and preserving the values of a liberal society.[17] Why does this follow? If one assumes that all members of society have an interest in life, bodily and mental integrity, and personal property, then (as Bayles explains) one may argue (e.g., via Rawls's original position) that all people have good reasons for accepting the values of a liberal society. These values include governance by law, freedom, protection from injury, equality of opportunity, privacy, and welfare. One may also argue that, to the extent that researchers in a profession promote or preserve these social values, the profession is properly constituted, and their members probably fulfill their responsibilities with respect to research.[18] Brown University philosopher John Ladd argues along similar lines. He maintains that the big question to ask professionals (including researchers) is ''What is the significance of professionalism from the moral point of view for democracy, social equality, liberty and justice?''[19] Tenet 9 of the code of ethics of the Ecological Society of America, for example, likewise appears to give implicit assent to the notion that professionals ought to be judged by how well they promote the values of a liberal society.[20]

However, not all professionals who have developed a code for scientific researchers recognize researchers' responsibility to promote the values of a liberal society. Jacques Monod, for example, spoke of objectivity as the only duty of scientists.[21] As an alternative to Monod's ethics of objectivity, A. Cournand proposes an ''ethic of development,'' an ethics for scientists that gives priority to promoting human welfare, to ''liberal and democratic traditions.''[22] Cournand objected:

> The scientistic technocracy which Monod appears to favor stands apart from liberal and democratic traditions and their associated values of freedom, the readiness to question established power, social self-regulation by virtue of shared values, and the principles of representative institutions and civil liberties, including freedom of thought and of expression and the rule of law—all of which as a citizen he defended during his life.[23]

If the earlier arguments of Bayles and Ladd are correct, then Cournand is at least partially right in believing that professional norms, especially prima facie responsibilities, ought to serve the interests of liberal, democratic society.

The Principle of Objectivity: Avoiding Biased Results/Reports

In the case of university-employed research scientists, the most significant prima facie ethical responsibilities appear related to objectivity and to promoting the public good, the values of a liberal society. If the researchers have no industrial or commercial clients, but merely governmental clients (like many academic researchers), then their clients' goals theoretically match those of third parties or the public. (Admittedly, however, in some cases of controversial research, the governmental clients of researchers may not have the same goals as members of the general public. In the case of research concerning the conservation of the spotted owl,[24] for example, the authentic public interests are controversial. If the public desires the economic benefits brought by increased logging of old-growth forests essential to spotted-owl habitat, then public goals parallel those of the logging industry, rather than those of environmentalists or the government agency charged with protecting the spotted owl. This raises the question of whether the public interest lies with governmental goals, with industrial goals, with environmental goals, or with something else. In each case, only analysis of the duties and consequences associated with a specific situation will enable us to answer this question.) If researchers have only governmental or public clients, then they owe responsibility only to members of the public and to the profession. To serve members of the public and the profession, researchers must (1) avoid doing biased research themselves, (2) promote nonbiased use of scholarly results by others, and (3) support the goals of promoting the public good and the welfare of third parties, such as present and future inhabitants of the planet. Perhaps the easiest way to clarify and defend these three responsibilities is to show that a reasonable person, behind the veil of ignorance, would support them.

As Jacques Monod affirmed, the first or most basic ethical principle guiding researchers is to avoid dishonesty and deception, to conduct and report research with as much objectivity as possible and with no deliberate bias or misinterpretation. Chapters one and two gave several examples of the way scientists sometimes bias their research, by failing to use women or blacks as research subjects, for instance, but drawing conclusions alleged applicable to all. Other researchers have practiced deception, for instance, by suppressing or denying information about the hazards associated with nuclear weapons testing. The responsibility to maintain as much objectivity as possible and to avoid deception is not unique to the researcher, of course. It is a general ethical responsibility. In fact, since ancient Greek times, truth and virtue have been connected.[25] Hence, apart from the particular ethical stance that one takes on any occasion, it is always prima facie wrong (wrong in the absence of rebutting considerations) to engage in deliberate dishonesty or deception. Because of its obviousness and wide acceptance, we include no lengthy defense here. Deception, particularly among professionals conducting or presenting their research, wrongs those who use the research or who are affected by it because they need complete and unbiased information; moreover, deliberate lack of candor and objectivity thwarts the purpose of the research. Or, as one scientist put it, truthfulness is the cement that holds the building of science together.[26] For these reasons, researchers clearly have a professional and a general ethical responsibility to follow a first prima facie principle, to avoid deliberately biasing research results or reports.[27]

This first principle resembles a number of responsibilities listed in various professional codes of ethics. The first responsibility of scientists, as stated by the AAAS Committee on Academic Freedom and Responsibility, is "to present their scientific opinions and conclusions accurately and carefully, to identify factors which could affect their judgments, and recognize (as practicable) the limits of uncertainty in those judgments; also to acknowledge . . . possible conflicts of interest. . . ."[28] As this statement reveals, the AAAS Committee on Scientific Freedom and Responsibility explicitly notes that one must identify "the limits of uncertainty" in scientific judgments in order to present scientific opinions accurately.[29] (Chapter six discusses uncertainty in more detail.) Tenet 4 of the code of ethics of the ESA, for example, requires members to discourage dissemination of biased statements concerning ecology, and tenet 19 of the same code requires members to "convey their findings objectively."[30]

How ought researchers to follow the principle of objectivity? Obviously they must avoid frauds such as plagiarizing information, fabricating it, and stealing ideas. Such acts employ and present research in a biased way and violate research principles of objectivity. These frauds likely stem from an unethical mentality of "success at any cost." More controversial kinds of deception or fraud in research include loose authorship (inserting or removing names of persons who may or may not have helped with the work) and duplicate publication. Duplicate publication is controversial. Although sometimes scientists simply wish to bring their results to a wider audience, in other situations the authors desire to increase the perception of productivity.[31] Although some cases of alleged research fraud or misconduct are controversial, many instances of possible bias or lack of objectivity require no discussion because they unmistakably violate research ethics: failure to give credit to individuals for work done; failure to carry out research in a conscientious manner; or failure to publish a retraction when conclusive evidence exposes error in one's earlier work.[32] Although all such cases of research misconduct fail to serve principles of objectivity and honesty, argument often occurs over whether a given situation is actually a case of plagiarism, for example, or deliberate exclusion of an author. In other words, opinions frequently conflict over whether a case in research ethics involves fraud or mere error, sloppiness, or overstatement.[33] Because of such conflict, it may be easier to spot error or misconduct in scientific research than to determine ethical culpability on the part of a researcher.

Objectivity and Value Judgments in Research

Bias in research often escapes assessment because there is no value-free research, even in ''pure'' science, if such a thing exists. Contextual values—in the form of personal, social, cultural, or philosophical emphases—typically influence research processes. As chapter one illustrated, and as Helen Longino argues in chapter eight, sexist and racist values or biases often compromise the objectivity of research. Likewise, cultural values such as the profit motive or financial constraints often influence the way studies are done. Although researchers can avoid allowing bias and cultural values to affect their work, methodological or epistemic values are never avoidable, in any research, because all scientists must use value judgments to deal with research situations involving incomplete data or methods. Even researchers in pure science are forced to use methodological value judgments to ''fill in the gaps.'' Although making some type of methodological value judgment is unavoidable, nevertheless some value judgments are less objective and reasonable than others. For example, whenever researchers make an inference—about how to deal with unknowns, about how to choose which statistical tests to use, about how to select sample size, about where the burden of proof goes, about which theory or model to employ, about whether a certain interpolation of missing data is acceptable, about whether to extrapolate from laboratory to field data, or about whether incomplete information about a phenomenon is an adequate basis for drawing a conclusion—they make a methodological value judgment, a subjective inference that may be incorrect or may compromise the objectivity of their work more than other inferences or value judgments. Because they must judge their own methods, they could be wrong.[34] Methodological value judgments often interpret research methods, inferences, data, premises, or theories—interpretations that rely on commitments to particular goals of research. For scientists, these goals might include simplicity, predictive power, external consistency, accuracy, and so on. Whenever scientists employ or apply inferences, data, or premises in research, they must decide how to interpret them and whether to apply them in a particular case. Moreover, as Saul Kripke noted, there is no rule for how to apply a rule.[35] Therefore, researchers must make value judgments every time they infer that a particular rule applies (or not) to certain data or to a particular situation. Typically these interpretations and applications take the form of methodological value judgments.

Because some methodological value judgments are more plausible, logical, or defensible than others and because scientists' research conclusions often are highly sensitive to methodological value judgments, objectivity requires researchers to make their value judgments explicit and to assess them carefully. As Helen Longino points out in chapter eight, because values shape the research process, we must try to understand them and to recognize them when they appear, either as part of racial and gender ideologies, for example, or as part of methodological judgments. Moreover, even though many methodological value judgments are defensible and reliable, they all are somewhat subjective because they interpret inferences, data, premises, or theories. We term methodological value judgments ''value judgments'' because of their subjectivity, because they are a function of methodological values or norms (predictive power and so on), and because they often stir up more controversy than judgments about empirical data. When a research conclusion relies on problematic value judgments, it renders these judgments suspect because they are based on erroneous or questionable *assumptions*. Assumptions are claims or beliefs that are taken for granted, often because it is impossible or impractical to confirm them. For example, one assumption underlying the current applied scientific research on the proposed Yucca Mountain repository (for high-level radioactive waste and spent fuel) is that safe, geological storage of high-level radwaste is possible in perpetuity.[36] Although evidence for this proposition exists, we cannot confirm it because of the long time period. Therefore we take it for granted; we assume it is true. We can substantiate assumptions and methodological value judgments but not fully confirm them; sometimes we are wrong. Generally, the more plausible methodological value judgments are based on more plausible assumptions. Due to varying plausibility and objectivity, researchers must determine whether logic and evidence tend to substantiate certain assumptions or to call them into question. By using more reliable assumptions and methodological value judgments and by becoming more aware of the value judgments they make, scientists can provide more reliable and hence more objective research conclusions.

Although research can be more or less objective, it can never be per-
fectly objective because methodological value judgments are never
avoidable even in pure science or pure mathematics. Some authors go
even further and argue that because all research serves an *end* (keeping
funding agencies satisfied; helping a professor gain tenure; curing a
disease), it will always be accomplished and evaluated on the basis of
these ends, often on the basis of factors extraneous to the research itself.[37] Ends and values appear in researchers' choices about topics to
address, about who shall participate in the research, and about the likelihood that particular applications will result from the research. One biologist, for example, has illustrated how employment with one laboratory
rather than another imposes certain values (and therefore choices of
research topics) on scientific work. Whether research receives funding
depends on the degree to which it serves particular governmental and
industrial ends, such as chemically intensive (rather than sustainable)
agriculture. Some scientists charge that "the very structure of scientific
research militates against developing products to help the environment,
the poor, and the hungry."[38] Recent reports of the NRC and NAS, however, urge researchers to develop agricultural products that benefit "the
small-scale farmer . . . rural and urban poor in developing countries"
and "sustainable agriculture."[39] To the degree that research tends to be
biased in particular ways, such as for or against sustainable agriculture,
researchers have the duty both to make these biases explicit and to evaluate them. Scientists attain objectivity in research only by ridding themselves of distorted views about the "purity" (that is, freedom from
values) of scientific research, and by discovering the "objective" view
that completely objective research is impossible, even though some research is more objective than others.

Another Principle of Objectivity: Promoting Unbiased Use of Results/Reports

Objectivity, accuracy, and acknowledgment of uncertainties in research
work do not impose merely the negative requirement that research scientists avoid deliberate bias in their own work. Objectivity also requires
that they attempt to meet a positive demand: to present results in such
a way as to avoid their misuse and misapplication by others and to speak
out when others appear to misuse or misinterpret them. An appropriate
prima facie principle in this regard might be: always present research
results in such a way as to avoid their possible misuse and misapplica-

tion, and always speak out against apparent bias in their presentation. The intuitive and rational grounds for the obligation to promote unbiased use of results are to promote objectivity and to protect people and their interests from injury by others.[40] If research scientists did not present research results in such a way so as to avoid their misuse, or if they did not speak out when research results appeared to be misused, then objectivity would suffer, and the interests of innocent people could be hurt. For example, the interests of innocent blacks could be hurt if one did not speak out when biased research results were misused so as to encourage prejudice.

If researchers' failure to speak out about possible misuse or misinterpretation of scientific research has little effect on the needs, interests, and rights of others, then of course researchers have less responsibility to do so. But as Harvey Brooks pointed out: "Scientists can no longer afford to be naive about the political effects of publicly stated scientific opinions."[41] One example of this point is the debate over the supersonic transport (SST). When Jeb Magruder, the director of the U.S. presidential administration's supersonic transport development project, spoke before the U.S. Congress, he claimed that "there is no evidence of likelihood that SST operations will cause significant adverse effects on our atmosphere or our environment." Yet, the presidential review committee for the SST came to the opposite conclusion, and because the committee criticized the SST, the administration attempted (unsuccessfully) to suppress the committee document. Had no scientists spoken up to correct Magruder's misuse of the research on the SST, his misleading statements would have been accepted, and environmental damages would have been ignored.[42] This case illustrates that researchers have a responsibility to "speak out" when misuse of results could harm the public. Moreover, lack of candor and objectivity thwarts the purpose of scientific research. For both these reasons, research scientists must not only avoid deception (the first prima facie principle of research ethics) but also promote unbiased use of research and reports.[43] Following moral philosophers' commitment to universalizability (see earlier parts of this chapter), it is easy to show that scientists' inaction in the face of biased use of research results would have disastrous consequences. Therefore, there must be a prima facie obligation to promote unbiased use of research.

By virtue of membership in a particular profession (geneticists, for example), research scientists have a general ethical responsibility to promote the welfare of the profession, in part because they derive a number of benefits from membership in it. If researchers did not speak out against misapplications of research and results, then their profession generally would suffer, and its members would lose credibility. As Carl Mitcham points out in chapter nine, engineering design researchers gained credibility in part because they ''spoke out'' in cases like that of the Bay Area Rapid Transit. This suggests additional reasons for subscribing to the second prima facie ethical principle, promoting unbiased use of research. If researchers have a responsibility to protect the profession from misrepresentation, they should avoid hasty, unconfirmed, or exaggerated statements and point out when others fall victim to them. They should refrain from intemperate or sensational modes of speech, and they should point out these biases when they occur.[44] The second ethical principle also enjoins researchers not to err through incompleteness (because omission of data can lead to misinterpreted and misused results) and to point out incompleteness or bias in the work of others.[45] Scientific researchers can follow the second prima facie principle and ''speak out'' about bias or incompleteness in research when they serve as peer reviewers of the work of others. Of course, peer reviewing can either help or harm research; the norm for good peer reviewing is the norm for objectivity. Research scientists do have the duty to be objective and to point out flaws in their own and in others' work. However, such a duty can be carried too far. For example, the Church was not the primary enemy of Galileo and his heliocentric views. Rather, his fellow professionals, academics, and researchers put up the most resistance to his new ideas. They refused to look through the telescope, ridiculed Galileo, and invoked the powers of the Inquisition against him. The educated public supported Galileo, but his fellow researchers did not.[46] To the degree that scientific researchers do not promote objectivity in the uses and interpretations of others' work, through activities like peer reviewing, they become culpable in part for research biases. As one biology editor put it, researchers who do not promote objectivity by tough reviewing of professional work, for example, allow themselves to become ''marks,'' ''dupes,'' ''patsies,'' ''accessories,'' ''weasels,'' or ''flatfoots.''[47] As ''marks'' (intended victims of swindles), ''dupes'' (stupid birds), ''patsies'' (persons easily fooled), ''accessories'' (to misdeeds), and so on, researchers could also contribute to greater objectivity in their professions by advocating a number of reforms. Some of these reforms include (1) setting up procedures for all journals to deal with fraud, (2) requiring researchers to deposit their raw data in a special archive to which other researchers would have access, and (3) conducting on-site audits of research data collected in various projects.[48] By helping to improve standards of peer review, researchers could thus enhance the objectivity of the uses and interpretations of their work and that of other professionals.[49] They could also help to eliminate the vested interests and biases that often accompany the processes and products of research—the biases briefly surveyed in chapters one and two.

Despite the merits of various ways, like peer review, to improve the objectivity of research, both the first and second prima facie responsibilities (to perform unbiased research and to promote unbiased use of research results) are open to at least two objections: (1) The principles suggest that we should submit research to a political test, because researchers have greater responsibility to avoid bias insofar as the research and results have greater potential to affect the public welfare; and (2) The two prima facie principles also suggest, contrary to many philosophers' views, the existence of an "ethics of belief." Let us consider each of these objections in turn to see why they do not jeopardize the status of the second prima facie principle. First, does requiring research scientists to promote unbiased use of research results amount to submitting research to a political test, because the degree of this responsibility relates directly to the potential effect of the biased results on the public welfare?

Epistemic Objectivity and Ethical Objectivity

The second principle of objectivity does not amount to submitting research to a political test because research, as such, is not submitted to the test. The principle affirms that one has responsibilities to promote recognition of research bias and misuse to the degree that such bias or misuse puts others at risk. Hence we submit bias and misuse, not scientific research, to a political test. Moreover, we submit the applications of research, not research itself. The second principle also suggests that scientific researchers should demand a higher standard of certainty and accuracy for conclusions with potentially dangerous applications. This double standard makes sense because not all applications of research carry the same level of risk to the public. Because the goals of applying scientific research are political and ethical, as well as epistemological, the use of a political test for the applications of scientific research makes sense.

Scientists' duties to promote unbiased use of research results relate directly to the risk of public harm, for the same reasons that we constrain the use of dangerous technologies. Just as a justifiable double standard exists (based on the threat to the public welfare) for speaking out against problematic scientific research, so also there is a justifiable double standard (based on the threat to the public welfare) for criticizing dangerous technologies. In both cases, the varying gravity of the threat creates the double standard. This is why risk assessors, for example, typically have a double standard for assessing hazardous technologies, e.g., liquefied natural gas or nuclear power. Those that pose a greater threat to society must have greater counterbalancing benefits and meet higher standards of scientific accuracy and predictability in order to be judged acceptable.[50] Admittedly, it may not be reasonable to have a political test for "pure research." However, to the degree that scientific research applies (that is, to the degree that its consequences affect public welfare), research ought to pass a "political" test. Moreover, to deny the need for a political test for the applications of scientific research would be to disregard the difference between research results with significant, as opposed to minimal, consequences for public harm. Hence the second prima facie principle does not appear susceptible to criticism on the grounds that it would erroneously sanction submitting science to a political test.

Because researchers' responsibilities to objectivity—to perform and to promote unbiased research—depend in part on the degree to which the research is applied and its potential for harmful consequences, it makes sense to distinguish epistemic and ethical objectivity. Epistemic objectivity appears close to what Jacques Monod described as the most basic ethical principle to guide researchers. *Epistemic objectivity* addresses the objectivity of our *beliefs*. It requires us to assess *hypotheses* and their practical or scientific *consequences* with no deliberate bias or misinterpretation. *Ethical objectivity* addresses the objectivity of our researchers' *actions*. It requires more than merely avoiding deliberate bias or misinterpretation. Rather, ethical objectivity requires us to take into account our obligations to the greater good when we assess the ethical desirability of acting on our belief in a particular hypothesis or its consequences. For example, we might follow *epistemic objectivity* and claim that a hypothesis (such as "this biotechnological experiment will not harm humans") was both probable and likely to lead to no costly or impractical consequences. Nevertheless, we might decide, following a principle of *ethical objectivity*, not to act on our belief in the probability or likelihood associated with the hypothesis. We might conclude that objective examination of the hypothesis also requires us to consider the public's rights to protection and to laws requiring disclosure of a potentially harmful experiment before it is undertaken. In cases of applied research that involve duties to others potentially affected by the research, objectivity requires not merely unbiased episte-mic assessment of belief, but also unbiased ethical evaluation of *action* premised on that belief. Thus at least two different accounts of objectiv-ity—one directed against epistemic bias and the other against ethical bias—relate to the performance of scientific research. Epistemic objec-tivity is more appropriate to less applied research; more applied re-search, which has potentially serious public consequences and applica-tions, requires both epistemic and ethical objectivity.

The Ethics of Belief and the Second Principle of Research Ethics

Someone might question our dual notion of objectivity because it sanc-tions an "ethics of belief." Are we *ethically* responsible for our beliefs, reasoning, and research? The most famous proponent of an ethics of belief, W. K. Clifford, argued that people have an ethical obligation to seek the truth.[51] Because the second prima facie ethical principle postu-lates a responsibility to promote unbiased interpretation and use of re-search results, then presumably it too follows an ethics of belief, an instance of the argument that ethics binds one both to recognize bias and misinterpretation and to promote unbiased use of results.

One of the most prominent objections to the ethics of belief is that it presupposes that belief is under voluntary control, that we can "de-cide" to recognize bias or misinterpretation, or that we can choose to be more or less objective. Only if we can voluntarily control such recog-nition and therefore belief, according to the objector, can we subject purely cognitive decisionmaking to ethical appraisal. Because strong grounds support the argument that belief (e.g., in whether research re-sults exhibit bias) is not voluntary and that failure to believe something often is not culpable, therefore (goes the objection) strong grounds sup-port the claim that belief is not subject to ethical appraisal. For example, one might argue that researchers' actions, beliefs, and results either appear biased or not, and that one cannot voluntarily "recognize" or decide whether they actually involve bias. And if so, then one cannot have a moral responsibility to promote unbiased use of research results. Ethics cannot bind one to perform actions not under one's voluntary control. William Alston accepts this line of reasoning, arguing that rec-ognition and belief are not subject to moral appraisal.[52] He appears to believe that we cannot decide to be more or less objective.

Alston errs, however, in applying this argument to the case of research knowledge, because all scientific research situations are (to some degree) empirically underdetermined. All scientific research contains some degree of incompleteness and therefore is subject to some interpretation. Therefore no uninterpreted facts of research exist, and all research is value laden.[53] Thus, accepting particular interpretations, values, and results is in part a matter of choice. In part, we can choose whether or not to accept a particular interpretation, for example, that a particular project appears racially or sexually biased. We can choose whether or not to be explicit about a racist interpretation, for example, being only one possible interpretation, and we can choose whether or not to be explicit regarding the grounds for one interpretation rather than another. If such acts are in part matters of choice, then the acceptance of an interpretation or value judgment is in part a matter of voluntary control and therefore becomes subject to ethical appraisal. Hence, contrary to Alston and others,[54] one may argue that there is an ethics of belief, at least in the sense that researchers have an ethical obligation to question the value-laden interpretations of alleged facts that they and others use. They have an obligation to remain both open-minded and critical.[55] An ethics of belief in this sense might require research scientists to appraise their professional opinions and judgments.[56] Oliver Cromwell's famous plea, already mentioned, to the assembly of the Church of Scotland provides a model: ''I beseech you . . . think it possible you may be mistaken.'' Following an ethics of belief and questioning one's evaluative judgments and interpretations (e.g., as to whether given evidence actually supports a particular research hypothesis) is one way to promote unbiased use of research results, as required by the second prima facie principle. As Carl Cranor argues in chapter ten, such objectivity requires a commitment both to evidentiary ideals and to moral ideals, both to epistemic objectivity and to ethical objectivity.

4

Basic Principles: Promoting the Public Good

Massachusetts law currently provides for fines and imprisonment for persons convicted of research fraud,[1] and U.S. Representative John Conyers has suggested a similar law at the federal level.[2] While famous cases of research fraud—such as painting ''tumor'' spots on laboratory mice with ''Magic Marker''—have drawn publicity, an equally serious ethical question is the degree to which scientific research has been subverted to serve ends other than the public good. An apt symbol of this subversion is a recent cartoon in the *Chicago Tribune* that shows a serpent slithering into a chemical laboratory.[3]

Both of the prima facie ethical principles discussed in the last chapter focus on researchers' duties to remain as objective as possible, to avoid bias, and to promote the unbiased use of research and results. These principles form the core of professional responsibility as determined both by major associations of scientists, such as the AAAS and the ESA, and by individual researchers like Monod and Pasteur. Even unbiased presentation of research results, however, often can leave much unsaid, much uncertain, and much implied. Because it does, research results sometimes can be misused or misapplied. For example, creationists seeking to support their position have misused Stephen Jay Gould's remarks about problems with the theory of evolution. Because of the potential for misuse and misinterpretation of research results, particularly in ways that could harm the public interest, research scientists also have a responsibility to society, to use their findings in ways that serve the public good. In other words, scientific researchers have a responsibility to society as well as to objectivity. But what are these responsibilities to society? Many of them can be determined by examining professionals' responsibilities to promote the values of a liberal society, as we discussed in the last chapter.

Justification for the Third Principle: Promoting the Public Good

The AAAS Committee on Scientific Freedom and Responsibility articulates research scientists' most basic responsibility to society. The Committee claims that ''members of the scientific community have a basic right and responsibility . . . to apply it [knowledge] to the best of their ability to the improvement of the quality of life for all present and future inhabitants of the earth.''[4] Affirming researchers' responsibilities to society often becomes difficult, however, because these obligations are collective; we cannot assign the ultimate moral responsibility to a single researcher because an individual person is usually not causally responsible for a particular research conclusion or for the effects of applying specific research results. As the number of people and processes involved in the production of an outcome increases, the relative causal contribution—and therefore the relative ethical responsibility—of each agent lessens.[5] Hence, problems arise in evaluating the level of each researcher's ''share'' of collective responsibility. It is difficult to define the set whose member acts are performed by agents responsible for the total effects of the research. Moreover, with respect to responsibility for complicated causal systems, negative causation counts as much as positive causation. As the Birmingham smallpox case shows (see the previous chapter), people bear as much responsibility for what they do not do to prevent a research-related accident as for what they do.[6] Despite such factors that complicate the notion of collective responsibility, the degree of research scientists' responsibility to society (for particular outcomes or effects) is inversely proportional to the degree to which other researchers also have collective and causal responsibility for a particular outcome. Such degrees of responsibility vary; determining the proper levels requires analysis on a case-by-case basis.[7]

Perhaps the primary reason for researchers' duties to society is citizens' related right to free informed consent (see chapters one and two) to decisions affecting their welfare, including decisions about scientific research. To help ensure citizens' ability to exercise this consent, we must specify responsibilities of researchers to society and charge professional organizations with improving their members' communication with the public.[8] The AAAS Committee on Scientific Freedom and Responsibility, for example, appears to have followed a similar line of reasoning. The committee concluded that:

> Since all beings have a basic right to participate in the making of decisions affecting them or to have appropriate proxies represent their interests, scientific workers have a special responsibility to take all steps possible to assure that potentially affected parties (or their proxies) have all information necessary to make fully informed decisions.[9]

To understand why helping to ensure citizens' free informed consent requires that researchers have responsibilities to society, consider what would happen if they had no such duties. Researchers without the responsibility to provide the public with information relevant to the common good would open the door to political repression. If scientific researchers did not communicate their findings to the people at large, some political leaders might claim whatever they wished about research matters relevant to public welfare. This is exactly what the SST example (in the previous chapter) illustrated.[10]

Research scientists also have duties to the public and its interests because they, as professionals with economic, political, and intellectual power, control much of what happens in society.[11] Their special knowledge and the dependence of society on them are two of the main sources of their power. Given our highly sophisticated and technocratic society, and given researchers' special knowledge of "the multiple and complex consequences of the actions that we take," therefore "the responsibility of scientists [and researchers] is obviously much greater than that of nonscientists [and nonresearchers]."[12] Carl Cranor's discussion of public health research (chapter 10) shows that the prevention of serious public harm depends, in part, upon scientists' special knowledge and responsibilities. Perhaps the most important source of research scientists' power and control arises because, as professionals, they exercise a monopoly over the services they provide. Because of this monopoly (as we mentioned earlier in chapter two), the pressures of a competitive marketplace cannot function to determine how they use their power. Research scientists, in particular, have special knowledge, power, and ability that lends them a degree of immunity from being discovered to be behaving in inappropriate ways. As the Scientific Research Society, Sigma Xi, put it:

> Because the pathways that we pursue as research scientists are infinite and unfrequented, we cannot police them as we protect our streets and personal

property. We depend on those other travellers—other research scientists whose work happens to take them along such lonely byways of knowledge—to assist in ensuring that the research environment is a safe one.[13]

Moreover, as Camenisch points out, the monopoly researchers hold over their provision of services makes them accountable not only when they use their power in harmful ways, but also when they fail to use it properly or with adequate energy and perseverance. In other words, the monopoly "enlarges the significance of sins of omission."[14] Researchers working for chemical industries such as Dow and Dupont engaged in questionable practices when, after doing extensive medical and genetic tests on workers, they refused workers' requests for personal medical information. Instead, employers have used the tests on workers to avoid liability, to avoid hiring and retaining workers who could present a liability threat, and to protect company interests. Because of researchers' monopoly on such information and because of workers' right to know how they are at risk, one may argue that the results of genetic and medical screenings should not be withheld from hundreds of thousands of workers, as they are now.[15] As Tom Beauchamp put it:

> It is unacceptable to fail to communicate the results of a study containing material vital to the health and welfare of the public because results turned out differently than expected or because of some arrangement with a funding source that requires secrecy or confidentiality of the data. Nor is it acceptable to terminate a study prematurely because the results appear to be heading in an unexpected direction, particularly when the unexpected direction is politically inexpedient to either an investigator, an institution, or a funding source . . . Researchers and institutional frameworks should likewise carefully avoid being placed in a situation in which their results might be suppressed or inappropriately edited by either internal or external influences.[16]

Former Yale University President Giammatti echoed this theme when he said that scientific researchers have a duty to ensure that patentable solutions to societal problems and that knowledge with a "potential benefit to our society at large will reach the public in a timely and useful fashion."[17] Even in cases in which professionals might be thought to have a duty to their clients (as in psychiatrists' duties to their patients), the courts have consistently concluded that client confidentiality ends where possible public harm begins. Even if a patient does not physically threaten other people, but either the physician or the patient is suspected of insurance fraud, for example, confidentiality can be violated in the name of the public interest. Hence strong reasons support the argument that, for research scientists, especially in more applied areas, the public good outweighs client privacy in cases of serious conflicts.[18]

Researchers likewise have great responsibilities to the public, not only because they have the knowledge requisite to help inform society about their research, but also because their efforts to educate often succeed. They have a responsibility through ability.[19] As Von Hippel and Primack point out, ''outsider'' scientists have been very effective in informing the public about the negative aspects of certain research.[20] ''Outsider researchers'' representing the Ecological Society of America (ESA) have been instrumental, for example, in warning the public about the possible dangers of genetically engineered microorganisms and about the laxness of proposed federal regulations regarding biotechnology.[21] Research scientists might also effectively point out racist or sexist bias in certain research methods or interpretations. Indeed, the list of research-related sexist and racist biases Helen Longino presents in chapter eight suggests that scientists could have been more effective in this area.

Responding to the notion that researchers have special obligations to society due to their ability to ''make a difference,'' Ladenson objects that being well-placed to harm or benefit others does not mean that one has special responsibilities. Rather, he claims, the supposition that ability generates such responsibilities is based on the erroneous ''failure to distinguish between causing evil, on the one hand, and preventing evil or promoting good, on the other.'' Hence, says Ladenson, researchers such as scientists and engineers have no special duties simply because they are scientists or engineers. They are primarily responsible for avoiding causing evil.[22] A number of considerations rebut Ladenson's argument. For one thing, if those with special abilities did not have special responsibilities to promote the public good, then serious harms would be much more likely to occur because the very group (researchers) able to prevent the harm would not be responsible for doing so. Moreover, as Ross, Frankena, Singer, and others have argued, one has a duty to accomplish good if it can be done at no great cost or sacrifice. They argue for a general obligation to beneficence.[23] Such an ethical obligation exists, at least in part, because all moral duties, including justice, presuppose it.[24] Even the courts have affirmed surprisingly wide obligations for scientists and other research professionals. A pharmacist, for example, may be liable to a patient for negligence in filling a prescription, even if the pharmacist correctly fills the prescription as written by the prescribing physician. *Riff v. Morgan Pharmacy* established that every professional has "a duty to be, to a limited extent, his brother's keeper."[25]

Another reason that scientific researchers have special responsibilities to enhance societal welfare is that the public needs their efforts. Researchers' efforts are needed, for example, in the area of sustainable agriculture because of the decline of productivity of soil and water systems in high-population-growth regions such as Asia, Africa, and Latin America. Roughly 40,000 infants die each day in the Third World because of nutritional stress. If we are to feed 5 billion people, a recent NRC/NAS report argues, scientific researchers must have a "change in vision." They must serve the public interest through sustainable agricultural research that recognizes the values of biodiversity, equitable distribution of agrosystem products, the importance of indigenous agricultural knowledge, and ecological welfare.[26] While it may seem unusual for an NRC/NAS committee to affirm researchers' duties to achieve ethical goals, one must recognize that their affirmation implicitly affirms a major point of the last chapter: that scientists ought to serve ethical, as well as epistemic, objectivity. In situations where researchers' tools, support, and materials are viewed as "public resources," it is more important for ethical goals and public needs to drive research. For example, medical research, especially in areas such as organ transplants, is not a commodity but rather a "public resource" that should be distributed according to ethical criteria and public need.[27] Similar arguments suggest that scientific research may be, in part, a public resource.

Research scientists also have special responsibilities to enhance societal welfare because of the powerful vested interests (in research-related disputes) that often block the public interest. As the AAAS put it, "the relative power of contending parties [in research-related disputes] is often grossly unequal; a powerful government agency, with strong political and industrial backing, can often prevail in its purposes."[28] The power of vested interests in research-related conflicts is especially evident in the case of pesticides. For example, one reason that the largely accurate work of Rachel Carson was so violently attacked was that many of the leading scientists of the day had financial ties to the pesticide industry. As Edsall notes:

> Many if not most of them had financial and career ties to the use of pesticides and to the industries that produced them. The Committees of the National Academy of Sciences that dealt with these matters in those days tended to be dominated by people who were biased in this way.[29]

Moreover, if recent studies are correct, then researchers' financial ties to certain industries often remain a problem, as we suggested in chapters one and two. A 1988 report indicated that, merely by reading the names of titles, authors, and financial supporters of certain scholarship, it was possible to predict the conclusions in 81 percent of the scientific investigations.[30] This finding suggests that scientists often have special responsibilities to protect public welfare, in part because of powerful vested interests.

Researchers likewise need to protect society because, as chapter two illustrated, professional ethical codes frequently warn against public criticism of colleagues, and journal editors often do not monitor research papers to ensure that the researchers follow ethical practices in their work.[31] Hence peer control of abuses in research, although necessary for ethical behavior, often is not sufficient.[32] And if it is not, then individual research scientists ought no longer remain apart from the conflicts of our time. Moreover, because professionals such as scientists and engineers are under pressure from their clients to hold down costs of investigations, to meet demands of stockholders or customers, and to exist within a competitive market, concern for the public's well being is likely to have a low priority. As Nicholas Steneck writes, "broader ethical questions either will not be asked or they will be asked and answered by persons who are not trained to consider them."[33] For all these reasons, society requires the help of researchers, especially scientists, to meet its needs. Social scientists who have studied the evolution of codes of professional ethics have pointed out that the principal effect of the early codes was to bar researchers from serving the public interest. This is understandable, in part because professional societies often began as interest groups defending the welfare of their members. As Carl Mitcham points out in chapter nine, several of the early codes of professional ethics provided that "technical discussions and criticism of engineering subjects should not be conducted in the public press, but before engineering societies, or in the technical press."[34] When one official, Morris Cooke, of the American Society of Mechanical Engineers (ASME), for example, wanted the ASME to have a meeting on air pollution in 1908, it was vetoed; Cooke proved correct in arguing that consulting and research engineers were getting rich by defending the utility industry. Yet, the ASME leadership argued that Cooke violated the ASME code of ethics; "all professional codes of ethics limit criticism by colleagues."[35] Obviously, however, Cooke's actions were defensible. His case and others suggest that it may be unrealistic to expect professional societies, rather than individuals themselves, to take the lead in defending the interests of the public and in criticizing researchers whose actions do not further the public interest.[36]

Researchers also have special responsibilities to society because research is a public good, and society confers on researchers whatever ownership of their research and data they have; as one biology editor noted: ''the principle that the public is entitled to every man's evidence was enunciated by the Supreme Court more than 50 years ago.''[37] Society also has ultimate ownership of research because—as we argued in chapter two—researchers' abilities have been created and enhanced in part through societal interdependences and professional contracts. In other words, their abilities exist and can be put to use, at least in part, because of societal opportunities and controls. Because researchers (including professionals such as historians, medical doctors, and lawyers) are not wholly self-made persons, their obligations are not completely self-generated. Researchers depend upon society, and society relies upon researchers. Because of this interdependence, research scientists have a responsibility to society through complicity.[38] Researchers not only use powerful tools and machines developed in part through societal resources, but they often live on grants and contracts that come either through taxpayer support or through industrial networks that could not exist without societal interdependence. Because they benefit from their interdependence and interaction with the rest of society, researchers owe the public something in return, something more than merely refraining from wrongdoing.

Researchers' societal responsibilities stem from society's investment in, and licensing control over, them. One of the greatest societal investments in researchers is education. Virtually no student, even in a private school, ever pays the full cost of education; taxes or donations usually supplement that cost. Because of this societal investment in professional education, as well as taxpayers' funding the salaries of many researchers, researchers clearly owe society something in return.[39] As Camenisch points out, the cost to society of preparing the researcher or of sustaining professional practice is significant; each scientific researcher represents a considerable investment by the society, an investment not received by other occupational groups.[40] Such investment activities of the society constitute unearned gifts given to the researcher; the acceptance of the gifts places the recipient under a responsibility to the donor, hence under some responsibility to society. Chiefly, the recipient must use the benefits in a manner consistent with society's intentions in giving them.[41] The public also controls the licensure of many professionals, who then owe a debt to society.[42] Even in cases where no license is involved, as with researchers in arts and sciences, their advanced degrees serve a similar purpose and the public has some control over their award.

Yet another foundation for researchers' responsibilities to society lies with professional codes of ethics, especially those for scientists, stipulating such responsibilities. Therefore, apart from whether such codes are complete or correct, professionals either explicitly or implicitly agree to adhere to the provisions of the code. Commenting on this responsibility, the AAAS Committee on Scientific Freedom and Responsibility emphasizes the "added responsibility of members of the scientific community, individually and through their formal organizations, to speak out."[43] The responsibility of individual scientists and their professional organizations to speak out (on behalf of the public or third parties) was quite apparent, for example, when three Bay Area Rapid Transit (BART) research design engineers were fired as a result of their protesting lax safety standards on the BART system. After they were fired, the Institute of Electrical and Electronics Engineers (IEEE) hired attorneys who submitted briefs when the engineers sued BART. The IEEE, through the briefs, explicitly stated that:

> the Court should rule that an engineer is obligated to protect the public safety, that every contract of employment of an engineer contains within it an implied term to the effect that such engineer will protect the public safety, and that a discharge of an engineer solely or in substantial part because he acted to protect the public safety is a breach of such implied term. . . .[44]

The brief pointed out that, in other cases, the courts have noted that all workers, including all researchers, are bound to obey the rule "that no citizen can lawfully do that which has a tendency to be injurious to the public or against the public order," even when his employers or clients direct him to do so.[45] Summarizing these court cases, the brief on the BART problem explicitly stated that "the engineer has an overriding duty to protect the public,"[46] and that all the codes for all engineers recognize this as the overriding duty.[47]

As the AAAS affirmed, scientific researchers have a responsibility to improve the quality of life for present and future inhabitants of the earth, and at least six different grounds justify this responsibility: society's rights to informed consent, researchers' ability to "make a difference," societal needs, researchers' interdependence with society, public investment in research, and researchers' (especially scientists') codes of professional ethics. We have gone to some length attempting to justify researchers' responsibilities to society (third parties), both because these responsibilities have so often been ignored in the past and because they are less obvious than are responsibilities to employers, for example, with which they often conflict.

Promoting the Public Good: Disseminating Research Results and Avoiding Paternalism

The question of researchers' responsibilities to society, however, raises the whole issue of the precise nature of these responsibilities. What are scientists' specific duties and obligations? Although there are many such duties, at least two seem necessary conditions for meeting their responsibilities to society already outlined earlier. One such duty is to avoid paternalistic treatment of the public and therefore to disseminate research results to interested laypersons as well as to professionals. Another duty is to engage in whistleblowing whenever the situation warrants it. These duties are important because they provide essential information, information without which the public is unlikely to exercise free informed consent regarding research-related decisions that affect their interests. Let's examine each of these duties in turn.

Researchers have a duty to disseminate their results, as the AAAS notes,[48] because research findings are a product of social collaboration and therefore belong to the community as a whole and not to any particular individual. Hence secrecy is the antithesis of this norm.[49] Admittedly, however, avoiding secrecy does not mean that researchers have the obligation to disseminate research results prior to their being peer reviewed, either internally by one's colleagues or by a journal. In the ecological controversy between Kangas and Noss during 1986–88, for example, peer reviewing might have avoided the subsequent conflict over the environmental-policy implications of using species-area curves to predict extinctions caused by development. If Kangas's arguments were scientifically unsound, as other ecologists claimed,[50] and if peer reviewing revealed their deficiencies to Kangas, then he might never have presented them. In that case, he would have avoided arguing that much land development does not cause species extinctions. And if Kangas had withheld his questionable evidence, then the whole ethics and public-policy controversy surrounding his claims might never have arisen. In other words, the Kangas case illustrates that, with appropriate peer reviewing, ethically and environmentally problematic results sometimes can be refuted before they do any damage. This suggests that, in many cases, asking how to deal with uncertain or harmful research results might be premature, especially if there has been no extensive effort to evaluate them. Hence scientists have no general obligation to disseminate research that has not withstood an initial evaluation by scientific peers. Scientists' duties to their employers to maintain confidentiality may also necessitate limiting dissemination of scientific research.[51] Whenever a conflict occurs between a client's desire for secrecy and the public's right to know, research scientists ought to engage in ethical analysis (see chapter five). The spotted-owl controversy revealed that even governmental clients disagree about what best benefits the public interest.[52] Hence, such complicated ethical analysis depends on the particulars of the situation.

Not all researchers recognize a responsibility to be open and to release their appropriately reviewed findings to the public. Jacques Monod, for example, as was already mentioned, spoke of objectivity as the only duty of scientists.[53] If objectivity were researchers' only duty, however, then paternalistic secrecy toward the public might be justifiable. (Paternalistic conduct involves a rationale based on doing something to or on behalf of another person, for that person's well-being.[54]) The AAAS gives two basic reasons that researchers must neither behave paternalistically toward the lay public nor fail to release information to society. One reason is that research scientists have no right to make decisions that affect the welfare of others. The second reason is that they are often biased.[55] Admittedly, curtailing paternalism would depose many research scientists from the thrones built by expertise. It would dispel part of their mystique. It might also limit their ability to determine their own compensation.[56] More important, paternalism is often justified on the grounds that professionals and researchers have superior knowledge, that clients or members of the public lack the ability to give free informed consent to a complex proposal, and that clients or members of the public will later agree that professionals' decisions, on their behalf, were correct.

In spite of these arguments favoring paternalism, there are at least four reasons that openness and researchers' duties to the public require them not to behave paternalistically in decisions having public consequences. *First,* people rarely are so incapacitated that they need others to make decisions for them.[57] The public does need information and education to enable them to make reasonable decisions. And scientific researchers and other professionals must remain sources of this information and education, rather than the ultimate decisionmakers themselves. Moreover, it does not seem reasonable to claim that a majority of members of society (all the non-experts) are incapacitated, and hence need researchers to behave paternalistically toward them. If one did make this claim, it would be difficult to justify the fact that non-experts, government officials and representatives, make policy decisions all the time.

Second, researchers' superior knowledge and skills do not justify paternalism on their part; research-related policy decisions (with consequences for the public interest) are not typically choices about the best scientific or technical means to given ends. Rather, as many authors have noted, policy decisions require balancing technical or professional considerations with other concerns, e.g., health, economic welfare, freedom, and consent. They usually concern ethics and public values. Because researchers, especially scientists, have no special training in such value choices, they have few grounds for behaving paternalistically toward the public or their clients. Moreover, even if they have had such training, they are unlikely to know what is best for given clients or the public.[58]

Third, because of the economic notion of consumer sovereignty, it is arguable that clients and the public have the right to make their own choices, including their own mistakes (so long as the mistakes do not jeopardize the life or liberty of other human beings). This is because clients directly pay for the research and professional expertise they obtain and because society indirectly (through monies for education, grants, and contracts) funds the work of such professionals. Scientists might object that in some cases (such as tropical deforestation or commercial nuclear accidents) public decisionmaking could have catastrophic consequences and that therefore scientists and other experts, alone, ought to make decisions about research-related policy. Such an objection, however, ignores the fact that whenever imminent danger is used as a rationale for limiting or forgoing democratic control, abuses typically occur. Virtually any loss of democratic control could be justified if the alleged catastrophe being averted were great enough. Yet imminent and catastrophic events rarely occur. Often informed people disagree, either about the magnitude or the immediacy of the alleged problem. This disagreement, as well as the dangerous precedent set by forgoing democratic control in serious situations, means that ethically questionable consequences will likely occur if researchers behave in paternalistic ways.

Just as the war power and national security have been used inappropriately to justify paternalistic and anti-democratic decisionmaking, it is conceivable that researchers' appeals to environmental catastrophe, for example, could also be used for unethical and anti-democratic purposes. Admittedly, the war power is a clear instance in which national security ought to coopt democratic decisionmaking, at least in part. Nevertheless, appeals to national security and the war power have been misused in the past. The war power has been used in peacetime, for example, to push nuclear power plants on states that did not want them. Also, in *Ashwander v. Tennessee Valley Authority*, the Supreme Court allowed the construction of a dam and electrical generating facility on the basis of the war power. The court claimed that the construction was necessary to "national security," even though it took place during peacetime. The Ashwander example illustrates that researchers or those with vested interests can define "national security" in an arbitrary way, so as to serve vested interests. Likewise they can define "environmental catastrophe" in an arbitrary way, also to serve vested interests. Such spurious definitions might lead to using erroneous claims of "national security" or "environmental catastrophe" to decrease public control of research having public consequences. Indeed, once "environmental catastrophe" were seen as justifying loss of democratic control of environment-related research, various burdens might be imposed on unwilling communities, all in the name of expert research and decisionmaking.[59] This suggests that there are good grounds for arguing that researchers may not be justified in behaving paternalistically toward the public. As Thomas Jefferson warned, "I know of no safe depositor of the ultimate powers of the society but the people themselves; and if we think them not enlightened enough to exercise their control with a wholesome discretion, the remedy is not to take it from them, but to inform their discretion."[60]

Fourth, scientific researchers working in applied areas also appear to have an obligation not to behave paternalistically (and instead to disseminate their results to the public) for some of the same reasons (already discussed) that they have responsibilities to society in the first place. For one thing, research scientists' informing the public about matters relevant to its interests often is necessary in order for members of society to give free informed consent to research-related public actions. The seventh duty mentioned by the AAAS Committee on Scientific Freedom and Responsibility explicitly states that scientists have the duty "to refuse to work on projects where individuals potentially at risk (or their appropriate proxies), as a result of participation in the project, have not given free and fully informed consent."[61] One way of insuring free informed consent is for researchers to provide information to the public.[62] When Richard Garwin testified about the SST at a congressional hearing, for example, he emphasized that the public has a right to free informed consent to research-related policies that affect it: "Since there are so few people familiar with these programs, it is important for me to give to Congress, as well as the administration, the benefit of my experience."[63] Likewise, Kenneth Pitzer, Chair of a Presidential Committee to investigate the safety of underground nuclear testing, wrote:

> the panel believes that the public should not be asked to accept risks resulting from purely internal governmental decisions if, without endangering national security, the information can be made public and decisions can be reached after public discussions.[64]

Researchers who keep information from the public ignore the fact that the ultimate responsibility in a democracy resides with individual citizens, and that denying them information pertinent to their own health and welfare effectively deprives them of the rights of citizenship. The writers of our constitution understood this very well. James Madison said:

> Knowledge will forever govern ignorance. And a people who mean to be their own governors must arm themselves with the power knowledge gives. A popular government without popular information or the means of acquiring it is but the prologue to a farce or tragedy, or perhaps both.[65]

Likewise, as Albert Einstein said: "The right to search for truth implies also a duty; one must not conceal any part of what one has recognized to be true."[66]

Apart from the ethical and political arguments for openness, epistemological concerns require keeping the research community open and disseminating policy-relevant research results to the public. One rationale for continuing the openness of dissemination is that professionals have traditionally argued that knowledge should be pursued wherever it leads.[67] If it makes sense to pursue knowledge wherever it leads, then it is arguable that such knowledge ought to be available to the public. Moreover, because knowledge is not a closed system and because it has virtually no absolutes, it is important for it to continue developing through criticism and experiment. This development cannot happen, however, without openness. Even when good grounds for secrecy exist (e.g., national security or trade secrets), knowledge itself is nevertheless hurt. (Of course, as we pointed out earlier, researchers do not have an obligation to be open about their results prior to their being peer reviewed or otherwise disinterestedly checked for errors.[68]) The case of J. J. Waterston, who did original work on the kinetic theory of gases, illustrates how secrecy hurts the growth of knowledge. Waterston submitted a major paper to the Royal Society in 1845, which the group rejected as "nothing but nonsense." Disheartened, Waterston abandoned his research altogether. Nearly 50 years later Lord Rayleigh found Waterston's manuscript in the files of the Royal Society and had it published. Unfortunately, it was too late; Clerk Maxwell, who knew nothing of Waterston's work, independently developed the theory much further, and along somewhat different lines.[69] Had other scientists publicized Waterston's work, after its secret and erroneous rejection, English science could have developed more rapidly and differently than it did, and a great scientist would not have given up his life's work as a result of unfair treatment. Just as secrecy prevented the acceptance of Waterston's work, so also secrecy could prevent the acceptance of important advances in other areas of knowledge.

Researchers' duties to disseminate policy-related results to the public also exist because society needs such information and has a right to it, because taxpayer and consumer monies directly or indirectly fund much research. Moreover, sometimes research results, as in the SST case cited earlier, are not disseminated by appropriate bodies, including government agencies. For example, the United States commissioned the Brookhaven Report (WASH-740) in the 1950s to establish that commercial nuclear power was safe and economical. When the experts concluded that property damage alone, in the event of a nuclear accident, could wipe out an area the size of Pennsylvania and could cost as much as $17 billion—apart from the 45,000 immediate deaths and the 100,000 later deaths, injuries, and cancers—those who commissioned the taxpayer-funded report suppressed it, lest its conclusions frighten the public about commercial nuclear fission. The first commercial reactors went on-line shortly after the Brookhaven Report was completed and then suppressed. Despite the suppression of the report, however, the government (the taxpayers) nevertheless underwrote insurance for the nuclear industry both because private insurers refused to do so (at a cost-effective rate) and because utilities feared bankruptcy in the event of a catastrophic reactor accident. The Brookhaven Report was not released until nearly 20 years later, as a result of the Freedom of Information Act; had the report not been suppressed, very likely the public would not have given its alleged consent to the development of commercial nuclear power.[70]

Cases of government suppression of information, like that of WASH-740, show that citizens often do not exercise free and informed consent to various risks affecting them. They frequently are deprived of knowledge their own tax dollars generate, because vested interests typically have the power to suppress data. An AAAS report concluded:

> We hold that, with rare exceptions, data representing a real advance in fundamental science should never be kept secret, except in a major war situation, such as the early stages of the development of the atomic bomb in World War II. Even in such cases, scientific information should remain classified only for a limited and specified time; it should then be released automatically, unless a strong and specific case can be made for withholding a particular piece of information for a further limited period of time.[71]

In other words, the burden of proof is on the person who wants to limit access to information or to control secrecy.

Promoting the Public Good: Whistleblowing

But if research scientists have a duty to disseminate important policy-relevant results to the public, what happens when employers or others with a vested interest either fail to do so or prevent researchers from doing so? In some cases, scientists have a duty to engage in whistleblowing, a duty necessary to meet the requirements of openness and public dissemination of research results. As the authors of a Sigma Xi (the Scientific Research Society) report put it: whistleblowing is "a necessary part of maintaining the integrity of scientific research."[72] Some researchers even claim that, in order to fulfill their "social contract" and to avoid having unqualified persons making research-related decisions,[73] they must engage in whistleblowing and take a political role in areas related to their research expertise. In fact, the AAAS Committee report, "Principles of Scientific Freedom and Responsibility," lists this as a sixth duty: "to speak out where significant information concerning possible significant risks is being withheld or presented in such a way as to deceive or mislead persons who may be affected, and to refuse to work on such projects."[74]

Because whistleblowing is a researcher's duty, it is important to understand exactly what it is. An act of whistleblowing is a special kind of organizational disobedience or, rather, obedience to a higher principle than loyalty to an employer. It involves "going public" with organization, employer, contractor, or government information, and it is done "in the public interest."[75] One commentator lists five characteristics of such acts of disobedience.

- The act disobeys an organizational policy.
- An employee of the organization in question performs the act.
- The act attempts to rescind an organizational policy or policies.
- To achieve this end, it tries to rouse a higher opinion against the organizational policy.
- The employee acts under the belief that the targeted policy threatens the public's or the organization's interest, and with the intention of protecting that interest.[76]

What circumstances would justify a researcher's engaging in an act of organizational disobedience or whistleblowing? According to one recent discussion, whistleblowing is morally justified if and only if it satisfies four general conditions: (1) The employee has reason to believe that the problematic policy or action cannot be overturned within a reasonable period of time through normal, internal channels; (2) The problematic policy or action seriously threatens the public interest; (3) There is reason to believe that whistleblowing will effectively overthrow the problematic policy in question; (4) There are good reasons for believing that the act of whistleblowing will not violate any authentic obligations.[77] The omission of any of these conditions is likely either to be unfair to the accused or to endanger the whistleblower.[78] One famous example of whistleblowing that involved public health and safety, as well as the right to know, concerns the effects of radiation. When research scientists and whistleblowers John Gofman and Arthur Tamplin argued, in the 1960s, that official standards for permissible exposure to radiation were too tolerant and would cause many additional cancer deaths in the United States each year, the U.S. Atomic Energy Commission (AEC) disputed and dismissed their claims. In large part because of Gofman's and Tamplin's whistleblowing, the NAS investigated the matter and ultimately resolved it. The NAS "report is in agreement with the view of Gofman and Tamplin that there is no safe level of radiation exposure and in disagreement with the AEC view that there is such a threshold."[79]

Just as the Gofman and Tamplin case illustrates a successful instance of how whistleblowing ensures the openness of research and protects public health and welfare, cases of failed whistleblowing show how damaging to the public such failures can be. Although many researchers were aware of the carcinogenicity of vinyl chloride years before the Occupational Safety and Health Administration mandated stricter standards for it, no one "blew the whistle." As a consequence, more people died.[80] Even when researchers do attempt to blow the whistle, as in the case of the faulty design of the Ford Pinto, sometimes not enough scientists and engineers can be mobilized to support the whistleblowing effort, and so it fails. In the Pinto case, more than 180 people died annually owing to rear-end collisions resulting in the automobiles' catching fire, and almost 400 others annually suffered fatal burns because of the delayed whistleblowing.[81]

The obvious critical response to these cases is that often whistleblowers are wrong, they politicize research, and they waste taxpayers' time and money with specious worries and inaccurate claims. Such flawed efforts, claim the objectors, can lead to scientific researchers' losing credibility, perhaps without justification. Scientist Alvin Weinberg holds such a position. He believes in limitations on the whistleblowing responsibility of researchers. He holds, for instance, that scientists (who believe they have evidence that current standards of environmental protection are too lax in some respect) should submit their findings to a refereed scientific journal before publicizing them. If the journal rejects the report, claims Weinberg, the researchers may honestly believe that the reviewers are biased. In that case they may be justified in bringing the matter before the public, while admitting that others disagree with them.[82] Other writers point out that ''sensible employees,'' operating on the basis of both common sense and loyalty to their employer, obviously go first to their superiors and urge correction of a problem before bringing the issue before the public.[83] Indeed, few justify whistleblowing unless it meets the first condition already mentioned: that the employee has grounds for belief that the problematic policy or action cannot be overturned within a reasonable period of time through normal internal channels.[84] Whistleblowers must first use normal internal channels to correct an alleged problem and only resort to public means once internal methods have either failed totally or failed to be effective within a time frame necessary to avoid great harm. The soundness of Weinberg's advice therefore depends on the individual case and on whether the potential whistleblower receives timely and just hearing through internal means. In cases with great vested interests, however, such as the agricultural chemicals industry, it is difficult to believe that potential whistleblowers will always have alleged problems corrected internally. If not, then after detailed ethical analysis, researchers owe it to society to speak out. Indeed their whistleblowing may be part of their basic duty to promote the public good. But because whistleblowing and other acts could harm innocent people, scientists must take care to assess ethically the relevant factors of each particular situation. In the next chapter we begin to discuss how to engage in such an ethical analysis.

5

Handling Conflicts Through Stage-Two Ethical Analysis: Giving Priority to the Common Good

On June 29, 1993, the U.S. National Academy of Science (NAS)/National Research Council (NRC) released a major scientific study on the impact of pesticides.[1] The research highlighted the effect of the chemicals on children who, by the time they reach one year of age, will have received (on average) the acceptable lifetime dose of eight cancer-causing pesticides from 20 commonly eaten foods. Although the study did not call for the United States to require a cutback in use of the chemicals, it did indict the safety of the food supply and call for better government test procedures to protect infants and children. Concluding that there is a ''potential concern'' that some children ingest unsafe amounts of pesticides, the report has fueled both industry and environmentalist arguments regarding the chemicals. Putting their own interpretation on the study, industry officials have emphasized that the NAS research cited only a ''potential'' concern. Using a quite different interpretation of the report, environmentalists have argued that the research calls for new tests aimed at protecting children. Just before the NAS released its study, the U.S. Environmental Protection Agency warned that both ''environmentalists and industry are 'primed and ready' to put their own 'spin' on the report and use it in arguing for [their own preferred] legislation.''[2] As the divergent responses to this study show, even the most prestigious reports fall prey to interpretation and to political manipulation. The frequency and variety of these subjective interpretations raise many ethical questions about how researchers ought to perform their work and present their results. Should researchers attempt to present their results with as little interpretation as possible? Or, in order to

81

avoid misinterpretations of their work, should researchers deliberately interpret their findings when they present them?

Similar questions regarding research ethics arose in 1986 and 1987 when a number of ecologists engaged in a research dispute over how to design wildlife reserves and how to predict species losses resulting from deforestation. Obviously, if the dispute could have been resolved purely on the basis of who best interpreted the facts, such a resolution would have been desirable. Unfortunately, the situation was uncertain. The battle, played out in the pages of the Ecological Society of America *Bulletin*, began in August 1986 when P. C. Kangas gave a paper at the meetings of the Fourth International Congress of Ecology, held in Syracuse, New York. Using data on trees in Costa Rica and the "objective approach" of species-area curves, Kangas argued that extinction rates due to deforestation in the tropics are actually much lower than most other researchers have alleged.[3] Ecologists in the audience disagreed with Kangas's claim and complained that his questionable results would be used to justify more rapid and widespread deforestation.[4] No uncontroversial ecological facts or theories were able to settle the dispute.

Ecologist R. F. Noss accused Kangas of "bad science" and of "encouraging the deforestation of the tropics."[5] Worried about the ethical consequences of Kangas's research results, Noss criticized Kangas for claiming that "you can deforest an area for a long time before you have a decline in species."[6] Noss argued that Kangas's conclusion failed on scientific grounds, because of his extrapolation technique and his ignoring minimum viable populations of trees and animal mutualists.[7] In subsequent issues of the *Bulletin*, other ecologists criticized Noss for suggesting "that scientists should shade their results to make sure that they come down on the "right" side of ecologically important issues." Instead, they argued for the "open expression of alternative points of view" as critical in maintaining the credibility of any scientific policy.[8] They criticized Noss for having a "moral stance" that is "myopic" and for assuming that only "dire predictions of extinction" would encourage conservation.[9] They also faulted Noss for ignoring the possibility that such dire predictions could lead to loss of scientific credibility and to subsequent problems for anyone defending conservation.[10] Still other ecologists claimed that ethical discussion of Kangas's actions was premature because the content of his remarks was never refereed and was highly questionable.[11] Kangas defended himself by claiming that he was not encouraging deforestation of the tropics.[12] Noss responded by asserting that he was not criticizing Kangas's right to present his

views, but rather warning that his ''simplistic study'' could lead to ''potentially dangerous conclusions.'' Noss argued not for censorship but
for prudence in the presentation of research results.[13]

Ecologists like Noss worry about Kangas's presenting his research
results in (what appears to be) an ethically questionable way, especially
given the scientific uncertainty surrounding the issues. Earlier, in chapter two, we sketched five rules for types of research one ought to avoid
because of the harm they cause. So much uncertainty revolves around
the Kangas–Noss case, however, that it is not possible to use these five
rules. Instead we need some general principles for dealing with research
situations with subtle harmful consequences. In chapters three and four
we began to develop additional general principles, based on scientists'
positive duties to objectivity and promotion of the common good. In
these chapters we also outlined the two stages of ethical analysis. We
illustrated the first, or deontological, stage by developing several general, positive principles of research ethics. These general principles include the following:

(1) One ought to avoid bias in one's own research.
(2) One ought to promote unbiased use of research generally.
(3) One ought to improve the quality of life for present and future
    inhabitants of the earth.

Continuing our first-stage, or deontological, analysis, we also argued in
chapters three and four that meeting the three responsibilities just listed
requires at least two specific duties:

(4) One ought to disseminate one's research to the public, profes-
    sionals, and employers.
(5) One ought to engage in whistleblowing when appropriate.

In the Kangas and Noss case just mentioned, Kangas appealed to
principle (1) to justify his position, whereas Noss appealed to principle
(3). Clearly, although this list of five general, positive principles covers
all thirteen responsibilities of scientists, as formulated by the American
Association for the Advancement of Science (AAAS),[14] the list has at
least two limitations. (1) The principles are *too general* to provide any
specific guidance in a given situation, like that of Kangas and Noss, and
(2) the principles are not *ranked* according to which takes priority in a
situation of conflict. This chapter uses a second-stage ethical analysis
in order to provide a more precise account of the duties these principles

require and to establish some rules of thumb for a priority ranking of the principles when they conflict. By evaluating the Kangas–Noss controversy, we hope both to clarify ethical behavior under uncertainty and to illustrate second-stage analysis of ethical conflicts.

The Need for Analysis of Specific Duties, Consequences, and Circumstances

The generality of the five prima facie principles (just listed) is a problem, as we mentioned, because often they do not provide sufficient guidelines for researchers' behavior in particular circumstances or in cases of conflicting principles, like that involving Kangas and Noss. For example, even if one accepts that researchers have a general responsibility to engage in whistleblowing, one must use interpretation and judgment in order to determine the appropriateness of whistleblowing in a given case. Because these general responsibilities require interpretation and judgment in specific situations, the AAAS Board has bemoaned the vagueness of its recommendations for scientific researchers,[15] warning that its rules sometimes are too general to provide much guidance.[16]

Another problem with the list of five responsibilities is that different principles governing research ethics can be used to justify conflicting behavior. As the AAAS Committee on Professional Ethics put it: "although not inherently inconsistent, in practice [lists of responsibilities] may present the scientist or engineer with conflicting obligations."[17] A common instance of conflict among general principles of research ethics occurs when one must choose between duties to one's employer and duties to the public interest.[18] For example, the codes of the Ecological Society of America (ESA), Registered Professional Entomologists (EntSA), and the American Fisheries Society (AFS) all have tenets requiring researchers to correct their colleagues' errors, in some cases because they must take account of the health and welfare of the public. Yet, the codes also enjoin researchers not to injure the reputation of other colleagues by criticizing their work. The codes give no clue (beyond the ESA injunction that members should be "guided by their conscience"[19]), for example, as to what to do when the words of an unscrupulous but unmanageable researcher encourage actions threatening the health of the public.

Given a conflict among general principles relevant to research ethics, one way to determine which takes priority is to use a second-stage ethical analysis and apply it to a specific case. Although all such cases involve epistemic or methodological value judgments (see chapter three), nevertheless analysis of duties, specific circumstances, and the factual consequences of a particular situation often provides some clues as to ethical priorities and recommended actions. In the case of Kangas's research (mentioned at the beginning of this chapter), one part of this second-stage critical analysis would be to assess factual consequences in order to gain insights on whether the first principle (objectivity) or the third principle (enhancing the common good) ought to take precedence, given the scientific uncertainty in the case. In his presentation, Kangas appealed to the first principle (avoiding bias), whereas Noss appealed to the third (promoting the common good). In other words, they disagree both about the scientific facts of the matter and about how to resolve conflicts over ethical behavior in a situation of uncertainty. By tracing the consequences likely following from Kangas's subscribing to the first principle and then comparing these to the consequences likely following from Noss's subscribing to the third principle, one might determine which of the two principles will likely lead to more desirable consequences.

On the one hand, if Kangas and Noss gave priority to objectivity (the first principle), emphasizing the uncertainty inherent in their conclusions about species losses caused by deforestation, then opponents of environmentalism could use the uncertainties in ecological data and theories as grounds for objecting to wildlife preserves. Such a situation echoes what happened when S. J. Gould stated clearly and objectively problems with Darwinian evolution, and creationists used his remarks as grounds for objecting to the theory of evolution. Hence, in attempting to be purely objective in presenting their findings and in following the first principle, researchers might not serve the third principle, promoting the common good. Their objectivity and openness about the flaws in their account might increase the chance that unscrupulous individuals would misinterpret the results and use them to threaten biodiversity and environmental welfare. Moreover, by promoting objectivity rather than preservation in an uncertain situation, they might cause policymakers not to recommend creation of a wildlife reserve. Being objective about uncertainties in biodiversity research could also cause policymakers not to purchase land for a reserve. This failure likewise could mean that scientists will have lost a valuable experiment that could help create successful reserves for other species in the future.

On the other hand, if Kangas and Noss gave priority to enhancing the quality of life of all inhabitants of the planet (the third principle), they would probably downplay their research uncertainties and instead recommend whatever actions (such as creating a nature reserve) seemed most likely to promote the public good, e.g., by reducing deforestation and species losses. As a result, the ''preservationist'' ecologists might have to fight tense battles with other researchers who might charge them with violating the first ethical principle (avoiding bias) because they downplayed the scientific uncertainty inherent in their interpretations. Moreover, researchers who gave priority to preservation and the third principle might have to live with their predictions about saving species being proved wrong. As a result, their status, as well as that of many other researchers, might decline. They might be dismissed as environmentalist advocates, rather than respected as reliable scientists. Also, their trying to promote biodiversity might be a lost cause, from an empirical point of view, if certain species present in a proposed wildlife reserve have too few members to sustain the population, or if inbreeding depression is already a problem. As this quick survey of consequences reveals, giving priority to either (of the two) ethical principles may lead to serious difficulties.

The End Does Not Justify the Means

Perhaps the crucial ethical question—raised by the possible consequences of giving priority to a particular ethical principle—is how much information researchers ought to withhold or interpret, in a situation of uncertainty, if they wish both to emphasize a legitimate goal (such as environmental preservation) and yet to remain objective. Ought they to manipulate the interpretation in ways to serve the public or environmental interest? And when do such manipulations lead to unethical consequences? Where is the line between advocacy and bias? What are researchers' duties?

The case of researchers' attempting to interpret a situation of scientific uncertainty for the public resembles that of a doctor attempting to decide whether to tell a patient the truth about the seriousness of his condition. Both the doctor and the researcher must decide what their duties and rights are and whether benevolence (the third principle) or honesty (the first principle) will lead to better consequences.[20] Traditional ethical theory sometimes accepts the withholding of partial truth; it does not accept lying. We have a general duty not to lie, in part because of the disastrous social consequences of accepting lying (see chapter three). But how much of the truth must one reveal, and how far can one be justified in interpreting it? In recent court cases in which representatives of victims killed by psychiatrists' patients sued the psychiatrists, the courts had to decide how much of the truth professionals are obliged to reveal to the public. In cases involving potential harm to the public, the courts have typically found on behalf of the plaintiffs whenever the psychiatrists appealed to client confidentiality as grounds for not warning potential victims about their patients. As one court put it: "The protective privilege ends where the public peril begins. . . ."[21] Although professionals, including researchers, generally have a duty to keep confidences, courts have forced them to take responsibility for the third-party consequences of their actions. This court finding suggests that intuitive precedents exist for limiting the scope of professionals' (including researchers') responsibilities to clients (when public harm is at stake) and for expanding the scope of their responsibilities to society.

Despite these grounds for expanding their responsibilities to society, however, researchers (like Kangas or Noss) cannot justify using any means whatsoever to achieve desirable societal ends or consequences, e.g., wildlife preservation. In other words, the (third) principle of benevolence or serving the common good binds one to maximize desirable consequences, but not at any cost. Not at the cost of ignoring certain duties and responsibilities to avoid deliberate bias. For instance, any reasonable person would claim that using the *means* of murdering humans is not justifiable in order to achieve a desirable *end*, e.g., conservation or preservation. Regardless of the end or consequence at stake, not all means are justifiable in order to attain it. This is what Oliver North may have learned and what much of the United States debated regarding the Iran-Contra hearings. Likewise one may argue that regardless of the end, using the means of torturing someone to death or organizing a homicidal project against an innocent person is not justifiable.[22] Some principles must be followed even when doing so does not lead to the best consequences in the particular situation.[23] Stephen Vincent Benet's *The Devil and Daniel Webster* illustrates the importance of such ethical principles or rules. Webster was allowed to plead in a court of the dead for the life of his neighbor who had lost a bargain with the devil. Pride and his wish to save his friend, however, tempted Webster to stretch the truth. As he began to do so, Webster realized that his own soul, not his neighbor's, was on trial. At the last moment, he realized the relevant ethical rule, told the truth, and saved both himself and his friend.[24]

As the Webster story illustrates, there are a number of reasons that researchers ought not do anything in order to follow the (third) principle of promoting benevolence or helping to achieve good ends or consequences: The end does not justify the means. Plato recognized one of the most important reasons when he had Socrates argue that he would not use illicit means to escape from an unjust death sentence. If people break the most basic laws of justice and fairness, so as to serve some desired end, he argued that they weaken the fabric of society. They weaken the rule and acceptance of justice. Likewise, the ends or consequences do not justify the means because illicit means often violate the legitimate interests of other persons.[25] Hence, the third principle generally cannot trump the first principle (objectivity) in the sense that the third principle generally cannot justify deliberate bias or misinterpretation of research. One reason it cannot is that everyone has a duty not to take away the necessary conditions of human action, such as physical security; if illicit means—such as deliberately misrepresenting research results—weaken the rule of justice, then they also could weaken people's physical security. Most important, some wrong means may subvert the minimal dignity of either the agent or the recipient and hence undermine the basic presuppositions of ethics itself.[26] Besides, ethics does not require us to achieve benevolence or desirable consequences at any price. Therefore, in ethics we often distinguish between the goodness of an action's end or consequences and the rightness of the judgment on which the action is based. We make the distinction between utilitarian and deontological ethics. Many moral philosophers claim that people can be morally good even if their actions lead to bad consequences (e.g., not attaining a desirable end), provided they have virtuous motives or protect an important right.[27]

Granted that some means (e.g., torturing innocent persons) ought not be used to achieve good consequences, regardless of how desirable the end, several important questions remain before us in the Kangas–Noss case and other situations of research uncertainty. Can researchers justify lying, for example, about the significance and possibility of preserving biodiversity by means of a particular type of nature reserve? Ought they lie in order to increase the chance of attaining the desirable end or consequence of preservation? In other words, would such an *end*, possible delay of an irreversible extinction, justify the *means* of lying or biasing one's research results? In an analogous case, Bayles asks whether a dentist might lie to a patient about the significance of his precancerous oral lesions, in order to get the man to stop smoking.[28] If the discussions of objectivity in chapters three and four were correct, then researchers must not lie because their responsibility to clients and to the public requires honesty. Short of lying or bias, however, they could prudently interpret ambiguous data in ways that might help to achieve desirable consequences. Noss,[29] for example, says that we should use "professional responsibility" when reporting on research results with important policy implications. He suggests that the *end* of preventing destruction of ecosystems justifies the *means* of prudence in reporting research conclusions that could jeopardize this end. Noss denies that he supports censorship,[30] but he appears to argue for pro-preservation interpretations of ambiguous data. Waide disagrees and says that such biases are "dangerous to the free expression of scientific results" because they amount to censorship.[31] Waide also claims that expression of alternative points of view is essential to the credibility of scientific policy.

Who is right, Noss or Waide? It is difficult to say because it is not clear exactly what Noss supports. If he opposes lying yet advocates a pro-preservation interpretation in a situation that requires some interpretation and in which the facts are unclear, then his recommendations are probably defensible. (He does not appear to support lying or intentional bias.) If he argues for lying, however, then his recommendations are not defensible, because lying is wrong. It is wrong for the same reasons that the use and promotion of biased results and reports is inappropriate (see chapter three). Also, society has no "strong right" to preservation.[32] Yet only something like protecting a "strong right," or what Gewirth calls an "absolute right,"[33] appears even potentially capable of justifying lying in research. Moreover, as we argued earlier, there are at least six good reasons for claiming that researchers are not justified in behaving paternalistically toward the public. Lying/intentionally misrepresenting the situation in cases like that of Kangas–Noss also is wrong because it is an instance of paternalism. As we argued in chapter three, lying and deliberate bias in research wrong everyone because they undermine the profession, public trust in it, and researcher–client relationships.

Another reason that researchers should not lie to achieve good consequences is that their technical or professional expertise does not guarantee their expertise in making value judgments. Hence they are justified only in making decisions about non-ethical, largely factual, means to research ends. Because it involves ethics and values, lying (as a means to the end of preservation) is not a largely factual means to a research end. Also, because most researchers have no special claim to expertise in value judgments, and because value judgments affecting the common good are the prerogative of the public, researchers do not have the right to make the value judgment that they may lie so as to protect an important public value. As Bayles puts it: "A professional has a strong claim to independence of judgment only for technical decisions not significantly affecting values, in which the element of particular knowledge and expertise dominates.''[34] Cases like that involving Kangas and Noss do not present such a claim. Moreover, there are prudential grounds for not lying or being biased: the lie will fail anyway, and people will discover the truth. Hence, there are a variety of reasons for believing that researchers' duty to society to help accomplish an end (such as wildlife preservation) does not extend to the use of unethical means to achieve this end.[35] But how does one know that some means are unethical? We need to understand more fully the constraints on achieving good consequences, on following the (third) principle of benevolence or promoting quality of life.

Duties, Consequences, and Third-Party Priority: Rethinking Objectivity

Generally speaking, one can evaluate the desirability of following a particular ethical principle by assessing the *obligations and duties* enhanced or threatened by following the principle or by assessing the *consequences* associated with following it. The former is a deontological analysis, while the latter is utilitarian. Once one accomplishes these two evaluations, one can tell which ethical principles generally ought to take priority over others. We shall use both types of evaluation. Within the utilitarian analysis, there are at least three tests of the ethical desirability of the consequences associated with following a particular ethical principle. As Bayles explains the three-part test,[36] it subjects professionals (researchers) to ordinary ethical norms and considers what people would want done for themselves in a particular situation if they were clients, affected third parties, or researchers. The test involves asking, in a particular case,

(1) What and whose values are at stake?
(2) What is the probability of one's being a researcher, client (sponsoring research), or member of society affected by a researcher's decision?
(3) Would one rather live in a society governed by one set of research-related rules or another?[37]

Let us examine each of the three steps. At each stage of our analysis, we shall also assess relevant duties or obligations.

What and whose values are at stake in the case of the Kangas–Noss conflict? If the analyses in chapters three and four are correct, the values of epistemic and ethical objectivity (required by the first principle) and serving the societal good of wildlife preservation (required by the third principle) appear paramount. On the one hand, epistemic objectivity seems to be required by researchers' responsibilities to their *profession* and to *society*. The profession requires epistemic objectivity because professionals are often necessary to evaluate expert knowledge and because adherence to objectivity promotes the welfare of both professionals and society. Research scientists likewise owe ethical objectivity to the *profession* and to *society*, again to advance the welfare of both the profession and society. On the other hand, the value of wildlife preservation appears to be required primarily by responsibilities to *society*, because wildlife and other environmental goods are part of the commons. On the basis of earlier arguments, we also can assume that researchers are not allowed, under any circumstances, to lie to other scientists, to the public, or to clients about any of their findings. They have a duty (to the profession and to society) not to lie. Hence, provided that they avoid deception, should researchers (such as Kangas and Noss) give priority to responsibilities to the profession and to society (through objectivity) or to society (through attempts at wildlife preservation)? Giving priority to the *first principle*, objectivity, would likely benefit researchers, the subset of society interested in development, and all of society that has a great social interest in or a need for objectivity. Giving priority to the *third principle*, preservation, would likely benefit present and future members of society generally, because it would protect the environmental commons. Hence, using criterion (1), giving priority to either principle serves societal values.[38]

Because the Kangas–Noss conflict potentially affects many people, the values of those affected must be weighted by the number of people involved. This is the second (2) phase of the test of consequences. What is the probability of reasonable persons' finding themselves, in the case of the Kangas–Noss controversy, in the position of the client, researchers, developers, or members of society affected by the research results? Because one is more likely to be an affected member of society than an affected client, developer, or researcher, a reasonable person (behind the veil of ignorance) would probably decide to give priority to societal interests. Yet both the first (objectivity) and the third principle (benevolence or preservation) serve societal interests. Admittedly, however, if researchers give priority to the third principle, and cause some habitat to be preserved, then the financial loss to affected developers would probably be greater for each individual. Nevertheless, the present and future members of society outnumber developers. Hence, according to criterion (2), one should probably give priority to societal, rather than clients', developers', or other private interests. But societal interests require that one serve both the first principle (objectivity) and the third principle (promoting preservation or the common good). Hence, according to both criterion (1) and criterion (2), neither principle appears preferable because both principles serve societal values and society generally. Perhaps a more precise analysis, more relevant to the particular case at hand, is required to resolve the Kangas–Noss controversy. Perhaps we need a closer analysis of objectivity in the light of the specifics of the Kangas–Noss case study.

So far, we have assumed that Kangas presented his unrefereed results—with potentially damaging consequences for preservation—objectively. Likewise we have assumed that Noss and others argued for less objectivity in Kangas's presentation and more emphasis on preservation values. Hence we assumed that the conflict between Kangas and Noss was analyzable as a controversy between the first principle (objectivity) and the third principle (promoting preservation or the common good). Perhaps these initial assumptions were wrong.

There are grounds for believing that, although Kangas's presentation was straightforward, revealed his own conclusions accurately, and served the principle of epistemic objectivity, it may not have served ethical objectivity. As we argued in chapter three, epistemic objectivity deals with the objectivity of researchers' *beliefs*, whereas ethical objectivity addresses the objectivity of their *actions*. As such, epistemic objectivity demands that we avoid deliberate bias in presenting conclusions. Ethical objectivity, however, requires us also to take account of obligations and the greater good in assessing the ethical desirability of acting on our belief in a particular hypothesis or its consequences. In Kangas's case, ethical objectivity seems to have directed him both to take account of the harm that could be done by acting on his beliefs in his findings and to take account of the obligations he had to society to help avoid such harm.

An analogy may help explain our new analysis of the types of objectivity in the Kangas–Noss situation: epistemic objectivity might require chemical researchers to outline, in an unbiased way, the hazards associated with use of a particular pesticide. If the researchers had reason to believe, however, that the pesticide might be used by those unable to read their warning labels or that people might not understand the significance and seriousness of the warnings on the labels, then ethical objectivity also might require the researchers and label writers to attempt to counteract this misinterpretation. Otherwise, the pesticide users might misunderstand the facts of the matter regarding the danger. In other words, acting in accord with (ethical) objectivity or acting in accord with ethical reality requires researchers to take account of all real aspects of the situation. The real aspects of the situation include duties and obligations. People's potential deaths as a consequence of misused pesticides are a reality. (The World Health Organization estimates that 40,000 people die per year of pesticide poisoning, mostly in developing nations.)[39] Hence, objectivity on the part of the chemists demands that they consider both epistemic and ethical considerations. Likewise, in Kangas's case, ethical objectivity might have required him, not merely to present his beliefs without bias, but to act to offset any danger that might arise if others acted on his beliefs. In other words, objectivity requires us to weigh the relevant epistemic and ethical conditions impartially, especially in areas of applied research or science. According to this latter interpretation, Kangas may not have erred in supporting the first principle (objectivity) rather than the third (promoting preservation), but rather in failing to serve both objectivity (in the full ethical and epistemological senses) and preservation.

What does this new analysis of the circumstances surrounding the Kangas and Noss dispute reveal to us about researchers' ethical conflicts over objectivity and the public or societal good? The case suggests that many apparent conflicts between objectivity and the public good may not be controversies in the sense we suspect. Rather, once we correctly understand objectivity (in cases of applied research having potentially serious consequences) to take account of ethical as well as epistemic factors, often objectivity and other values do not conflict. Hence, in the Kangas–Noss case, to serve both objectivity and the public good, Kangas should have presented his results in a way that acknowledged their uncertainty and their threat to preservation, rather than in a manner that ignored these aspects of the ''real'' situation.

But would the conclusion just stated hold true for all similar cases? Is it universalizable, as most ethical conclusions should be (see chapter three)? Although we might agree with giving priority to Noss rather than Kangas, and although we might say that Noss's response serves both objectivity and the common good (first and third principles), is there any more to the alleged conflict? Supporting Noss rather than Kangas might mean we support preservation rather than development. Following part (3) of our test of consequences, would a reasonable person rather live in a society that gives priority to benefitting developers or to benefitting society at large? And when does development benefit society at large?[40] A reasonable person, having a higher probability of not being a developer, would presumably rather give priority to benefitting society at large. This is because the decision likely would benefit more people and serve the liberal societal values of promoting equal opportunity and welfare. Hence, according to criterion (3), although researchers ought not engage in any deception, Noss seems correct, in this case, to serve preservation rather than development. More generally, in situations of uncertainty researchers probably ought to interpret findings more in the way required to serve preservation rather than development. In subsequent paragraphs, and especially in chapter seven, we explain and defend this conclusion.

A number of objections can be made in response to this conclusion (giving priority to third-party or public responsibilities in situations of uncertainty). The first recognizes that although *many people* would benefit from enhanced environmental preservation, they each receive a very *small benefit*. Supporters of this objection prefer to serve the interests of a *few people*, e.g., developers, each of whom receives a *large benefit* from complete objectivity and from developing wildlife habitat, rather than to serve the interests of a large group, each of whom receives a small benefit from environmental preservation. In other words, someone might object that the type and magnitude of benefits obtained, not just the number of people receiving them, are crucial to the consequence-oriented segment of our second-stage ethical analysis.

Such an objection correctly presupposes that some benefits, given only to a small number of individuals, may be so important that consideration of other benefits affecting a larger number of people cannot override them. For example, suppose one were able to spend x dollars to clean up a polluted municipal water supply. Suppose that the x dollars could be spent either for chemical additive y, which would destroy the effects of a pollutant responsible for human cancers—in 2 out of every 1,000 people per year—or for chemical additive z, which would remove the unpleasant (but harmless) taste from the water drunk by 5 million people. Even though a larger group would experience the unpleasant taste than by the cancer, obviously it would be more important to prevent cancer than to avoid unpleasant-tasting water. Because protection from injury has priority over aesthetic considerations, regardless of the numbers of individuals involved, some duties, values, and benefits carry more weight than others. But if some values have more importance than others, then how were we able to conclude, in situations of uncertainty like the Kangas–Noss case, that Noss appeared to serve the values of both objectivity and the common good (preservation)? There are at least two reasons. *First,* we argued for an important duty. We argued that researchers reporting their results must not engage in deliberate deception. *Second,* we argued that no loss of basic human rights was involved in supporting preservation or failing to support development. That is, no one would gain or lose life or political liberty as a result of either decision in the Kangas–Noss case. Hence, the choice between preservation versus development became a choice between maximizing two values or ideals, one environmental and one economic. Because the choice did not involve rights or rights claims, neither *type* of beneficial consequences (preservation vs. development) can "trump" the other.[41] Hence, in the Kangas–Noss case, it makes sense to choose the option that appears to promote both the best consequences and recognition of our ethical duties and values. Moreover, it appears that more people have their welfare enhanced when the researchers follow societal responsibilities (such as protecting public interest in preservation) than when they promote development.[42]

A critic might object, however, that economic development would enhance the welfare of more people than would habitat or wildlife preservation. Thus a critic might claim that development would serve society as a whole, not just researchers and developers. In response, one must consider a number of reasons that researchers often serve authentic public interest through environmental preservation, rather than through economic development, when they cannot pursue both values. Provided that economic development is not essential to human security or survival in a particular case, the economic benefits of development of a given area will likely affect only a few people (developers) over the short term, whereas the environmental benefits of preservation will likely benefit virtually everyone, over the long term. Admittedly, how to calculate and evaluate such benefits is a matter of argument and a function of the particular case; nevertheless, if human security or survival is not at stake, it would be difficult for the critic to make the case that development should take precedence over preservation. The critic's argument weakens further when one considers that the long-term consequences of conservation include economic benefits like eco-tourism.[43]

Still pursuing the argument, objectors might claim that society prefers economic development to preservation and that, regardless of the public's genuine *interests,* its *preferences* lean toward economic welfare, deforestation, and consequent development of tropical areas like those discussed by Kangas and Noss. For such an objection to succeed, however, the proponents would have to show not merely that current short-term preferences support development over preservation but that future long-term preferences, overall, do so as well. The objectors would have to show that *future* people (assuming that their welfare requires consideration) would most likely favor *present* development. If they cannot establish such claims about future preferences, then the objectors cannot prove that development represented the greater good for the greater number of people, present and future. If development did not represent the greater good and if it were not essential to human security and survival, then a reasonable person could presuppose that preservation, rather than development, represented the better way to serve third-party or societal interests.

A number of codes of ethics of professional societies agree with our analysis of the responsibilities of researchers. Many codes give priority to third-party or societal considerations, and virtually all codes recognize a responsibility for the public good.[44] For example, for engineers and for members of the American Society of Biological Chemists,[45] third-party or public responsibilities receive the highest priority.[46] (See Carl Mitcham's discussion of the ethics of engineering research in chapter nine.) *The Code of the National Society of Professional Engineers* explicitly states (in sections 2a and b) that "he [the engineer] will regard his duty to the public welfare as paramount. He shall seek opportunities to be of constructive service in civic affairs and work for the advancement of the safety, health, and well-being of his community."[47] The *Code of Ethics for Government Service* also places third-party responsibility as the highest in priority. This code applies to "any person in government service," and requires one to "put loyalty to the highest moral principles and to country above loyalty to persons, party, or government department."[48] If such norms are typical, as they seem to be, then researchers' primary responsibilities, like those of other professionals, generally are not to special groups, such as developers, but to members of the public and to public welfare.

Third-Party Priority and Freedom to Choose Research

If researchers' primary responsibilities are to third parties, to members of the public, then are they free to choose whatever research contracts, grants, and topics they desire? Or do researchers have an obligation to do some work in the public interest, just as attorneys might have some obligation to do "pro bono" legal work? To some extent, the degree to which researchers are constrained in choosing their work is determined both by who their employers are and by how much public support of their training and subsequent work they have received.

One alleged justification for university researchers' accepting corporate funds, for example, is that professors ought to have academic freedom to pursue research funded by vested interests. University scholars, however, even at private institutions, directly and indirectly receive much of their support from the public. Taxpayers fund them by virtue of colleges' and universities' being tax-exempt and accepting government grants. Hence, if citizens pay, in part, for university research, then they ought to have some say in what research is done and whose interests are served. If the *public* cannot completely withdraw its tax support for research, then *researchers* ought not be completely free to do whatever work they choose. Only wholly self-supporting scholars ought to have full control over their choice of research contracts. Moreover, selling oneself to the highest industrial, technological, or private-interest bidder—in cases involving extensive amounts of money and consequent restrictions—hardly argues for the freedom of the person being sold.

Another argument for researchers' freedom in performing work for private interests is that serving corporate interests amounts to serving the public interest. This too is a false rebuttal, because industry usually strives for short-term, applied research for profit maximization, whereas academia seeks long-term, basic research for the sake of knowledge. History also suggests that we not assume the automatic beneficence of vested interests like corporations. Many industries campaigned against child labor laws. Many industries continue to campaign against increased environmental, safety, and health regulations. The nuclear industry in the United States, for example, has successfully campaigned for protection against 99 percent of liability damages, in the event of a catastrophic nuclear accident.[49] The chemical industry, at least in the United States, successfully lobbied both to protect itself against the liability provisions of the toxic waste superfund legislation and to cut industry cleanup funds by two-thirds. Likewise, Johns Manville exposed 4 million U.S. workers to asbestos, even after the company officials knew the health effects, and they fought to prevent disclosure of the danger. Metropolitan Edison Company falsified the cooling system tests at Three Mile Island prior to the nuclear accident.[50] Such examples are widespread and part of the reason that nearly a quarter of a million occupationally induced fatalities or permanent disabilities occur in the United States every year. Most of these industrial accidents are preventable.[51] Of course, not all industries or private interests behave in a reprehensible manner or cause public harm. Obviously they do not. Industry makes up an integral part of the engine that drives the economy and ultimately serves the public good. But the examples point out that a *special* interest group does not always and automatically behave in the *public* interest, especially if pressures from competitors and shareholders motivate it to serve private interests. And if so, then university researchers' being beholden to private interests is not always a benevolent or socially desirable situation.

But doesn't the public benefit when a new product, like the cancer drug interferon, is developed and marketed through industry funding of university research? This response unfortunately fails to recognize that sometimes the public *benefit* is disproportional to the public *investment*. The discovery of interferon, for example, resulted from research sponsored by the National Institute of Health: taxpayers. The financial rewards for developing and marketing the drug will go to Hoffmann-LaRoche and to the University of California. Such rewards mean that the public will have paid three times for interferon: first for the research to make it; second for the tax credits for laboratories, wages, and equipment; and third for the commercially produced product. Yet the public benefits only once, by having the product. The drug company and the university, however, benefit twice: they have the product and they have the profit made by commercializing the product. Because such a situation could be inequitable,[52] perhaps industry should sometimes pay a higher price (to society) for the intellectual capital it extracts from university researchers.[53] Industry ought not be able to transform a public-sector social resource into a private-sector preserve with little public accountability.[54] Otherwise the *public* ends up subsidizing *private* interests, often without consent. Likewise researchers ought not participate in the transfer of a public resource to private interests.

Arguments in favor of laissez-faire industry control over segments of academic research sometimes incorporate feigned naivete. University administrators and researchers want the industry dollars, but they might believe that the funds never compromise their autonomy. As one university administrator quipped: we want "to get pregnant without really losing our virginity."[55] Universities sometimes may have allowed higher education to become "hire education" in the name of productivity. The situation may be reminiscent of what Tacitus said of the Romans: "they made a desert and called it peace."[56] To the degree that university researchers have benefitted from public support, they have a greater responsibility not to create a research network that makes a "desert" of public needs. As beneficiaries of public largesse, they have some responsibility to act as guardians of the public interest. Thus they might answer the question of Juvenal: "Quis custodiet ipsos custodes?"[57] (Who shall guard the guardians themselves?) The answer, in part, is researchers, scholars, disinterested intellectuals. Scholars can help to guard the public interest by refusing to preside over the demise of the public-spirited, altruistic professor. They can provide a structure that encourages researchers to follow the example of Cesar Milstein, the co-inventor of monoclonal antibodies. He shared his cells with other researchers, and he asked that they not seek patents.[58]

Researchers should encourage universities to provide guidelines to ensure that outside funding and control neither exceed a certain financial level nor threaten departmental autonomy, pure research, or the interests of students and the public. Committees composed of both faculty and representatives of the public should also scrutinize all major contracts with universities, at least in part to determine whether the proposed contracts follow something like the *American Civil Liberties Union Guidelines on University and Contract Research.*[59] Although cooperation between university researchers and outside groups is desirable, university committees ought to have guidelines requiring either very large or very restrictive funders to perform compensatory actions or to pay for programs that present "the other side"—such as a discussion of the social and ethical dangers associated with controversial research. In other words, the university ought to attempt to prevent a monopoly in the marketplace of ideas. When laboratories at the University of California began developing 90 percent of the nuclear warheads in the U.S. arsenal, for instance, California professors demanded that the taxpayers and the university fund a massive research and teaching Center for Global Peace and Disarmament.[60] At the national or governmental level, providing articulate spokespersons for "the other side" might mean researchers' lobbying for creating a funding agency for interdisciplinary university projects that deal with ethical and values issues in science and technology. In the United States, the "Ethics and Values" program of the National Science Foundation (NSF) has served this end, despite its limited government funding.[61]

If private interests seek to buy the intellectual capital of university scientists, then researchers must make sure that these interests do so under public scrutiny and at prices that reflect the prior public and taxpayer investment in the research.[62] Otherwise, scientists and engineers may sell our common intellectual birthright. Because this intellectual birthright belongs to all people, researchers' primary duties—especially in uncertain cases of applied science—must be to the public good. Carl

Mitcham discusses this issue in more detail in chapter nine and uses examples from engineering design research. In chapter ten, Carl Cranor makes similar points and argues for more consideration of the public interest in cases that involve consequences to public welfare.

6

Research and Uncertainty

Thomas Edison's extensive biological and chemical laboratories, near Fort Myers, Florida, contain hundreds of unmarked bottles of substances, some harmful. Busy with his research and blessed with an almost flawless memory, Edison never needed to mark any of the bottles, each of which he kept in a distinct place on a distinct shelf in a distinct room of one of his laboratories.

If anyone (other than Edison) took an unmarked bottle from one of the Fort Myers laboratories and told us to drink the contents, we would protest. We would object that being forced to accept a risk—when the exact nature of the risk is uncertain or unknown—is dangerous and unfair. Although no members of the public are forced to drink from Edison's unmarked bottles, we are often compelled to accept the unknown consequences of research, some of which can harm us. As chapter one suggested, military research—especially nuclear testing, for example—has caused massive and catastrophic consequences. However, scientists ought not avoid all work that involves unknown or uncertain consequences. How should researchers respond to such situations of uncertainty?

Scientific Responses to Uncertainty

Perhaps the classic scientific response to a situation of uncertainty in research is to do more research. For example, if epidemiologists are uncertain about the precise level of harm associated with a particular pesticide or food additive, they may do additional work using more sensitive tests, in order to reduce the level of their uncertainty. Instead of measuring parts per million of a toxin, they may do additional work that enables them to measure parts per billion of the toxin. When uncertainties about research data arise because of the limited size of the sample considered, further studies with larger samples help to increase the precision and reliability of our knowledge of a phenomenon. For example, if researchers draw conclusions about the effects of background radiation on 100 people, the results would be more precise and reliable if they performed further studies on 1,000 people or if they conducted the studies over a longer period of time.

Simply doing more research, however, does not always reduce the uncertainty inherent in study results because much uncertainty derives from unavoidable methodological value judgments (see chapter three) inherent in all research. If all data are empirically underdetermined, to some degree, then researchers must use value judgments to bridge the gaps between what they know and don't know, and those value judgments often result in continuing uncertainty despite further research. For example, despite continuing research, heated controversies still occur over the safety of food additives such as nitrates and saccharin.[1] In the United States, the government has sanctioned the use of saccharin but banned the use of cyclamates, arguing that research shows that cyclamates pose more risks. Canada, however, permits cyclamates but not saccharin, on the grounds that research shows that saccharin presents more of a threat.

Another strategy is to attempt to specify the nature and level of the uncertainty so that people will not be misled about the reliability of particular findings and can make their own value judgments about the significance of the uncertainty. In other words, the philosophy behind explicitness about uncertainties in one's research is not only that honesty and objectivity (see chapter three) are desirable but also that "the devil you know is better than the devil you don't know." In order to make uncertainty explicit in research, however, we need to know some of its sources. As mentioned in chapter three, methodological value judgments cause some uncertainties in research.

Experts and Laypersons Deal Differently with Uncertainty

Especially in the area of applied research having public risks—such as testing nuclear weapons or developing genetically engineered crops—researchers and laypersons often make different methodological value judgments about the adequacy of evidence and safety and about how to deal with uncertainty. In particular, scientists' and lay views about the acceptability of dangerous consequences of research frequently diverge, as the discussion of nuclear weapons testing revealed in chapter one. Many industrial researchers attribute public opposition to research on new technologies to lay ignorance, mass paranoia, and anti-industry, anti-science, or anti-government sentiments. Alvin Weinberg, a prominent proponent of commercial nuclear energy, claims that the public has been misled by "environmental hypochondria," hysteria similar to what drove the witch hunts of the fourteenth through sixteenth centuries. Weinberg claims that contemporary researchers need a new "Inquisitor" who can bring the public to its senses. Laypersons, however, often claim that scientific experts frequently have vested interests in conducting certain research, even when it threatens societal health and safety. Spokespersons for public-interest groups maintain that the catastrophic potential of many technological and research-related risks, imposed on society without its consent, has caused widespread feelings of impotence, rage, and depression and an epidemic of human-caused cancer. Sheldon Samuels calls these psychological and physical consequences a result of "industrial cannibalism."[2]

Who is right about the potentially dangerous consequences of research- and technology-related risks, the scientific experts (researchers) or the public? On the one hand, experts may be correct in claiming laypersons are ignorant about many of the technical details of the consequences, technologies, and research that they fear. Indeed, studies of lay risk probability estimates often err by a wide margin. On the other hand, laypersons are correct in arguing that decisions about research safety—how safe is safe enough—are essentially questions about values and ethics, not technical or scientific questions. Therefore, members of the public argue that they have the right to decide the risks that others will impose on them, precisely because the justifiability of risk imposition is an ethical, not merely a technical, issue. In a democracy, citizens and not only experts ought to make the ethical judgments and the decisions that affect public welfare. Hence there are strong ethical grounds for arguing that the public has the right to determine how much and what kind of research and technological risk they will accept.[3]

Ethical Principles for Controlling Research Risk to the Public

At least five ethical principles are at the heart of citizens' rights to control the risks that others impose on them. First, citizens argue that, in the face of research-related environmental and technological uncertainties, the government must take an active role to ensure that members of the public have the best available information so that they can help make knowledgeable policy decisions. As we argued in chapter one, because alleged free choice is free only to the degree that it is informed, the public has a right to know research-related uncertainties and their potential consequences.[4]

Second, the public contends that laypersons, not researchers or implementers of technology, have the right to exercise free informed consent to the risks imposed on them. (See chapter one for a discussion of free informed consent.) For example, government already requires medical researchers to obtain written informed consent from all subjects involved in experiments, to have independent institutional committees to review all proposed research, and to allow audits and site visits to determine the conditions under which they perform research. The government attempts to protect the freedom and security of experimental subjects because researchers have a conflict of interest. They wish to obtain information and to advance knowledge and yet they have to protect subjects' welfare.[5] Because of this conflict of interest, it is ethically suspect for the welfare of experimental subjects to depend solely on the good will of researchers. Similarly, the public must also be protected against experimenters' conflicts of interest. The single best protection is to insure that all those potentially affected by some research or technology give genuine free informed consent to the possible consequences.

Third, society has the duty to use its regulations and laws to protect members made vulnerable to research risks through lack of information, poor education, or poverty.[6] The rationale for protecting the most vulnerable members of society from dangerous effects of research is that everyone has rights to equal protection of life and bodily security. Because equal protection does not mean sameness of protection, but whatever degree of protection will ensure equal levels of health and safety for all, society has a special obligation to its most vulnerable members.[7] Members of many prominent research groups recognize this obligation. For example, in recent studies on the effect of pesticides on children, as the previous chapter noted, a subcommittee of the U.S. NRC/NAS recommended that because of uncertainties in our data about pesticides, scientists should use an additional ''uncertainty factor'' to protect children. The subcommittee's rationale was that children are much more vulnerable to pesticides than adults are. They specifically recommended that, when there is evidence of postnatal toxicity or when data regarding children are incomplete, researchers should take the current "no-effect" dose of a pesticide and divide it by a factor of up to 10 to obtain the presumed no-effect dose.[8] By using more conservative data in the face of risk uncertainties, researchers thus protect the most vulnerable members of society.

Fourth, hazards imposed by society ought to be distributed according to principles of fairness. For example, certain groups of people (such as black subjects of syphilis experiments) ought not bear the risks associated with research, while other groups (such as whites) receive most of the benefits. Rather, fairness in allocating research burdens and benefits requires that people be treated equitably and that researchers recognize their full human rights. Many of the research abuses detailed in chapter one occurred because scientists did not practice fairness.

Fifth, government has the duty not to assume that unknown or uncertain risks are either zero or unimportant. Such a way of dealing with uncertainty is ethically questionable, especially from the point of view of the public who may be at risk. Yet a recent study by the NRC appears to have handled uncertainty in this manner. The authors of the study admitted the need for more research both on patterns of fluoride exposure from foods and dental products and on fluoride's effects on bone strength and tooth enamel. They also noted limited data on possible links between fluoride and the risk of hip or other bone fractures. Yet, despite the uncertainties, the committee concluded that "no basis" exists to recommend that the Environmental Protection Agency lower the current standard for fluoride in drinking water.[9] Drawing such a conclusion about fluoride risk in a situation of research uncertainty is problematic. The committee could just as well have concluded that there is "no basis" for believing that fluoride's effects on bone strength, tooth enamel, and bone fractures are completely benign. Logically, if one has not done research relevant to bone strength, tooth enamel, and bone fractures, then one does not know whether current fluoride standards ought to be lowered. Hence, to note the uncertainty of, or even ignore, certain data relevant to public health standards—and then to claim that "no basis" exists for changing public health standards—is misleading. It begs the question. Such question-begging conclusions seem an inappropriate response to uncertainty.

Likewise, the Department of Energy (DOE) studies on the proposed Yucca Mountain (Nevada) repository for high-level nuclear waste disposal include a number of cases of the DOE researchers' assuming, in the face of inadequate data and uncertain results, that the facility will be safe for thousands of years. Indeed, many of the key methodological value judgments (see chapter three) in research address how to deal with situations of uncertainty. In its research on Yucca Mountain, the DOE admits it operates under the principle that if ''current information does not indicate that the site is unsuitable, then the . . . suitability finding could be supported.''[10] Clearly, however, the inability of researchers to show the unsuitability of a site does not mean that they ought to support a suitability finding, particularly if the site could cause millions of cancers over thousands of years and massive contamination of land and groundwater. Logical and ethical problems arise when researchers decide that their inability to prove that a site is unsuitable, in the face of short-term, limited data, allows them to assume that the site is suitable. The logical problem is that failure to disprove something is not adequate to prove it. The ethical problem is that—in a situation in which a majority of the population believes that permanent disposal of radioactive waste is unsafe and in which 80 percent of Nevadans oppose the repository at Yucca Mountain,[11]—government ought to take account of public preferences. Moreover, given the opposition of the state and the nation, basing conclusions of site suitability on uncertainty merely gives the DOE an excuse to impose a potentially serious risk on an unwilling public. These considerations suggest that researchers may not be justified in imposing unknown risks on the public. Absence of evidence is not evidence of absence.

Uncertainty, Research Risks, and Types I and II Error

If, in situations of uncertainty, researchers may err in forcing unknown research risks on the public, then some of the basic norms that researchers follow may be wrong. In the remaining sections of this chapter, we argue that—in situations having potentially serious public consequences or applications—researchers' traditional methods of dealing with uncertainty, especially with respect to types I and II error, are ethically questionable. To illustrate our points, consider the 1986–1987 deforestation/extinction controversy discussed in the previous chapter. The conflict among Kangas, Noss, and others showed that ecological researchers were divided on the issue of how to interpret uncertain ecological studies that could be used to justify destruction of the tropical environment. In the Kangas–Noss dispute, researchers on different sides of the controversy invoked the notion of statistical errors of types I and II, respectively, to defend their positions. Noss argued that, in situations of ecological uncertainty, the desirable and conservative course of action would be to risk type-I errors (false positives), rather than type-II errors (false negatives).[12] Simberloff (following a widely used norm) argued that "risking type-I rather than type-II error is not the most conservative course."[13] We explain types I and II error and then attempt to determine the correct view. We also draw some *prima facie* ethical conclusions to use in other cases that involve uncertain research data or interpretations.

Consider the case of research engineers who must assess the uncertain consequences of developing a liquefied natural gas (LNG) facility. In chapter nine, Carl Mitcham will assess several general cases in the ethics of research design. Given a volatile situation, with many vested interests and policy consequences, what ethical principles direct how they ought to interpret the results of their studies to the public, to developers/industry, and to environmentalists? If the researchers overemphasize the LNG risk, the community and industry could suffer serious economic losses in avoiding development of a LNG facility. In a situation of uncertainty, however, if they underemphasize the risk, the community might face an LNG accident that could kill many people. How should they decide? At least two facts complicate the decision. One is that expert estimates of risks to people living near LNG terminals vary by a factor of 100 million.[14] Another complicating factor is that much of researchers' disagreement regarding uncertain probabilities and consequences, like LNG risks, originates from limited experience and therefore limited data on new technologies.[15] For example, before the Browns Ferry nuclear accident occurred, government experts said that the mishap had the same probability of occurrence as a large meteor's striking the earth. Assessors likewise called the Chernobyl accident "highly improbable" before it happened.[16] A variety of similar uncertainties force researchers to make value judgments (see chapter three) in order to interpret their conclusions and to provide requested input to policymakers. They must judge whether, in a situation of uncertainty, type-I or type-II error is more preferable. We shall argue that, in part, the correctness of our value judgment depends on how "applied" the research is, whether it has potentially serious practical applications and consequences.

When researchers make a decision about a statistical hypothesis, at least two different types of error may occur. Type-I errors (false positives) occur when one rejects a true null hypothesis; errors of type II occur when one fails to reject a false null hypothesis.[17] In the Kangas–Noss controversy, one null hypothesis might be, for example, that conservation corridors—strips of land designed to allow species to migrate from one wildlife reserve to another—will not delay the extinction of the Florida panther, *Felis concolor*, beyond the year 2014. Statistical procedure dictates that we make assumptions about the tolerable size of each of these types of error, and on this basis we choose a testing pattern for our null hypothesis. The concept of *significance*, for example, is often defined in terms of a type-I risk of error of either 0.01 or 0.05, where there is not more than a 1 in 100 or a 5 in 100 chance of committing the error of rejecting a true null hypothesis. Determining significance, however, is not sufficient to determine the more serious error, type I or type II. An analogous issue arises in law. Does one err more in acquitting a guilty person or in convicting an innocent person? In evaluating potential consequences and applications of their work, ought researchers strive to minimize type-I error (rejecting a true null hypothesis)? Churchman says that if we minimize type-I error when we consider a hypothesis with practical consequences, we minimize the possibility of rejecting a harmless development. He calls this the "Producer Risk." Or, in such a situation, ought one to minimize type-II error (not rejecting a false null hypothesis)? Churchman likewise claims that when considering a hypothesis with practical consequences, in a situation of uncertainty, when we minimize type-II error, we minimize the error of accepting a harmful development. He calls this the "Consumer Risk."[18]

In the case of the Florida panther, Churchman's "Producer Risk" and "Consumer Risk" might be better termed, respectively, "developer risk" and "public risk." In this revised terminology, minimizing developer risk amounts to minimizing the chance of rejecting the null hypothesis, minimizing the chance of rejecting the hypothesis, for example, that conservation corridors will not delay extinction of the Florida panther beyond the year 2014. But minimizing the chance of rejecting it means increasing the chance of accepting it. And to the degree that researchers accept this null hypothesis, to that same extent will there be no argument for conservation corridors (at least in the case of the panther). If no one makes other arguments for conservation corridors, then presumably the land set aside for the corridors can now be developed. Such a commercial enterprise would likely benefit developers and presumably reduce their risk, although it would likely increase the risk to the public as a whole, if one assumes that the public at large has an interest in conservation rather than development. Hence minimizing developer risk (in Churchman's sense)—in situations of uncertainty where research hypotheses have real-world consequences—appears to increase public risk.[19] An analogous argument can show that minimizing public (type-II) risk—in situations of uncertainty where research hypotheses have real-world consequences—increases developer risk. In the panther case, minimizing type-II error increases the chance of establishing the corridors, which presumably would benefit the public at large (rather than developers).

How does one decide, in a situation of uncertainty, whether to run the developer or type-I risk of rejecting a true null hypothesis, for example, that conservation corridors will not delay extinction of the Florida panther beyond the year 2014? Or, in cases of uncertainty where the research hypotheses have practical consequences, ought one run the (public or type-II) risk of not rejecting an allegedly false null hypothesis, for example, that conservation corridors will not delay extinction of the Florida panther beyond the year 2014? In such cases of applied research, decreasing developer risk might hurt the public, whereas decreasing public risk might hurt the developers, as the previous paragraph illustrated.[20] In subsequent paragraphs, we argue that researchers have a *prima facie* obligation to minimize public risk in evaluating possible consequences of applied research, especially work that involves potentially serious consequences to public ethics and welfare.

Many Researchers Minimize Type-I Error

Especially in "pure" science (if there is such a thing) researchers usually make the value judgment to prefer type-II errors over type-I. That is, they elect to take the risk of not rejecting a false hypothesis rather than the risk of rejecting a true hypothesis. Consumers and the public generally, however, especially with more applied research, probably prefer type-I (over type-II) errors, false positives over false negatives. That is, on Churchman's account, researchers in applied areas tend to prefer the risk of not rejecting harmful developments to the risk of rejecting harmless developments or consequences. The public, however, tends to prefer the risk of rejecting harmless development or consequences to the error of not rejecting dangerous development or consequences.[21] After examining some of the reasons that many researchers tend to minimize type-I errors, we argue that—in situations of uncertainty where research hypotheses have potentially serious consequences—a stronger case can be made for minimizing type-II errors.

Preferences for minimizing type-I risks might arise in part because they appear more consistent with scientific practice. Hypothesis-testing in science operates on the basis of limiting false positives (assertions of effects where none exists) or limiting rejections of a true null hypothesis. In order to minimize type-I errors, researchers design studies to guard against the influence of all possible confounding variables, and they demand replication of study results before accepting them as supporting a particular hypothesis. They apply tests of statistical significance that reject results whose probability of being due to chance, whose p value, is greater than, for example, 5 percent. As a result, there is a certain conservatism or inertia in the research enterprise, often rationalized as the healthy skepticism characteristic of a ''scientific'' approach. Preferences for minimizing type-I errors are also consistent with the standards of proof required in criminal cases, as opposed to cases in torts. Our law requires the jury in a criminal case to be sure beyond a reasonable doubt that a defendant is guilty, before deciding against him; standards of proof in criminal cases thus also reveal a preference for type-II error, a preference for not rejecting the null hypothesis (innocence). The standards accept the risk of acquitting a guilty person.[22]

Researchers' preferences for type-II error might also arise in part from the fact that many studies are done by those who have a vested interest in the outcome, applications, or consequences. Such researchers typically underestimate risks,[23] at least in part because they are difficult to identify and because these researchers assume that unidentified risks are zero. Researchers' preferences for minimizing type-I risk, in a situation of uncertainty, may also arise as a consequence of the fact that experts almost always use widely accepted Bayesian decision rules rather than the maximin decision rule. The Bayesian rules are based on expected utility and subjective probabilities, whereas the maximin rule forces one to choose the option where the worst outcome is better than the worst outcome of all the other options.[24] In situations of uncertainty where research hypotheses have potentially serious consequences, using a Bayesian decision rule (especially when those sympathetic to development provide the subjective probabilities) typically generates a choice in favor of a low probability, but potentially catastrophic, scientific, technological, or environmental impact of research. In the same situation, however, using a maximin decision rule likely produces a verdict against an uncertain (but potentially catastrophic or irreversible) consequence.[25] In other words, different norms for rational decision-making under uncertainty produce conflicting evaluations about the acceptability of the potential consequences of research. Contrary to most assessors, we argue that there are *prima facie* grounds for minimizing type-II error or public risk in situations of uncertainty where the research has potentially serious consequences.

Why We Should Minimize Type-II Errors in Applied Research

Arguing that, in general, there are grounds for reducing public (type-II) risks associated with applied research amounts to showing that, in cases with potentially serious consequences, the burden of proof (regarding risk acceptability) should be placed on the person wishing to reduce developer (type-I), rather than public (type-II), risk. If this argument is correct, then, in the absence of evidence to the contrary, one may assume that, in situations of uncertainty where there are potentially serious consequences, researchers (like Kangas and Noss) ought to minimize type-II risks. In chapter 10, Carl Cranor argues for a similar conclusion in the area of public health research.

There are a number of reasons for holding that, in many areas of applied work, researchers generally have the duty to minimize type-II errors, viz., (in Churchman's terms) to minimize the risk of not rejecting a potentially dangerous action that puts the public at risk. First, minimizing the chance of not rejecting false null hypotheses with important practical consequences—that is, minimizing judgments that a potentially harmful research-related impact is harmless—is reasonable, in general, on grounds of protecting the public. Most political theorists, regardless of their persuasion, would probably agree that protecting the public from serious harm (e.g., loss of species, nuclear accidents) takes precedence over enhancing welfare (e.g., by permitting land development or by providing electrical power on demand). This is in part because the right to protection against those who cause harm outweighs rights to heightened welfare. Society must strive to prevent acts that cause serious harm before it promotes acts that enhance welfare. As part of the Hippocratic oath states: "First, do no harm."

But why is protecting society against loss of a species or a unique habitat—as in the Kangas–Noss case—a case of protection against harm, rather than one of enhancing welfare? One important factor is that a species or a unique habitat contributes to diversity, which at least benefits humans aesthetically. Species and unique habitats are also essential on utilitarian grounds because of their medicinal and economic importance and because they contribute to human health, food, industry, or shelter. Moreover, even for species and habitats with no known economic benefits, medicinal or otherwise, future scientific discoveries leave room for the possibility that they may be useful at a later date. Also, apart from economic considerations, species and habitats have both inherent worth and a variety of intrinsic and instrumental values for humans. Because species and habitats contribute to well-being in all these ways, causing their extinction or disappearance is an act that, generally speaking, harms that well-being. To cause extinction or disappearance of a habitat is also questionable because the act destroys something that already exists. Presumably if one brought a new species to some area or introduced a new habitat, a case could be made, under some circumstances, that the act constituted an enhancement of welfare. But if one causes a species to go extinct or a habitat to disappear, then one has destroyed something already in existence. As a consequence, humans could no longer enjoy the species or habitat. One has failed to protect against loss of a good, the species or the habitat. If one fails to allow economic development or application of some research-related activity, however, one does not reduce welfare (taking away something, like a species, that already exists there) but enhances welfare. Hence to permit implementation of actions based on research—such as using nuclear fission technology—is more a case of enhancing welfare than of protecting against harm. And therefore, all things being equal, it is more important to protect the public from type-II errors (not rejecting potentially harmful research-related consequences and applications) than to protect it from type-I errors (rejecting harmless impacts). This is at least in part because enjoying other freedoms seems to require protection from serious harm.[26] Bentham,[27] for instance, in discussing an important part of liberalism, argued that government's sole goal ought to be the greatest happiness of the greatest possible number of the community, and that happiness consists of maximum enjoyment and minimum suffering. However, he cautioned, much as Nozick (and others who argue for only minimal ethical obligations) might, that ''the care of providing for his enjoyments ought to be left almost entirely to each individual; the principal function of government being to protect him from sufferings.'' In other words, Bentham established protection from serious harm as more basic than enhancing welfare. If he is right, then it is more important for researchers—indeed everyone—to protect from harm (via preservation, for example) than to enhance welfare (via economic development of some rare and threatened habitat). Of course, it is difficult to draw the line between what enhances welfare and what avoids harm. Nevertheless, just as there is a basic distinction between negative rights and welfare rights,[28] so also there is a basic distinction between protective laws (e.g., prohibiting infringements on already existing persons, species or habitats) and welfare laws (e.g., providing some economic good such as development of a particular parcel of land). Likewise, philosophers distinguish between killing versus letting die, and between acts of commission and acts of omission.[29] Therefore, to the degree that minimizing type-II risks prohibits positive harm, protects rather than enhances welfare, and governs commissions rather than omissions, to that extent researchers ought to minimize type-II (rather than type-I) risks in applied situations characterized by uncertainty.

Another reason for minimizing public (type-II) risks in such situations is that those who fund particular research, e.g., on a new drug, typically receive more benefits from the research than do members of the public. Whoever receives most of the benefits of research ought to bear most of its risks and costs. For one large group (the public) to carry most of the risks of particular research (e.g., on a hazardous technology like chemical pesticides), while a small subset (chemical producers and users, for example) receives more of the benefits, defies fairness. Ethically asymmetrical, it amounts to a gerrymandering of the concepts of justice.[30] Of course, in many cases the public does receive potential benefits from research. The point here is that those who bear the risks of research ought to be those who receive most of its benefits. Researchers working in applied areas ought not violate the basic ethical rule— prohibiting the use of some persons (the public) as a means to the ends of other persons (researchers or their sponsors) or as a means to the end of economic welfare. Most moral philosophers presuppose this rule, as do tort law and the legal guarantees of the Fifth and Fourteenth Amendments to the U.S. Constitution.[31] If people ignored this rule and discriminated against others whenever it was economically expedient, the concept of rights would have no meaning. Because people do have rights to bodily security and to equal protection, ethical rules must forbid using people merely as means to the ends of others, even when those ends are valuable research or its economically desirable consequences. Under such rules, maximizing economic welfare cannot justify a preference for type-II or public risk in a situation characterized by uncertainty and potentially serious consequences.[32]

The public typically needs more risk protection than do promoters of particular research having potentially catastrophic consequences, which supports the limitation of type-II rather than type-I risks. They need more protection because members of the public usually have fewer financial resources than developers or promoters of a new technology or research application. Laypersons also have greater needs because they usually have less information about how to deal with societal hazards created by applied research and because they often face bureaucratic denials of public danger or threats to their interests. Laypersons' vulnerability in this regard has been confirmed repeatedly. When the toxic polybrominated biphenyl (PBB) was accidentally used in cattle feed in

Michigan, for example, it was the most widespread and least reported chemical disaster ever to happen in the western world. Strong evidence pointed to contamination in September 1973, but extensive research and detailed articles on the problem did not appear, even in the local papers, for two more years. Larger newspapers, like the *Detroit Free Press* and the *Detroit News*, did not examine the crisis until fours years after its appearance. The reason for ignoring the problem for so long was that the local bureaucrats denied the farmers' claims. This bureaucratic denial of danger led to the PBB-caused deaths of tens of thousands of farm animals and to the contamination of nine million people who ate tainted meat.[33] The mercury poisoning in Japan likewise illustrates the typical failure to protect against public risk because of bureaucratic denials, industry indifference, and the isolation of the afflicted. In Japan, the dangers of mercury poisoning were identified in 1940, deaths were reported in 1948, and Minimata poisoning occurred in 1953. Only in the 1960s, however, did public awareness of the problem motivate officials to take action against mercury contamination. Because of these and similar instances of whistle swallowing (rather than whistle blowing) in cases involving hazards such as asbestos, biotechnology, and chemical dumps, a strong possibility exists that new research-related public risks will be ignored. These examples argue that in many cases of applied research characterized by uncertainty, the public, rather than an industrial or technological sponsor of research, has a greater need for protection.[34]

Yet another reason for minimizing public risks—especially in cases characterized by research-related uncertainty and potentially serious consequences—is that the public ought to have rights to protection against researchers' decisions that could impose incompensable damages. These rights arise out of the consideration that everyone has an obligation to compensate those whom he harms. Applied researchers who minimize type-I (rather than type-II) errors can cause uncompensated harms—like death—as some of the examples in chapter one show. Some research can also harm the environment. Both types of harms may be incompensable if they destroy something (like life) that cannot be replaced. Also, to the degree that environmental benefits, such as biodiversity and clean air, belong to the ''commons,'' then to that same degree do we all have rights to it. As Aldo Leopold put it, in his introduction to *A Sand County Almanac*: ''the chance to find a pasqueflower is a right as inalienable as free speech.''[35] To the degree that Leopold is right, applied researchers ought to minimize public risks, risks to this ''commons,'' rather than developer or industrial risks, when they face situations of uncertainty. But if so, then those who impose or increase public risk through their research have a duty to minimize the risk, to protect people from it, or to compensate the public for its imposition. The ethical grounds for preventing potentially serious research-related dangers are that, in cases where those responsible cannot redress or compensate the harms done to others, the risks should be eliminated. Causing a species to become extinct or a person to contract cancer is not like causing a car to be wrecked. The car is replaceable and compensable; the species or the person is not. And if not, then the risks to the public because of research-related threats like species extinction and use of carcinogenic chemicals should be minimized. In other words, if all people have rights to redress for harm done to them, and if people (facing a situation of uncertainty) make faulty research-related decisions but cannot make good on their injuries to others' interests or welfare, then they ought not be allowed to put the interests of others in jeopardy. To do so, when they cannot meet claims against them, is to deny in-principle rights of victims to compensation or redress of damages. If we consider Judith Jarvis Thomson's notion of ''incompensable harms,'' harms so serious that no amount of money could possibly compensate the victims (e.g., for a loss of a species or habitat), then it appears that extinction and death, at least, are obviously ''incompensable harms.'' One cannot compensate a dead person or reverse species extinction. As Thomson puts it, speaking of another case, ''however fair and efficient the judicial system may be, . . . [those] who cause incompensable harms by their negligence cannot square accounts with their victims.''[36] This means that anyone who imposes a significant risk (e.g., death) on others, without their free informed consent, imposes an incompensable, and therefore morally unjustifiable, harm.

If imposition of incompensable risks might be justified in cases in which potential victims—of research-related experimentation, for example—give free informed consent, then this suggests another reason for minimizing type-II, as opposed to type-I, risk in situations characterized by uncertainty and by potentially serious consequences: The public is less likely than the sponsors of research to have given free informed consent to the imposition of research-related risk. Yet imposition of risk should not occur without the free informed consent of those who must bear it. This dictum holds true in medical research and experimentation, and can easily be shown to have an analogue in other research as well.[37] The public is less likely to have given free informed consent because research sponsors often have scientific or technical information that they do not share with the public. Patents, profits, and competition with other businessmen often keep them from providing data about research-related risk to the public. The public as a whole is also less able than industrial sponsors of research to give free informed consent to a dangerous environmental impact, both because laypersons usually have less scientific and technical expertise than risk imposers and because researchers often behave paternalistically toward the public. The government's occasional suppression of information about new scientific and environmental hazards further jeopardizes the public's right to free informed consent to research-related risks. Evidence shows that most of those bearing high levels of public risk have not given free informed consent. For all these reasons, there are strong grounds for minimizing type-II, rather than type-I, risk in situations characterized by uncertainty and by potentially serious consequences.

Strong economic grounds likewise support minimizing type-II (rather than type-I) risk whenever this minimization reflects consumer preferences. In situations characterized by uncertainty and potentially serious consequences, consumer sovereignty justifies letting the public decide the fate of very risky, proposed new research and research-related activities (and therefore to minimize public risk). This justification is a revered one: "no taxation without representation."[38] Citizens themselves, as Schelling[39] notes, have safeguarded consumer sovereignty by means of "arms, martyrdom, boycott, or some principles held to be self-evident. . . . [I]t includes the inalienable right of the consumer to make his own mistakes." Minimizing type-II (rather than type-I) risk, in situations characterized by uncertainty and by potentially serious consequences, is also justified in the name of public self-determination and consistent with most ethical theories about when one might justify paternalism. Sponsors of applied research thus ought not behave paternalistically toward the public in alleging that impositions of research-related risk further the public interest, even when members of society do not consent to the risk. In his classic discussion of liberty, J. S. Mill[40] makes it clear that it is acceptable to override individual decisionmaking only to protect others or to protect someone from selling himself into slavery. Any other justification for a limitation on individual freedom, Mill claims, would amount to a dangerous infringement on individual autonomy. If Mill is correct, paternalistic decisions should only prevail in the situations Mill describes. Thus, in general no grounds support the use of paternalism to justify research-related decisions having consequences that threaten either the public or its legitimate interests. Minimizing type-II risk in uncertain and potentially dangerous situations also might be less likely to lead to social disruption and political unrest than minimizing type-I risk. This is because effective management of societal risks, as many assessors have pointed out, requires the cooperation of a large body of laypeople. Otherwise accidents, costly publicity, and civil disobedience may result. Hence there are sound practical reasons, in applied research characterized by uncertainty, for minimizing public risk.

Conclusion: Give Priority to the Public

The ethical analysis in this chapter argues that in general there are reasons for giving priority—in situations characterized by research-related uncertainty and potentially serious consequences—to public welfare and public decisionmaking. In emphasizing the priority of third-party obligations in such cases, we are emphasizing the primacy of public, democratic control of research having the potential to cause dangerous results. In chapter 10, Carl Cranor argues for a similar point. Both conclusions reemphasize a point that Jefferson made: the only safe locus of power in a democracy is the people. Public accountability also helps researchers become more sensitive to the ethical dimensions of research-related impacts and applications.

7

A Case Study in Conservation Research: Uncertain Science in Controversial and Litigious Times

Why should we worry about species extinction? Individual species have always come into, and gone out of, existence. Because of factors such as natural selection, adaption, and climate change, some species have evolved into new taxa, while other species have gone extinct. Extinction is thus a ''natural'' process, even though it is forever.

What is disturbing about more recent, human-caused extinctions, however, is that they are occurring much more rapidly than earlier, non-human events. Harvard biologist E. O. Wilson, for example, estimates that current rates of species extinction are between 1,000 and 10,000 times greater than they were before any human intervention in nature.[1] Consider the case of mammalian extinctions in the Americas after humans arrived here during the Late Pleistocene. Shortly after the arrival of human hunters, 38 percent (120 genera) of South American land mammals became extinct, and 28 percent (114 genera) of North American land mammals vanished. These human-induced extinctions occurred at two to four times the rate caused by earlier, nonhuman events.[2] In our own era, economic development of wildlands has accelerated extinction to an incredible degree. Wilson belives that we humans destroy approximately 140 invertebrate species every day.[3] Because a majority of species live in tropical forests, and because half of these forests are already gone,[4] extinctions are increasing at an exponential rate. In nations like Brazil and Madagascar, where roughly 90 percent of the species are endemic (occur nowhere else),[5] where humans destroy one to two percent of forest land each year,[6] and where only about two percent of total land is protected,[7] the losses are dramatic.

Such escalating losses are disturbing not only because species are unique and irreplaceable products of millions of years of evolution, but also because species have such beauty and scientific value. Because species are like the rivets that hold "spaceship earth" together, destroying them might also jeopardize the natural systems they secure. Mangroves cut for firewood cannot protect coastlines from erosion, and earthworms killed by pesticides cannot aerate soils. Likewise, willows bulldozed by developers cannot provide an organic molecule for aspirin, and sea squirts destroyed by chemical runoff cannot provide antiviral medicines. Indeed, ten percent of the GNP of the United States is directly traceable to wild species used in agriculture, industry, and medicine.[8]

Applying Research Ethics to Four Specific Cases: Overview

Given the importance of preventing massive extinctions, what are the ethical obligations of biological researchers who face a situation of scientific uncertainty regarding their ability to save a particular species or subspecies? Consider the case of the Florida panther, a natural symbol of Florida in much the same way that the bald eagle is a natural symbol of the United States. Only about 40 members of this endangered subspecies remain, largely in the swampy, southern parts of Florida. Is it possible to save the Florida panther in the wild? In this chapter, we discuss this question and illustrate how to solve some problems faced by applied researchers dealing with ethically and scientifically uncertain situations.[9] In the case of the Florida panther, scientists face an ethical dilemma between advocacy and objectivity, between promoting environmental welfare (by trying to save the panther) and admitting objectively that saving the panther will be difficult if not impossible. The researchers must make the ethical decisions not only about how to interpret uncertain scientific research about the status of the Florida panthers, but also about how to assess and present research results that could lead to desirable or undesirable consequences for the public and the environment, particularly if they are misinterpreted. In this chapter, we investigate how our earlier conclusions—about the primacy of public good (chapter four) and about type-I and type-II errors (chapter six), for example—apply to research ethics in conservation biology. Perhaps the most basic question we address is researchers' responsibilities to interpret their results when they know that they are likely to be used "by the powerful for the direct manipulation of the powerless."[10] This issue is one of the central ethical problems facing the researcher, as our earlier examples of studies of pesticide harm to children and tropical deforestation reveal (chapter five).

This and the next three chapters present other case studies, addressing research in conservation biology (chapter seven), in psychology, anthropology, and physiology (chapter eight), in engineering design (chapter nine), and in public health (chapter ten). Chapter eight shows how the sexist and racist biases of our cultural values unethically influence research methods and practices. Here Helen Longino demonstrates that the *cultural values of researchers themselves* can make their research ethically questionable. As this case study on gender and racial bias illustrates, if professionals like researchers do not promote the public good (chapter four) and make every effort to establish the values of a liberal society (chapter five), then their own research can be twisted by faulty ethical values. In chapter nine Carl Mitcham shows how various vested interests (manufacturers, military contractors) can unethically influence the types of products that research in engineering design makes available to us. In other words, because the *partisan and economic values of those who fund/sponsor research* can be ethically questionable, the case study exemplifies points we made in chapters four through six, that researchers' first duties are typically to promote public welfare, to disclose questionable research practices in industry, and even to act as whistleblowers when necessary. In chapter ten Carl Cranor illustrates how *research methods themselves* contain implicit ethical commitments that are questionable, particularly in the area of public-health research and toxicology. This chapter illustrates some of the same ethical principles that we developed in chapter six and that Cranor discusses in chapter ten. For example, in situations of uncertainty affecting public welfare, both of us argue that researchers ought to minimize type-II, rather than type-I, error. All four case studies should show the importance of the ethical principles developed earlier in the volume. Consider first a case dealing with biological research, that of the Florida panther.

Research and the Florida Panther: Background

What we call the "cougar" or "mountain lion" (*Felis concolor*) has 15 recognized subspecies in North America, one of which is the Florida panther, *F. concolor coryi.*[11] The Florida panther is a medium-sized subspecies whose members have golden brown, short, stiff hair.[12] It has distinctive long limbs, small feet, and a rich ferruginous color.[13] Three external characteristics often observed on Florida panthers are not found in combination on other subspecies of *F. concolor:*[14] a right angle crook at the end of the tail, a whorl of hair (like a ''cowlick'') in the middle of the back, and irregular white flecking on the head, nape, and shoulders.[15] Although the cougar or mountain lion once ranged widely throughout North America, the species' range is now fragmented, and substantial populations remain only in parts of the West.[16] Likewise, the Florida panther formerly ranged throughout much of the southeastern United States, from eastern Texas to South Carolina,[17] but now it lives only in remote areas of southern Florida.[18] The total number of individuals remaining in the wild probably is less than 40.[19] The Florida panther and one other subspecies, *F. c. costaricensis* (found only in southern Central America and probably Colombia), are listed as endangered by the U.S. Fish and Wildlife Service in 1986.

Like many other large, warm-blooded predators, the Florida panther occupies a precarious ecological position.[20] Because it is a relatively large mammal, it must expend great energy to obtain food. Therefore the Florida panther must hunt prey items with a high enough energy content—such as the white-tailed deer and the ferral pig—to offset the energy expended to acquire them.[21] High energy demand and expenditures also mean that even transient shortages of deer and pigs may strongly affect populations of the Florida panther. Because of the panther's high energy demand and its low per capita reproductive output (between two and three young per female biennially), population sizes of the subspecies have never been very high.[22] Thus, even before extensive human settlement of its natural range, probably only 1,400 individuals lived in Florida.[23] The Florida panther population declined even more after the arrival of European settlers.[24] Settlers viewed it as a competitor and eliminated most populations even before 1900. Those populations that survived did so because of their remoteness from humans; eventually, survivors remained only in southern Florida.

Reduction of high-quality prey populations as a result of human activities and land development has exacerbated the direct hunting pressure on the Florida panther. Adult Florida panthers ordinarily need to consume one deer (or similar-sized prey item) per week and pregnant females need to consume two such prey items.[25] From these numbers, one can see that a wild population of about 50 panthers would require a very large and accessible prey population.[26] Populations of large prey items, however, have become increasingly rare in the southeastern United States. In southern Florida, low habitat quality seems to have promoted chronically low densities of deer.[27] The most severe current threat to the survival of the Florida panther, small population sizes, [28] increase both the vulnerability of an organism to adverse environmental change and the chance of depressed genetic viability because of too much inbreeding.[29] The Florida panther itself displays a higher percentage of abnormal sperm than other subspecies of *Felis concolor*.[30] Expansion of human activities such as agriculture, industry, water management, and housing has likewise jeopardized the future of the Florida panther because they have reduced and fragmented available habitat lands. Fragmentation of their habitat thus has forced panthers to cross inhospitable terrain and to expose themselves to additional risks. Between 1980 and 1986, for example, we know that 10 panthers died on Florida roads after being struck by vehicles.[31]

Because so little is known about the panther,[32] including the minimum viable population size needed for its survival, it is not possible to specify sufficient conditions for guaranteeing the survival of the panther in the wild for 20 years (the estimated mean time to extinction).[33] One major scientific uncertainty is whether genetic inbreeding has already doomed the subspecies. Another uncertainty is whether the state could set aside enough protected land—approximately 50,000 acres for each panther.[34] For a viable population of about 50 panthers, an acceptable wild habitat with enough prey would amount to nearly 3 million acres.[35] In part because there are not 3 million acres of contiguous lands available in Florida to serve as panther habitats, many researchers have argued that any effort to preserve the Florida panther will fail without the use of captive breeding and reintroduction of the panthers propagated in captivity.[36] Other biologists, however, have argued that a system of land corridors, connecting small tracts of panther habitat, would enable the panther to survive in the wild.[37] Still other researchers say the corridors would not work and would be too expensive; hence they argue that saving the Florida panther should not be a high ethical priority.[38] What are the ethical obligations of biological researchers in such a situation of scientific uncertainty? How should they present and interpret their research and conclusions? As one researcher put it,

> two analysts can legitimately come to two different . . . conclusions from the same raw data. Although there are standards of good practice to help researchers make these judgments, there are no simple, unambiguous rules about what to do at each step. The . . . conclusions . . . often involve a

combination of scientific evidence and personal judgment that might not be apparent to readers of research reports. This kind of problem is probably much more prevalent than outright cheating, and it has a bigger effect on science.[39]

Ethics, Economics, and Panther Preservation

In a situation of scientific uncertainty regarding panther preservation, some researchers might claim that the benefits of developing panther habitat outweigh the benefits of attempting to preserve the subspecies. In other words, researchers might emphasize the uncertainties in their panther work, in part because they might believe development and its associated impacts may produce a net benefit for the public. The general ethical question their belief raises is how great the human benefits must be to offset seriously harmful environmental impacts and associated development—e.g., building the Aswan Dam, or causing massive extinctions. This is a difficult question because representing hypothesized public or environmental interests does not necessarily represent all the interests of various members of society. Hence, in this case, both environmentalists and developers each could claim to represent the public interest.[40] In general, however, as we argued in chapter five, a number of reasons argue that environmentalists, not developers, more accurately and more often represent the public and hence that researchers ought to follow their account of ''public interest.'' One reason is that, if a law or policy involves no violation of the basic rights of any individual and benefits the public as a whole, then one ought to follow it, rather than those laws and policies that benefit only a subset of the public, e.g., developers. Once one realizes that biodiversity or conservation benefits everybody, *present and future*, whereas development of an area benefits primarily present developers and those present people who benefit from development, it appears that often a greater number of people gain from conservation. For example, each year Americans spend more than $14 billion on nonconsumptive wildlife-related recreation.[41] If the figures for consumptive, wildlife-related recreation were included, the numbers would be many times higher. They illustrate that conservation may be desirable, even on purely economic grounds.[42] And if so, then researchers need not believe that their scientific uncertainties (regarding the panther) argue for development rather than preservation of the panther habitat.

True, the current economic benefits of development, at least for some, may overshadow the current environmental benefits of preservation. Nevertheless, such a situation does not make development morally preferable, because no one has a *moral right*, as such, to develop a particular area. Although developers may have a *legal right* to certain land, by virtue of purchasing it, people have no moral or legal right to develop it any way they wish. For one thing, ''police power'' and ''takings'' impose legal limits, as does the fact that exclusionary property rights would be incompatible.[43] There also are moral limits imposed on property rights by the fact that property is only a weak, and not a strong, right.[44] Weak rights are those whose exercise is contingent on whether they serve the common good; they can be overridden when the common good demands it. Strong rights are those that can never be overridden for any reason. Legal and philosophical scholars have reached virtual unanimity that property is not a strong right.[45] Development also is not generally preferable to preservation because everyone has moral rights to equal opportunity to obtain and use environmental resources such as land. Because of these rights, developers and researchers who slant uncertain research conclusions toward development shoulder the burden of proof that their appropriation of land leaves ''as much and as good'' opportunity or land for others. Moreover, as we argued in chapter five, the developer and the researcher—or anyone else who potentially threatens the public good—must show that, even if a majority of people appear to prefer actions that threaten the environmental commons, these represent *authentic* preferences. For example, even if a majority of present people appears to prefer destruction of Florida panther habitat, the burden of proof is on them to show that their preferences are authentic indicators of welfare for both the present and future. Because using land as a conservation corridor or reserve, by definition, leaves it available for the use and enjoyment of all (including future) people, in general conservation appears better able than development to leave ''as much and as good'' for others.[46]

In uncertain cases where biological researchers must attempt to serve the public good, preservation takes precedence over development in light of the fact that those bearing high levels of public or environmental risk often have not given free informed consent to imposition of the risks.[47] This is obviously true for future people who will bear the environmental impacts of present generations, but it is likewise correct for many of us in the present. Because developers impose some risks on the public, along with possible benefits, developers ought to bear the burden of proof in justifying the risk imposition, particularly because citizens typically have not given free informed consent to the imposition. In the absence of such proof, it is not clear that development (with resultant public risk) is more beneficial than conservation or preservation. Likewise, technologies or developments with questionable environmental impacts have at least the potential to cause economic harm and reduce public welfare. Nuclear technology, for example, has jeopardized the economy in the sense that if the government did not guarantee a liability limit for catastrophic accidents, then no major U.S. atomic interests would have gone into nuclear generation of electricity.[48] The upshot is that, although nuclear utilities have been relieved of the burden of competing in the liability market, they nevertheless have the potential to cripple the economy with a dangerous accident. Regardless of the benefits of commercial nuclear power, its liability limit could easily contribute to public and economic harm.[49] Land development likewise could cause public and economic harm. Because species extinctions and damage to habitats are not priced on any market but instead are externalities, benefit-cost analyses typically ignore them. Such analyses consequently misrepresent welfare and economic measures of it. As a result, policies based on such misleading economic analyses have the potential to encourage uneconomical decisionmaking.[50] Hence, unless researchers facing a situation of uncertainty can assess the authentic costs of both biotic damage and preservation, environmental preservation is preferable to development, even in cases like that of the panther, in which prevention of extinction is not guaranteed.

Another reason researchers attempting to support the public good (in such a situation) ought to favor preservation over development is that ''reasonable environmental measures reduce more environmental damages than they cost.''[51] For every dollar spent to clean up the air, for example, we save from $3 to $15 in avoided environmental damage.[52] Not acting so as to preserve air, water, species, and habitats also causes economic losses. Annual environmental damage in western countries is typically 6 percent of the GNP. In West Germany, for example, this is DM 103 billion per year.[53] Habitat destruction reduces both marketable products, e.g., fish, minerals, medicines, and the genetic resources of valuable species for potential use in areas such as agriculture. Habitat preservation likewise provides quantifiable benefits in terms of pest control, pollination, recreation, aesthetic enjoyment, and study. It provides watershed protection, regulates climate, and keeps options open for the future.[54] Most important, habitats generate benefits by virtue of the interdependence of their species and their organic and inorganic individuals, benefits such as photosynthesis; breaking down and absorbing pollutants; cycling nutrients; binding and producing soil; degrading organic waste; controlling radiation, climate, and gases in the air; and fixing solar energy. Preservation also provides even more easily measured benefits of a largely economic nature. The resale dollars lost on U.S. homes near polluted rivers and lakes is $5 billion annually; in West Germany the annual figure is DM 1 billion.[55] The National Wildlife Federation discovered after a recent study, for example, that a mere $200 investment in backyard habitat management can increase real-estate values anywhere from 3 to 10 percent.[56] This study suggests that, because people value nature, they willingly pay more for environmentally managed real estate. This means that destructive development of a habitat can cause environmental and economic damage that costs both the property owner and the public. When a habitat becomes unhealthy, society incurs numerous costs, e.g., providing waste-water treatment facilities after wetlands are destroyed. One group of researchers calculated the cost of artificially duplicating natural waste-water treatment facilities and fisheries by other means at $205,000 per hectare (and this figure does not take into account the value of the site for sulfate reduction, carbon-dioxide fixation, oxygen release, and waterfowl support). Another ecologist arrived at a minimum annual value of $1.8 million for a Georgian river-swamp-forest habitat that ''performed'' ecological services such as ground-water storage, soil binding, water purification, and streamside fertilization.[57] Others have calculated that wetlands, for example, perform functions worth between $50 and $80 thousand per acre per year.[58]

Apart from the economic value of these functions, an additional reason (for researchers in uncertain situations) to define public good in terms of preservation rather than development is that damage to habitats and the expense of repairing them are expensive. The value of a potential development site ignores these amounts, and repair costs for ecological damage can run quite high. For example, in West Germany, the *annual increase* in the cost of drinking water, because of development of watersheds and increasing pollution, is DM 6 billion,[59] and the figures are even worse for the United States. Likewise, some ecologists, studying absorption of air pollution by soil and vegetation, have calculated a net loss of pollution absorption of 440 kilograms of carbon monoxide per hectare per year for every hectare of San Bernardino Freeway built through pasturelands. Yet this figure represents only the partial costs of the loss of pasture. Air-pollution damage alone from the San Bernardino Freeway has been estimated at $27 million per year, although admittedly some alternatives to the freeway might cost just as much. This damage occurs in part because of the freeway's interfering with plants' ability to absorb other pollutants, bind the soil, and control radiation.[60] In practice, of course, not all the damages to habitats can be repaired. We can repair neither species extinction nor loss of a unique habitat, for example, and so these losses need to be prevented. Although utilitarian and economic reasons are not the only basis for arguing against species and subspecies extinction, it is important to point out that most of our medicines come from the wild, and that over 9 percent of U.S. agricultural produce derives from non-native or wild species.[61] Hence even on economic grounds we may be undervaluing benefits of environmental and species preservation.[62] Once we recognize these full values, even economics may justify preservation over development, especially over the long term.[63]

But what makes development often seem beneficial to applied researchers who must evaluate the consequences of their work? Because many people view land development as a good, without placing any market-based costs on its harmful environmental impacts, a given development could be uneconomical but appear desirable. Roads (highways) and canals typically seem economical, for example, until one tallies all the costs and benefits and discovers that the market-based costs are often twice as great as the benefits.[64] This is because the opportunity costs of development are usually ignored, and development is controlled by the idiosyncracies of how an individual wishes to exercise property rights. Some of the opportunity costs of developing land are that it can never again sustain the same aesthetic worth. It can never again contain the same species, habitats, and ecosystems. Policymakers and individual property owners alike tend to ignore the economic effects of such foreclosed opportunities and their effects on future generations. Also, because benefit-cost analyses often misrepresent environmental goods as free goods, developments that are uneconomical over the long term are often represented as economical (if at all) over the short term.[65] Each year in Florida, for example, timber sold from national forests amounts to about 95 million board feet, and timber cut totals approximately 122 million board feet, for which the state receives approximately $5 million. Although the $5 million is counted as a benefit of logging, no dollars are calculated for the opportunity costs of logging, costs that include, for example, destruction of part of the habitat for 38 threatened, endangered, and sensitive plant species and 61 threatened, endangered, and sensitive animal species living on national forest land in the state. Likewise, no dollars are calculated for the opportunity costs of logging that include threats to watershed protection. National forests in Florida produce nearly 2 million acre feet of water annually for surface and groundwater systems, and logging endangers not only this water production but also the purity of 36,000 acres of lakes and four of the state's largest rivers.[66] Were the value of all these ecological services of forests calculated, as well as the opportunity costs of logging and the costs of government subsidies to the logging industry (through road building to remove timber, for example), the results would probably justify preservation as more economical than logging.

Even if researchers employed purely economic definitions of "public interest," if they costed all actions (including environment-related ones) close to their real value, they might conclude that development frequently threatens the public interest because it is uneconomical. It often only appears economical because developers do not "pay their way" in terms of liabilities, subsidies, externalities, and providing needed services in the developed areas.[67] One Florida study showed, for example, that 1,000 new residents—attracted by developers—would include 270 new families, 200 school children, 19 blind persons, 68 aged persons, 11 juvenile delinquents, 16 alcoholics, and 30 mentally retarded persons, all of whom would require special government services.[68] If all these services were actually costed, then development could well be a net loss, not a gain, in actual economic terms. One author was able to show, for instance, that it would save Lexington, Massachusetts, taxpayers money if they would buy up 2,000 acres of vacant land rather than develop them.[69] The conclusion to draw from such considerations is not that we ought never develop lands but that development often is a net loss, even on economic terms.[70] Hence scientists (whose research serves development) need to assess their work very carefully.

Another problem with the objection (that development generally is more economically desirable than preservation) is that it appears to sanction using humans as means to the end of economic development. Such means/ends arguments are always morally questionable. For example, the same means/end presuppositions central to this objection also dominate several erroneous lines of reasoning: (1) "We can't abolish slavery, because that would destroy the economy of the South." Or (2) "We can't pass the Equal Rights Amendment (ERA), because women won't stay home and take care of their children, and that would hurt the family." In (1) slavery is assumed justifiable because it is a means to the end of promoting the southern economy. In (2) opposition to the ERA is assumed justifiable because it is a means to the end of achieving childcare. A peculiar characteristic of these means/end arguments is that they all pit important values, like family and economic well-being, against moral values, like citizen welfare or abolishing racism and sexism. The arguments are troubling because they force us to choose between two goods and because they suggest that one can use unethical means to achieve an ethical end, provided that the end is important. Arguments like (1) and (2), arguments about environmental degradation, slavery, and women's rights, all err because they propose using humans—whether citizens at risk from environmental degradation, or blacks who are victims of slavery, or women who are disadvantaged by sexism—as *means* to an economic or social *end*. Yet, if Kant was correct, as most moralists maintain, humans ought never be used as means to an end of other individuals,[71] even when the ends are economic development. The only justification for the failure to treat one person as equal to another, as Frankena has pointed out, is that the discrimination will work to the advantage of everyone, including those discriminated against. Any other attempt to justify discrimination fails because it would amount to sanctioning the use of some humans as means to the ends of others.[72] We can apply this insight about justified discrimination to the case of uncertain environmental or public impacts and researchers' facing issues of preservation versus development. A necessary condition for discriminating against the public generally—especially citizens who prefer preservation and strict environmental standards—would be proof that rejecting such standards, in a given case, would work to the advantage of everyone. In other words, the burden of proof lies with the developer or researcher—indeed anyone—who attempts to put the public at risk. Researchers in a situation of uncertainty thus bear the burden of proof if they interpret uncertain results in ways that threaten public goods such as preservation.[73]

Researchers and Credibility

But suppose researchers fear that, if they interpret scientifically uncertain results in ways that favor preservation, rather than development, they will lose credibility. Suppose, following our arguments in chapter six, researchers studying the panther choose to interpret their studies so as to minimize public risk or type-II error; if so, then they will be choosing to minimize the chance that a potentially false null (no-effect) hypothesis will not be rejected. One such null hypothesis, for example, is that creating conservation corridors will have no effect, that it will not delay extinction of the Florida panther for at least 20 years.[74] On the one hand, if researchers minimize the chance of type-II error (false negatives), of not rejecting this particular null hypothesis, then they increase the chance of type-I error (false positives), rejecting the hypothesis. Rejecting this hypothesis, however, makes it more likely that conservation corridors will be created. But if those corridors do not delay panther extinction for at least 20 years, the researchers who argued for them might lose credibility as a consequence of their attempting to minimize type-II error. On the other hand, if researchers attempt to minimize type-I error, they might jeopardize panther preservation by arguing against corridors. Their rationale might be that the effectiveness of corridors is uncertain, that comparable time and money could better be spent on other conservation projects, and that panther survival depends more on ''minimum viable populations and minimum critical sizes of ecosystems.''[75] Researchers who argue against corridors could likewise claim that those who support them may lose the ability to affect future research-related policy actions.[76] In other words, loss of credibility could cause loss of species in the future, by jeopardizing researchers' ability to affect preservation policy.[77]

Simberloff appears to believe that attempting to minimize type-I error could cause both researchers' loss of scientific credibility and future reductions in species, because policymakers might not listen to scientists.[78] Contrary to Simberloff, however, much evidence suggests that perhaps we ought to take the risk of researchers' being wrong because their loss of credibility (by virtue of their making mistakes) does not always lead to serious consequences. For example, disproving the scientific foundations of the Endangered Species Act did not cause the act to be repealed. The main scientific underpinning for this act was the traditional version of the diversity-stability thesis,[79] as both a number of authors and the congressional debate reveal.[80] Within a decade after the act was passed, however, many ecologists questioned the diversity-stability hypothesis. Depite the hypothesis's loss of credibility, neither the public nor Congress rejected the Endangered Species Act. This counterexample illustrates that the consequences of researchers' being wrong are not always disastrous. Moreover, possible loss of credibility is not merely a function of one's errors, as Simberloff appears to presuppose, but also a function of the severity of one's errors relative to those of others, and a function of the political climate in which those errors occur.

Assessing errors made on the ''pro development'' side puts Simberloff's worries about researchers' credibility into perspective. Consider the egregious mistake made by Cal Tech founder and Nobel winner,

Robert Millikan.[81] He erred in calling belief in nuclear power a "myth" less than a decade before the existence of fission energy was proved. Yet Millikan did not lose credibility afterwards. Likewise, if the work of Kahneman, Tversky, and others is correct, then experts chronically err, even in their own fields of expertise, when they reason probabilistically. In employing necessary heuristic strategies to render their problems malleable, they fall victim to the same errors as laypersons, e.g., the representativeness bias.[82] This means that expert errors are nothing new. If making serious errors were a sufficient condition for researchers' losing credibility, few of them would be credible. Consider the case of scientists' assessing failure rates of subsystem components in commercial nuclear reactors in the most comprehensive assessment of such risks ever accomplished, the U.S. Rasmussen Report, WASH-1400.[83] When Dutch researchers compared failure frequencies from operating experience to the WASH-1400 calculations for failure rates for seven key reactor subsystems, they discovered some startling facts. Amazingly, *all* the failure-frequency values from operating experience fell *outside* the 90 percent confidence bands in the WASH-1400 study. However, there is only a subjective probability of 10 percent that the true values should fall outside these bands. Moreover, a majority of the values fell above the upper confidence band, suggesting that the WASH-1400 calculations, the product of 30 experts working together, are too low.[84] If the Dutch studies are correct, then the allegedly best risk assessment (the Rasmussen Report, WASH-1400) ever accomplished contains a flagrant overconfidence bias. Despite this loss of credibility, the United States has not closed its nuclear plants, just as it did not repeal the Endangered Species Act after the diversity-stability thesis was abandoned.

Perhaps researchers—who fear loss of credibility because of their attempts, in situations of uncertainty, to make research decisions likely to serve the public interest—forget something. They forget that scientists and other researchers often err without losing their credibility. Scientists were wrong when they said that irradiating enlarged tonsils was harmless. They were wrong when they said that x-raying feet, to determine shoe size, was safe. They were wrong when they said that the Titanic would not sink. They were wrong when they said that irradiating women's breasts, to alleviate mastitis, was harmless. They were wrong when they said that the Tacoma Narrows bridge would not collapse. And they were wrong when they said that witnessing A-bomb tests at close range, in the western United States and in the Pacific, was harmless.[85] Likewise, geologists were proved wrong, by six orders of magnitude, ten years after they calculated that hazardous waste at Maxey Flats, Kentucky, would not migrate offsite.[86] Despite this geological error, the government did not stop employing scientists to assess site potential for hazardous-waste facilities. When allegedly reliable assessments of the environmental risk associated with the LNG facility in Oxnard, California, differed by three orders of magnitude,[87] the Oxnard City Council did not shut down the facility. And when government assessments of the risk of a serious accident at Three Mile Island (TMI) differed by two orders of magnitude,[88] the U.S. Nuclear Regulatory Commission did not close TMI. It took an accident, not loss of scientific credibility, to do that. Likewise, when 500,000 U.S. G.I.'s were exposed to injurious levels of radiation (levels called "safe" by government scientists) during the "Smokey" weapons tests in the United States in the 1950s,[89] the scientists did not lose credibility. Even though many servicemen died of testing-induced leukemia, the U.S. Atomic Energy Commission and the U.S. Nuclear Regulatory Commission continued to seek the advice and support of the very researchers who had misled them in the weapons-testing debacle. All of these examples suggest that researchers' *being wrong* may be less important in the credibility issue than being on the "wrong" side, i.e., the side with the least political and economic power. Even if being wrong were a sufficient condition for researchers' losing credibility, however, it is not clear that this credibility loss would be likely to jeopardize the chances of most or all researchers to influence public policy. Rather, the loss of credibility, if it occurred at all, would likely accrue only to some of the errant researchers.[90] Another problem with the presupposition (that researchers ought to take environmental, or type-II, risks in order to avoid loss of credibility) is that it ignores the importance of the researchers' intentions. Loss of credibility might be more positively correlated with deliberate intent to deceive, rather than with error alone. If so, then researchers ought neither deceive nor give the impression of deceit. They ought to remain conservative in how they interpret their conclusions, analyses, and interpretations. This is undoubtedly true. But what counts as conservative?

Public Good, Ethical Rationality, and Epistemic Rationality

In one policy-related debate over interpreting research in conservation biology, Simberloff stated quite clearly: "risking type I rather than type

II error is not the most conservative course.''[91] Presumably, the most conservative course, in a situation of uncertainty characterized by potentially serious consequences, would be the course least prone to error, all else being equal. Simberloff believes that risking type-II error (when both types of error cannot be avoided) is more conservative, at least in some cases, because this type of risk amounts to not rejecting a false null hypothesis. For example, it leads to not rejecting the hypothesis that conservation corridors will have no effect on the extinction of the Florida panther for at least 20 years. Some biologists question this hypothesis on biological grounds, such as whether corridors can offset problems of inbreeding depression and whether minimum viable panther populations still survive.[92] Hence, Simberloff concludes that ''it is not automatic that large and connected reserves ensure the fewest extinctions.''[93] Simberloff's conservative course avoids positing an effect (the importance of corridors in delaying panther extinction), in a situation of uncertainty, and shies from type-I error, rejecting the null hypothesis.

Of course, there are both scientific and legal precedents for researchers to follow Simberloff's allegedly conservative course of risking type-II (environmental or public) errors and for minimizing type-I (developer or industry) errors. In both research and in law, we wish to limit false positives. Hence, Simberloff correctly affirms that *epistemic rationality* is conservative and hence supports being scientifically cautious, viz., avoiding positing an effect. In its broadest sense, when researchers use epistemic rationality they employ scientific theory to assess hypotheses and their consequences. Epistemic rationality—following our account of epistemic objectivity in chapter three—thus is primarily a rationality of *belief*. It assesses the various degrees of *probability* associated with researchers' competing hypotheses and the practical, economic, and scientific *consequences* following from their acceptance of alternative hypotheses. Hence, on this view, epistemic rationality focuses on both epistemic and practical considerations. It often encompasses the use of some type of *decision theory* to assess the various degrees of *expected utility* (probability times outcome utility), and the various costs and benefits associated with competing hypotheses.[94] Epistemic rationality, in a situation of uncertainty, requires that the burden of proof be on the person positing the effect and risking type-I error. The important question, however, may not be the nature of *epistemic* rationality, and whether it helps minimize type-I error in a situation of research uncertainty, but whether *epistemic* rationality is the most appropriate basis for researchers' interpretations of their work on the panther. If not, then

Simberloff may be giving the right answer to the question about epistemic rationality, but he may be asking the wrong question. The most appropriate question may be whether epistemic rationality provides the best model for assessing the ethical aspects of research cases related to public and environmental policy.

When researchers use *ethical rationality*, they employ *ethical theory* to assess the moral goodness or badness of alternative actions. Ethical rationality—following our account of ethical objectivity in chapter three—is primarily a rationality of *action*. In a situation in which researchers' decisions have important consequences, but their data are uncertain, epistemic rationality in its fullest sense might dictate deciding in favor of a hypothesis with slightly lower probability but with an expected utility (benefits over costs) that significantly outweighs that of another hypothesis. In a similar situation, ethical rationality might dictate deciding in favor of a hypothesis that would lead to the greatest ethical good. For example, suppose researchers were attempting to determine whether it was more rational to claim that an unknown chemical were highly toxic or not. Suppose the latter hypothesis appeared to have a slightly higher probability than the former, but the former hypothesis had a significantly higher outcome utility than the latter. The utility of the former hypothesis might be higher because its acceptance would result in taking actions to prevent possible loss of lives and property. In such a situation, considerations of epistemic rationality might dictate accepting the hypothesis that the chemical was toxic. ''Accepting'' this hypothesis, however, would not mean ''taking to be true,'' because the utility associated with a potential state of affairs has no bearing on whether that state of affairs is actual. Hence, ''accepting'' this hypothesis (on grounds of epistemic rationality) means ''being prepared to act as if it were true.''

Suppose, however, a researcher were faced with a slightly different case. Suppose one were attempting to determine whether the unknown chemical was toxic or not. Likewise, suppose the hypothesis that it was not toxic appeared to have a slightly higher probability than the hypothesis that it was toxic. Suppose, too, that the former hypothesis had a much higher utility, because accepting the latter hypothesis would result in researchers' having to notify safety authorities, and thus might cause massive negative publicity for the research lab. Hence, purely *epistemic rationality* might dictate our choosing the former hypothesis (chemical is nontoxic) because of its higher utility. *Ethical rationality*, however, might dictate choosing the latter hypothesis (chemical is toxic), because it takes account of citizens' rights to know, rather than merely the hypothesis associated with the higher utility. Even if the utility were lower, even if the probable damage were minimal, and even if current regulations did not require notification of safety officials, a researcher might be obliged ethically to recognize the rights of those likely to be affected by a potentially toxic substance. If others have the right to protection against the adverse effects of potential toxins, however slight, and if judging that a chemical is not toxic decreases the probability that people will be informed of potential dangers and hence protected, then it is rational (from an ethical point of view) to guarantee their protection.[95] In other words, in any case in which a researcher's judgment about a hypothesis affects the interests of, and duties to, other people, what is rational is not merely a matter of epistemic rationality. Rationality is also a matter of moral and legal obligation, fairness, consent, voluntariness, and so on. When one moves from *pure* to *applied* research affecting public welfare and policy, what is rational moves from epistemological considerations to both ethical and epistemological concerns. Likewise, when one moves from considerations of *utility* to those of *ethics*, one moves from epistemic rationality to ethical rationality. Or, as Carl Cranor emphasizes in his case study in chapter ten, one moves from serving a purely evidentiary ideal to a moral ideal.

Returning to conservation cases—like the one discussed by Simberloff, Kangas, and Noss—a crucial question is whether, given a situation of uncertainty, researchers ought to employ epistemic or scientific rationality. Because the questions about whether conservation corridors will help protect the Florida panther and whether certain land ought to be preserved, for example, have social and policy consequences affecting the interests of many, the questions do not appear to be either a matter of pure science, utility, or epistemic rationality. Instead, the social and policy consequences dictate that one needs to assess (1) the outcome utilities, (2) the probabilities that the corridors will or will not delay extinction, and (3) the probabilities that preservation will or will not enhance the common good—and meet ethical obligations—more than will development. Following the model of epistemic, versus ethical, rationality, it is arguable that—just as we suggested in the previous chapter—epistemic rationality dictates minimizing type-I errors and not rejecting the null hypothesis in situations characterized by uncertainty. It is also arguable, however—just as we emphasized in chapter six—that in situations of uncertainty involving potentially serious consequences and obligations, ethical rationality dictates minimizing type-II errors and rejecting the null hypothesis in cases like that of the Florida panther. If loss of a species is more important than loss of credibility, as

Simberloff suggests,[96] and if preservation of a species or subspecies enhances ethical obligations and the common good more than does development, as many have argued,[97] then what follows? Ethical rationality might dictate minimizing type-II errors and rejecting the null hypothesis in cases of uncertainty in which research is used to make public or environmental decisions. In other words, the ethical obligations and consequences associated with loss of a species, subspecies, or habitat could be so great that, even if the probability (for example) that conservation corridors would delay Florida panther extinction for at least 20 years is low, it might still be rational (in an ethical sense) to attempt to avoid species or subspecies extinction.[98]

One could also argue, using decision theory, that in situations of probabilistic uncertainty and potentially catastrophic or irreversible consequences, researchers have grounds for following the Maximin decision rule,[99] because of their duty to promote public welfare (see chapter four). In other words, whenever potential losses are especially great, there might be general grounds for behaving conservatively and for following the Maximin rule, rather than the Bayesian rule, according to which we maximize expected utility. Because the Maximin rule enjoins one to be ethically conservative, to avoid accepting the hypothesis leading to the worst policy consequences, it dictates minimizing type-II errors and rejecting the null hypothesis in situations of uncertainty. In cases of extinction, presumably the worst policy consequence would be losing species or subspecies, and presumably this consequence could follow from acts or omissions such as failure to establish conservation corridors. Therefore, in cases of ethical rationality, the most conservative course of action is frequently to ignore uncertain probabilities and instead to focus on the ethical quality of outcomes or consequences. Hence, one may argue that if ethical rationality (rather than epistemic rationality) applies to cases like that of interpreting panther research, then researchers might be misguided to focus on the allegedly low *probability* of saving a particular species, for example, as the sole grounds for risking species extinction.[100] If the situation is one in which we ought to use ethical rationality, then the ethical quality associated with the *obligations* and *consequences* related to an act may hold more importance than probabilities and utilities. Hence, the conservative course of action in such a case would be to minimize type-II, rather than type-I, error. This means that Simberloff's claim (''that risking type I rather than type II error is not the most conservative course'') is correct only if researchers ought to use only epistemic rationality, and not include ethical rationality, when they make decisions under uncertainty.[101] From the general arguments already given, it is clear that the panther case (and any applied research situation like it) ought to involve considerations of ethical rationality, not merely epistemic rationality. Unlike Noss, Simberloff and other researchers appear to make no explicit appeal to ethical norms. In this, we believe they err.

If the arguments in this panther case are correct,[102] then epistemic rationality supports minimizing developer risk (errors of type I) in a research situation of probabilistic uncertainty. Ethical rationality, however, places the burden of proof on the person whose actions present the greatest threat to ethical norms and to the common good (see chapter four) and thus supports minimizing public risk (errors of type II) in situations of probabilistic uncertainty characterized by potentially serious obligations and consequences. One reason that ethical rationality is so important in applied or controversial research cases is that it recognizes that, where welfare, ethics, and vested interests are concerned, researchers ought to have a predisposition in favor of the vulnerable parties (the public, the environment) at the expense of the powerful parties (polluters, developers, those who put others at risk). This amounts to a general predisposition in favor of minimizing public risk and type-II errors. The predisposition warns against *overemphasizing epistemological errors* resulting in bad research and *underemphasizing ethical errors* resulting in bad policy and bad applications of research. Because of its practical and applied uses, most research requires both concepts of rationality. In the next three chapters, we examine other cases in which researchers face ethical issues. In all of them, a crucial conclusion is that researchers are obliged not merely to do good work, by following *epistemic rationality*, but also to employ *ethical rationality* in the way they choose their methods and interpret their conclusions.

8

Gender and Racial Biases in Scientific Research[1]

Helen Longino
Rice University

Members of the research community often exhibit the same social values and ideologies inherent in the social context within which research takes place. As a consequence, this chapter argues that researchers ought to attend to the way contextual values, especially gender bias and racial bias, occur in research. It also argues that the scientific research community, as a whole, has a duty to create a research context in which problems of bias are likely to be exposed.

Constitutive and Cultural Values

According to a standard conception of the relation between science and values, ethical issues are in an important sense external to the sciences. While those points of contact between science and the values of the social and cultural context in which it is done may determine the directions of research or of its applications, within the boundaries so determined scientific inquiry itself proceeds according to its own rules. The points of contact with the social and cultural context determine to what areas the rules will be applied. The effect may be a broad one that determines what questions to investigate, for example, in astronomy or mechanics, or which practical applications of knowledge to pursue and which to neglect, for example, nuclear technology or conservation technologies. The effect also may be more narrow, determining what paths to follow, which tests and experiments to permit, and which not.

The rules of scientific inquiry, on the other hand, are a function of the *constitutive values* of science, themselves a function of the goal of science, which in this model is simply assumed to be the development of an accurate understanding of the natural world. While the choice of which areas or aspects of the world application of the rules will illuminate is a function of social and cultural *contextual values*, the conclusions, answers, and explanations reached by means of their use and guidance are not. Even those contextual values that do affect science remain external to the real thing, to the doing of science. When they do not, we have a case of bad science. This represents the classical understanding of the relation of knowledge and values, of the connection between science and ethics.

On this analysis, paradigmatic cases of an ethical dilemma arise when satisfying a researcher's desire to acquire knowledge poses a danger to any of those within our ethical universe.[2] Debate about such cases focuses on what constitutes a harm and to whom, whether the benefit to be gained from a certain research program is comparable to the potential harm it might produce. In general, the role of ethics is perceived to be to restrain researchers. Morally based restrictions on experimentation are not new (as the old prohibition on the dissection of human cadavers reminds us), are not always imposed when they should be (as the fate of syphilitic black men in Tuskegee reminds us),[3] and are not always obvious (as the histories of both the Milgram obedience experiments and the NIH guidelines on recombinant DNA research make clear).[4] As the risks of harming subjects (as in various types of drug research) or violating their rights (such as that to privacy) have become better appreciated, professional associations have developed guidelines for their members.

Not all ethical or value issues are external to the productive aspects of research, however. On a contextual account of reasoning and argumentation in science, the construction of knowledge requires the integration of contextual as well as constitutive values. Ethical issues are transformed from relatively straightforward questions regarding what counts as reasonable constraint, or the costs and benefits of proceeding with a given project, to more elusive and complex problems of assessing the background values of empirical knowledge claims. The boundary between ethics and epistemology becomes less distinct. At least five elements of the research process can be shaped by contextual values:

Practices:	Contextual values can affect practices that bear on the epistemic integrity of science.
Questions:	Contextual values can determine which questions are asked and which are ignored about a given phenomenon.
Data:	Contextual values can affect the description of data; researchers may employ value-laden terms in the description of experimental or observational data, and their values may influence the selection of data or kinds of phenomena they investigate.
Specific assumptions:	Contextual values can be expressed in—or motivate the background assumptions facilitating—inferences in specific areas of inquiry.
Global assumptions:	Contextual values can be expressed in or motivate the acceptance of global, framework-like assumptions that determine the character of research in an entire field.

One of the most pervasive and, until recently, invisible contextual influences on scientific research has been that complex of norms, values, and attitudes that constitute our gender ideology. Scholars in the last 15 to 20 years have exposed a variety of areas in which European-American gender ideology has shaped Western scientific knowledge. More research needs to be done on the role of racial ideologies in the sciences, but the work that has been done shows some parallel with the role of gender ideologies. Because my own research has been on the latter, I have more to say about that, but the parallels between racial and gender ideologies help to put both in perspective. I use this scholarship to provide examples of each of the five categories listed.

Research Practices Shaped by Race and Gender Ideologies

Biases against women scientists have been manifest in a number of ways, ranging from the outright exclusion of women from scientific professions to devaluing their accomplishments, once admitted. Historians of science, including Margaret Rossiter and Londa Schiebinger, document the exclusion of women from scientific professions.[5] Less blatant, but nevertheless exclusionary, practices include male researchers' failure to listen to female colleagues, hierarchical laboratory organization which silences the many women who are research associates, and the exclusion that springs from choosing to hold informal meetings at sites where women colleagues are unwelcome or would feel uncomfortable. African-Americans, although they can count both applied and theoretical scientists among their numbers, have been discouraged from pursuing careers in the sciences, have experienced a similar devaluation and neglect of their contributions, and have been similarly marginalized within their professions. While such practices hurt individuals, they also have epistemological consequences. Perhaps the most obvious is the loss of ideas and of critical perspectives that results from limiting participation in science to one category of person.

Yet another aspect of gender ideology may be the devaluation of research styles that have gender connotations. Evelyn Keller argues that Western sciences have been characterized by an ethos of domination attributable to patterns of individual psychological development imposed on males in Western societies. This ethos expresses itself in the concept of knowledge acquisition through a certain type of interventionist experimentation and in the view that scientific understanding equals ability to control.[6] Western gender ideology treats initiative, activity, and control as masculine, and passivity and receptivity to control as feminine traits. Research styles that stress letting the material speak for itself, that result in representations of nature as complex and not susceptible to human control, may or may not be more frequently adopted by women. The avoidance of such styles by European men as unmanly (and unscientific), however, and their derogation when others employ them, result in a loss of information and impoverishment of understanding.[7] The work of Barbara McClintock was ridiculed because of her unorthodox conclusions concerning the mutability of the genome and the alleged idiosyncrasy of her research methods. For example, she is quoted as describing herself ''getting down in there'' and as imagining herself a chromosome, which seemed to involve a (forbidden) empathic identification with her research material. Subsequent events have shown that she was not wrong, in substance, and was ahead of her time in emphasizing diversity and individuality rather than uniformity among her samples.

The practices that impede research development thus include the blatant and the subtle. Blatantly sexist and racist practices appear in various forms of exclusion and silencing; the more subtly biased practices include ignoring and derogating research styles and results associated with ''feminine'' traits. Both impede the development of knowledge, and both produce moral and epistemological injury.

Research Questions Shaped by Race and Gender Ideologies

The focus on Caucasian males as the standard in biomedical research results in a failure to formulate research questions about diseases that Caucasian women or women and men of other racial groups represent more highly or in different ways. Hypertension, for example, exists more among African-American women than among European-Americans.[8] The research focus on interventive cures neglects the corrigible environmental basis of many disease states, particularly environmental factors consequent to poverty. Average Caucasian males have also been taken as the standard when framing questions regarding the effectiveness of certain therapies or the appropriate dose of prospective medications. Such framing makes consequent research of questionable relevance to women, whose physiology (due to endocrine balance, tissue density, etc.) differs from that of men, as well as to men from ethnic and racial groups who, on average, are smaller than Caucasian men. Two sorts of harm are perpetrated here. The marginalization of issues distinctive to nonwhites and women of any race means unwarranted suffering for those whose illness might otherwise have been prevented or cured. It also illustrates the unfair distribution of society's benefits and burdens because women, as well as African-Americans and Asian-Americans, also pay the taxes that support the NIH.

Thanks to the efforts of the Congressional Women's Caucus, the lack of research on women's health is beginning to be remedied by the establishment of an Office for Women's Health in the National Institutes of Health.[9] This office will initiate research on distinctively female health issues—such as breast, uterine and ovarian cancers—and oversee other NIH-sponsored research to ensure that women are represented in clinical trials. No comparable office yet exists to ensure adequate attention to the health needs of racial minorities.

Even when research does attend to women's issues, sexist values can allow other considerations to outweigh the interests of promoting health in the development of research questions. The development of oral contraceptives provides an example. Carol Korenbrot argues that in the selection of ''side effects'' to be measured, known hazards were downplayed and mentioned against a background of health benefits (apart from avoidance of pregnancy).[10] She takes as her text Gregory Pincus's *Control of Fertility*, an account of the history and biology of oral contraception by one who was deeply involved as a major researcher and developer of the product ''Enovid.''[11] While it is true that Pincus was supported by a drug company and so may have been influenced by commercial considerations, the one sociocultural theme he continually names is that of the dangers of unchecked population growth and the necessity for its control. Korenbrot suggests that his explicit commitment to the need for an effective method of limiting population growth strongly influenced how he tested Enovid for effects other than its inhibition of ovulation. In spite of the availability of data showing a relationship between estrogens and reproductive-tract cancers and between estrogens and blood coagulability, the chapter in Pincus's work entitled "Some Biological Properties of Ovulation Inhibitors in Human Subjects" emphasizes their prophylactic and therapeutic properties and minimizes their hazards. The tests he reports and the tables he presents concern, to a great extent, conditions that improve, might improve, or might be prevented by oral contraceptives; conditions such as dysmenorrhea, endometrial dysplasia, endometritis, and even breast cancer. He presents data on conditions that may deteriorate—cervical erosion and thromboembolism—with extensive qualifications and explanations that tend to exonerate Enovid as a causal factor.

Thus, gender or racial bias can result in excluding the concerns of members of given social categories from a research agenda or in downplaying such concerns relative to other, competing, values. A society might collectively decide that the benefits of a course of action outweigh the risks to one or the other sex or to a racial group. This could well constitute a social injury to the members of that group, but the preemption of such a political decision by a single researcher or a research community epitomizes bias in action.

Research Data Shaped by Race and Gender Ideologies

To illustrate the remaining three aspects of research, data, specific and global assumptions, I discuss several research programs that either explain or employ notions of behavioral sex differences or cognitive racial differences. Here gender and race ideology impacts less directly on individuals' lives. To the extent that its influence on research outcomes wrongly suggests a factual justification for gender and racial bias, however, it participates in perpetuating sexist attitudes and behaviors in society in general.

Perhaps some of the most notorious instances of racial ideology in the sciences are the various research efforts alleging a genetic basis for group differences in I.Q. African-Americans score, on average, about

20 points lower on I.Q. tests than European-Americans. One problem with this research is the treatment of performance on I.Q. tests as a measure of intelligence. As Stephen J. Gould has shown, the tests themselves have traditionally reflected white-middle-class culture, thus guaranteeing the poor performance of working class immigrants and native-born African-Americans.[12] Additionally, the assumption that intelligence is unitary in nature has supported treating I.Q. test performance as an unequivocal way to grade intellectual and cognitive ability. Researchers treat the data as marks of inherent difference rather than as marks of a difference produced by the imposition of one kind of screen rather than another.

Behavioral neuroendocrinology studies the role of hormones on behavior.[13] One subarea studies the effects of prenatal gonadal hormones on sex differences in behavior and cognition. The data used are from animal experimentation as well as from observation of individuals treated for the consequences of abnormal prenatal levels of gonadal hormones. One category of such individuals is girls with congenital adrenocortical hyperplasia (CAH), which involves overproduction by the adrenal glands of androgens in utero (and underproduction of cortisone throughout life). Researchers studying these individuals determined that they exhibited higher levels of what they called "tomboyism" than control subjects. The researchers characterize "tomboyism" as a behavioral syndrome involving preference for active outdoor play (over less active indoor play), greater preference for male over female playmates, greater interest in a public career than in domestic housewifery, less interest in small infants, and less play rehearsal of motherhood roles than that exhibited by "normal" young females. The correlation of tomboyism with high fetal androgen levels in these CAH cases is used as evidence for the claim that gonadal hormones are causally implicated (via their role in brain organization) in the expression of gender role behavior generally. So boys' preference for active outdoor play and relative disinterest in small infants and in parenting is explained by their fetal exposure to androgens. And girls' preferences are explained by their fetal hormone exposures.

A range of experiments in non-human animals, primarily rodents, showing that certain sexual behaviors and variations in "aggression" depend on gonadal hormone exposure during critical periods in development, provide part of the background supporting these causal inferences. The appeal to rodent experiments—taking the "zoocentric" view, as one researcher charmingly put it—assumes that the rodent and the human situation are similar enough that demonstration of a causal connection in one species is enough to support the inference from correlation to causation in the other. This presupposes that the behaviors the several species exhibit—human, other primates, rodents—are the same phenomenon, just as, say, reproduction or digestion in these species is the same phenomenon. Gender role behaviors, however, are much more complicated.

First, it is not at all obvious that the behaviors of experimental animals sufficiently mirror those of the human children and adults studied. Fighting behavior in a laboratory cage does not clearly represent either rough and tumble play or active outdoor play. Nor is frequency or intensity of rough and tumble play a dimension that matches propensities to athleticism as opposed to propensities to reading. The human child and adult behaviors, for instance, all exhibit a degree of intentionality not characteristic of the stereotyped rodent behaviors studied.

Second, the experiments with rodents all involve single-factor analysis. The conditions of the animals' lives can be highly regulated (more than those of human life, at least), making possible experiments that attempt to vary only one factor at a time and that make no attempt to understand interactions among factors. The human situation, including that of the CAH girls, is always interactive. Humans live in a social context from the first moments of their lives. We have no way of isolating the variables operating in real life, in which any one feature is a function of a multiplicity of interacting factors. Thus, the larger contexts in which the behaviors are observed cannot permit treating them as identical across species.

The analogy between the human behaviors and the stereotyped non-human behavioral dimorphisms seems obvious if one expects sexual dimorphism and classifies behavior as masculine or feminine. Without this expectation or the assumption that behavior is so gendered, however, the behaviors of the children seem more diverse and classifiable under different schemas. Hand-eye coordination, for example, cuts across indoor and outdoor, feminine and masculine, behavioral classifications. The assumption of dimorphism makes certain features of the behaviors—for example, level of expenditure of physical energy—more salient than others, and thus makes the behaviors appear suitable as evidence for the hormonal hypothesis. In addition, the sample results themselves are never uniform. The assumption of gender dimorphism makes the clustering of individuals around certain behavioral poles more significant than the amount of individual variation that is as much a feature of the data as the clustering, or than other variations, e.g., in degree of intentionality, that might appear if sought for.

At the level of description of data, gender ideology influences both description and selection, particularly by a sexual essentialism that assumes sex-appropriate and sex-inappropriate behaviors. The assignment of lively activity to one sex and the relegation of the other to quiet, domestically oriented play, is cultural mythology, although admittedly mythology acted out in many lives. The language used to describe the CAH girls' behavior—for example, "tomboyism"—reflects uncritical acceptance of this mythology from the start. This description implies the inappropriateness of the behavior. The myth it expresses may also influence the selection of data; that is, it may lead investigators to highlight the presence or absence of certain behavioral factors and overlook others, to design studies that look for culturally assigned masculine qualities in hormonally unusual females, and the converse for males. Finally, if sexual differentiation were a less central concern, other aspects of the observed behaviors might become more salient and lead to a reclassification of the data.

Specific Research Assumptions Shaped by Race and Gender Ideologies

The androcentric point of view has perhaps been most evident in ethology and evolutionary theory. Researchers take the male as the standard for the species, treat him as the locus of variation for the species, and assume him to be the pivot of social structure in innumerable species.[14] Nineteenth-century Europeans of both sexes considered themselves more highly evolved than women and men of other races, who were regarded as vestiges of an earlier stage of human evolution. The work of geneticists like Dobzhansky effectively discredited such ideas among practicing biologists. The research on intelligence mentioned earlier, however, has been shaped by similar assumptions of African inferiority, which prevented researchers from attending to flaws in the reasoning used to support hypotheses of a genetic basis to group differences in I.Q.[15]

Gender bias has been equally persistent, although the influx of women into ethological, archeological, and paleontological fields has produced challenges and changes to the traditional male bias. One of the best known examples has been the substitution of woman-the-gatherer for man-the-hunter.[16] Both accounts of the evolution of a distinctly human species from ancestral primate species regard the development of tool use as a pivotal behavioral change. It provided a selection pressure for bipedalism and upright carriage and hence for the anatomical changes required for the new postures. Both accounts also link tool use and its invention to the development of human intelligence and sociability.

The stones identified as early tools are found in the vicinity of hominid fossil remains, or massed in streambeds. But what were they used for? Perhaps early humans used them to kill small animals, scrape pelts, section corpses, dig up roots, break open seed pods, or hammer and soften tough roots and leaves in preparation for consumption. In attempting to give a specific use (which then serves as the basis for more elaborate accounts of the behavior of their users), anthropologists often have recourse to analogies with contemporary populations of hunters and gatherers. The difficulty is that, unlike the distinctive features of human anatomy, the behavior and social organization of these contemporary peoples varies so widely that, depending on the society one chooses, very different pictures of *Australopithecus* and of *Homo Erectus* develop. Man-the-hunter theorists will describe the role of the chipped stones in the killing and preparation of other animals, using as their model the behavior of contemporary hunting peoples. Woman-the-gatherer theorists will describe their role in the preparation of edible vegetation obtained while gathering, relying, for their part, on the model of gathering behavior among hunter/gatherers. Similarly, the fact that some contemporary primates use sticks to dig in ant and termite nests does no more than establish the possibility that creatures as much like them as like us could have done the same.

None of the admissible data thus provides any sort of decisive or even unequivocal evidence for or against either of the two accounts. How one interprets the data depends on whether one is working within the framework of man-the-hunter or woman-the-gatherer. On their own, the data are dumb, requiring such assumptions in order to function as evidence. The frameworks belong to ways of seeing and being in the world that assign different degrees of reality and value to male and female activities. If female gathering behavior is taken to be the crucial behavioral adaptation, the stones are evidence that females began to develop stone tools in addition to the organic tools already in use for gathering and preparing edible vegetation. If male hunting behavior is taken to be the crucial adaptation, then the stones are evidence of male invention of tools for use in the hunting and preparation of meat.

In time, a less gender-centric account of human evolution may eventually supersede both of these current contending stories. Such an account would focus on elements common to both sexes, perhaps on communication. At this point, however, a great value of the female-centered framework is that, in addition to telling a compelling story, it shows the extent the man-the-hunter story depends upon culturally embedded sexist assumptions. This case differs from the work on the genetic basis of group differences in I.Q. because the issue is not one of bias-induced mistakes. The available data require a story about human (or hominid) behavior in order to acquire evidential status. What is striking is not the reliance on assumptions but the congruence of those assumptions with socio-political status and interests. Unlike the behavioral neuroendocrinology case, values affect not the selection and organization of the data, but the assumptions in light of which the data acquire evidential relevance for one hypothesis or another.

Global Research Assumptions Shaped by Race and Gender Ideologies

Many of the global assumptions structuring research seem far removed from gender politics. A number of feminist critics, however, have drawn attention to the pervasiveness of an active/passive duality in the analysis of natural processes. This duality encodes an assumption that for any activity a non-active substratum upon which the agent acts must exist. So the active gene acts on the passive cytoplasm, and the active sperm acts on the passive ovum. Recent research shows the cytoplasm involves itself in gene activation and the ovum works to attract and unite with sperm. Why should an active/passive model be preferred to a model of co-activity? Although the gender associations of fertilization are fairly evident, they are less so in intracellular relations. Given the present likelihood of mutuality rather than dominance, i.e., the possibility of an alternative account of the relations between gene and cytoplasm, gene and organism, and given the cultural association of activity with masculinity and of passivity with femininity, the supposition that a reflexive preference for active/passive models expresses androcentric bias is not out of the question.[17] My own view is that such a preference is part of a concept of causality that has a variety of conceptual and axiological sources, among them a model of interaction derived from gender relations in male-dominant societies. Substantiation of this view, however, requires a much more extensive analysis of causation than is possible here.

Conclusion

Gender and racial ideologies support assumptions of difference where they do not exist and the neglect of differences that do exist. The various roles that these ideologies can play in inquiry present several different kinds of ethical issues. Practices of exclusion, whether blatant or subtle, are the most familiar. They cause identifiable injury to identifiable individuals. In addition, when practiced against an entire social category, they deprive the research community (and society in general) of the critical perspectives and insights flowing from the experiences characteristic for members of that category. The failure to formulate research questions in such a way as to make the consequent research relevant to women and women's concerns or to those of members of racial minorities also causes injury. While it is harder to see the injury as individually directed as opposed to class directed, individuals will suffer if doctors do not understand their diseases as well as they would have if the research had studied a wider variety of subjects. In addition, such failure reduces the amount of information available in the community. The moral harm consequent upon the use of sexist or racist assumptions in selecting and organizing data, or in facilitating inferences from data to hypotheses, is similarly double-edged. To the extent that sexist and racist research legitimizes sexist and racist practices in society, reliance on such assumptions perpetuates gender and racial injustice.

It should not be surprising that the assumptions of a research community should exhibit the same social values that characterize the social context within which it exists. Nor can we expect individual researchers to police themselves for contextual values and ideological commitments which may not be apparent to them as such. Researchers do, however, have an obligation to attend to critiques of their work that expose the role of values and social commitments in it. While not bound to abandon assumptions, the commitment to seek truth (or avoid error) requires that researchers reexamine the bases of their critical assumptions, and that the assumptions themselves be either better supported, abandoned, or treated as hypothetical. The analyses that feminist scholars have offered in the last 15 years serve to put the entire scientific community on notice that unsuspected gender biases may play a role in data gathering and interpretation. While any particular analysis may turn out to be incorrect, the bulk of this work has been substantiated by more than one scholar. This accumulated work confers a prima facie legitimacy on critiques of particular research programs and hence an obligation on the part of researchers (men and women) whose work has been critiqued to take it seriously. Individual responses, however, require a research context that rewards reflection and change as well as the production of results. It is the responsibility of the scientific community as a whole, and not of any single individual, to create such a context.

9

Engineering Design Research and Social Responsibility

Carl Mitcham
Pennsylvania State University

Although human beings have since antiquity undertaken projects that might be interpreted as engineering works, the first engineers as such did not appear until the Renaissance. If one dates the birth of modern science as an institution from the founding of the Royal Society in 1660, engineering as a profession is best dated from the formation of the Society of Civil Engineers (or Smeatonians) some hundred years later in 1771. Since then three distinct ideas have developed about engineering ethics, each of which can influence how engineering research is done. The first emphasizes company loyalty, the second technocratic leadership, the third social responsibility.

History of Ideas in Engineering Ethics

One idea is that engineers have a basic obligation to be loyal to institutional authority. An ''engineer'' was originally a soldier who designed military fortifications or operated engines of war such as catapults.[1] The first school to grant the engineering degree was the Ecole Polytechnique, founded in 1794 by the Directorate shortly before Napoleon became Brigadier General of the Revolutionary Army. In the United States, the Military Academy at West Point (1802) was the first school to offer engineering degrees. Within such a context, engineers' emphasis on duty is not surprising. During the same period as the founding of professional engineering schools, a few designers of "public works" began to call themselves "civil engineers."[2] The creation of this civilian counterpart to military engineering initially gave no cause to alter the basic sense of engineering obligation. Civil engineering was simply peacetime military engineering, and engineers remained duty-bound to obey their employer, often some branch of the government. The late eighteenth and early nineteenth centuries also witnessed the formation of the first professional engineering societies. Early in the twentieth century such organizations began to adopt formal codes of ethics. On analogy with physicians and lawyers, whose codes prescribe a fundamental obligation to patients and clients, the early ethics codes in professional engineering—such as those formulated in 1912 by the American Institute of Electrical Engineers (later to become the Institute of Electrical and Electronic Engineers or IEEE) and in 1914 by the American Society of Civil Engineers (ASCE)—defined the primary duty of the engineer to be of service as a "faithful agent or trustee" of an employing company.

There is undoubtedly some merit in engineers adopting the related principles of obedience and loyalty. Loyalty especially is a widely recognized virtue under many circumstances. But the problem with any obediential ethics is that it opens an adherent to manipulation by external powers that may well be unjust. Even in the military, for instance, it is now common to say that one is obligated to carry out only legitimate or just orders. Physicians and lawyers, too, must be loyal to their patients and clients only to the extent that patients and clients pursue health and justice, respectively. Attempts to meet this weakness in the principles of obedience and loyalty, and to articulate a substantive or regulative ideal for the engineering profession comparable to those in medicine and in law, gave rise to what has become known as "the technocracy movement."

Technocracy is at odds with both the implicit code of obedience and the explicit code of company loyalty; it is the ideology of leadership in technological progress through pursuit of the ideal of technical efficiency. In 1895, in an ASCE presidential address, George S. Morison, one of America's premier bridge-builders, spelled out this ideal in a bold vision of the engineer as the primary agent of technical change and the main force behind human progress. In Morison's words:

> We are the priests of material development, of the work which enables other men to enjoy the fruits of the great sources of power in Nature, and

of the power of mind over matter. We are the priests of the new epoch, without superstitions. . . .[3]

During the first third of the twentieth century such a vision of expanded engineering activity spawned the technocracy movement and the idea that engineers should have political and economic power. Economist Thorstein Veblen, for example, argued in *The Engineers and the Price System* (1921) that freeing engineers from subservience to business interests so they could exercise their own standards of good and bad, right and wrong, would result in a stronger economy and better consumer products.[4]

Again, there are evident truths in arguments for technocratic leadership and the pursuit of efficiency. Certainly the subordination of production to short-term profit-making without any concern for the good of the product is not desirable in the long run, and inefficiency or waste readily seems to be another denomination of badness. Moreover, in a highly complex technical world it is often difficult for average citizens to know what would be in their own best interests. Nevertheless, technical decisionmaking as an end can easily be separated from general human welfare. The pursuit of technical perfection for its own sake is not always the best use of limited societal resources—such as when engineers design cars to go faster and faster, despite the speed limit of 55 miles per hour. The ideal of efficiency also virtually requires the assumption of clearly defined boundary conditions that easily exclude relevant factors, including legitimate psychological and human concerns.

The World War II mobilization of science and engineering for national purpose and the North American post-war social recovery contributed to a temporary suppression of the tension between technical and economic ends, efficiency and profit, highlighted by the technocracy movement. But opposition to nuclear weapons in the 1950s and 1960s, together with the consumer and environmental movements of the 1960s and 1970s, provoked some engineers to challenge both national and business directions. In conjunction with a renewed concern for democratic values—especially as a result of the civil-rights movement—this challenge led to new ideas about engineering ethics. In the United States the seeds of this transformation were planted in 1947 when the Engineers' Council for Professional Development (ECPD, later the Accreditation Board for Engineering and Technology or ABET) drew up the first trans-disciplinary engineering ethics code. It committed the engineer "to interest himself [or herself] in public welfare.'' Revisions in 1963 and 1974 strengthened this commitment to the point where the first of four ''fundamental principles'' requires engineers to use ''their knowledge and skill for the enhancement of human welfare,'' and the first of seven ''fundamental canons'' states that ''Engineers shall hold paramount the safety, health and welfare of the public. . . .''

Because the third distinct emphasis in engineering ethics, social responsibility, meets many objections that can be raised against the first two, it has been widely adopted by the professional engineering community. It also allows for retention of the most desirable elements from the two earlier theories. Engineers can maintain loyalty, for instance, but within a more inclusive framework. Now loyalty is not to an individual or corporation but to the public as a whole. Leadership in technical development likewise remains, but it is now subordinated to the common welfare, especially in regard to public health and safety.

The idea of engineers' social responsibility, however, does not necessarily involve any citizen participation in decisionmaking. An engineer committed to the promotion of public safety, health, and welfare may make decisions about technical issues in a paternalistic manner at odds with democratic ideals. Indeed, recognition of the reality that technology often brings with it not only benefits but also costs and risks argues for granting all those affected by technical decisions some say in them. As a result, some have argued for the principle of ''no innovation without representation.''[5] Such representation does not imply veto power, but rather intelligent and relevant lay involvement. In accordance with this participation principle, the role of the engineer as technical specialist would become less that of independent decisionmaker and more that of participant in an educational dialogue and contributor to various regulatory processes within appropriate democratic governmental structures and guidelines. Acceptance of the idea of social responsibility, especially as modified by the participation principle, has nevertheless been surrounded by considerable practical and theoretical debate. Three cases from recent engineering ethics discussions highlight these practical questions.

Three Case Studies in Engineering Design Research

A fundamental practical problem for the engineering community has been how to develop an autonomy that would enable engineers to practice a professional commitment to the primacy of public safety, health, and welfare without making them independent arbiters of the public good or subverters of democratic process. The truth is that engineers often have the power to make technical decisions for the public that can easily lead to the promotion of non-public interests. One of the most influential of these ''conflicts of interest'' is exemplified in the Hydrolevel case. At the same time, in comparison with scientists, engineers are ''more on tap than on top.'' This fact has been driven home by case studies of disasters associated with design flaws in the cargo bay doors on the DC-10, the Goodrich A7D airbrakes, the gas tank on the Ford Pinto, the skywalks at the Kansas City Hyatt Regency, and so on. Two of the most widely influential cases of design flaws concern the Bay Area Rapid Transit (BART) system and the space shuttle Challenger.

In the mid-1800s, in response to an increasing number of public fatalities resulting from steamboat boiler explosions, the U.S. government undertook to regulate boiler manufacture and operation. As they evolved, the resultant regulatory agencies became the enforcers of technical standards that by the early 1900s had become the responsibility of the American Society of Mechanical Engineers (ASME). In the process, research engineers, in a benevolent technocratic manner, had clearly taken on a responsibility for helping to protect public safety and welfare.[6] By the mid-1900s this responsibility and relationship had become perhaps too well established. In the late 1960s research at a small engineering firm, Hydrolevel Corporation, developed a new type of low-water fuel cutoff device for steam boilers that threatened the business of McDonnell and Miller, Inc. (M&M), the primary supplier of such devices. When an appeal was made to the ASME for an interpretation of section HG-605a (a 43-word paragraph) in its 18,000-page *Boiler and Pressure Vessel Code* in order to certify the new Hydrolevel design, ASME members who were also involved with M&M acted to secure a negative response. The result was a lawsuit that went all the way to the Supreme Court, which in 1982 ruled that ASME had violated the Sherman Anti-Trust Act. (Hydrolevel also eventually went out of business because it could not market its new product.)[7] A commitment to protect public safety and welfare through technical ideals and engineering autonomy had been used as a subterfuge for protecting the welfare of a private corporation.

Another famous case of design flaws arose in the late 1960s when metropolitan San Francisco decided to create the Bay Area Rapid Transit (BART) system. Designed to provide the most advanced rapid transit in the world, BART would eliminate both operators and conductors in favor of an automatic train control (ATC) technology. Construction began in 1964. At the end of 1971, almost three years behind schedule and considerably over budget, BART was finally nearing the first stage of completion. However, Holger Hjortsvang, a research engineer working on the ATC, became seriously concerned about BART's design and testing—especially the attempt to deal with design problems in a very complex project on a piecemeal rather than a systemic basis. Beginning in 1969 he expressed these concerns to management, and by late 1971 he found himself supported by two newly hired engineers: Max Blankenzee, a senior program analyst, and Robert Bruder, an electrical-electronics construction engineer. For months these three engineers expressed their concerns to management both orally and in writing, only to be consistently ignored. Finally, in early 1972 the engineers contacted a member of the BART District Board of Directors and gave him papers documenting their concerns. Soon afterwards, newspaper stories appeared, followed by a February meeting of the Board that yielded a split vote of confidence in BART management. Management then undertook to identify the sources for certain critical documents acquired by the Board, and fired Hjortsvang, Blankenzee, and Bruder at the beginning of March.

The engineers, however, appealed to the California Society of Professional Engineers (CSPE) for support, arguing that they were only attempting to live up to a professional code of obligation to hold ''the public welfare paramount'' and to ''notify the proper authorities of any observed conditions which endanger public safety and health.'' In June CSPE submitted a report to the California State Senate that largely supported the engineers. Then in October, in dramatic confirmation of their concerns, an ATC failure caused a BART train to overrun a station, injuring four passengers and an attendant.

In 1986 the need for engineering independence again came to public attention because of the explosion of the space shuttle Challenger. Once more a major, high-tech, government-funded project was years behind schedule, considerably over budget, and thus subject to strong economic and political pressures to meet new and unrealistic deadlines. As came to light afterward, Roger Boisjoly, the Morton-Thiokol mechanical engineer in charge of research and design for the field joints on the solid rocket booster, had been questioning the safety of the Challenger's O-ring seals for almost a year. And the night prior to the January launch Boisjoly and other engineers had explicitly opposed continuing the countdown, only to have their decision overridden by senior management. Because of their testimony before the Presidential Commission during its post-disaster investigation, these engineers came under severe pressure from Morton-Thiokol. But Boisjoly, who ultimately resigned, also became an outspoken advocate for both greater autonomy in the engineering profession and the inclusion of engineering ethics in engineering curricula, thus helping to promote development of engineering ethics courses in engineering colleges throughout the United States.[8]

Uniting these three cases is not only the practical problem of promoting the right kind of engineering autonomy, but also what might be called the principle of public disclosure—a principle clearly related to that of public participation. Supporting such a principle is the argument that public good is served by a duty to disclose especially to those who might be affected by the full process of technical decisionmaking, as well as by shortcomings in areas of safety, health, and welfare.

The Perspectives of Research and Design

The problems that typically call for whistleblowing are not equally apparent in the general practice of engineering and in engineering research. Indeed, this is probably one of the things that makes research attractive to many: it avoids moral dilemmas. It is ''only'' research. But the term ''research'' can have weak and strong meanings. It can refer to (a) that aspect of the investigation of a problem that plays a continuing subsidiary role in any project, (b) the initial conceptualization and planning of a project, or (c) the specialized activity that constitutes the systematic deepening and elaboration of the engineering sciences. Of course, engineering research in the stronger senses referring to (b) and (c) is only a small part of engineering.[9]

It is worth noting that the very term ''research'' is distinctly modern, derived by way of the French *rechercher* (*re-*, intensifying prefix + *cercher*, to seek for) from the late Latin *recercare*. There are no classical Latin or Greek forms of the word. The ''intensive searching'' that implies an active or ''pushy'' inquiry contrasts with the more leisured and detached, observational study exhibited by premodern learning. Indeed, the term first became prominent in English during the 1600s in conjunction with the rise of modern experimental science. But not until the early 1900s did ''research'' become associated with engineering to designate work directed ''in an industrial context'' toward ''the innovation, introduction, and improvement of products and processes.''[10] Research directly for ''making'' is almost 300 hundred years younger than research for knowing.

From the perspective of engineering research in this strong sense, the codes of professional ethics appear singularly weak if not irrelevant. They focus on what most engineers do, which is simply not research. Unlike scientific research, engineering research occurs on the margins—at one end of a spectrum of activities ranging from research and development through construction or production to operation, management, and maintenance. Only a few engineers engage primarily in research, although a much larger proportion no doubt include research as some limited component of their engineering work.

Design, not research, unifies the various engineering activities. The research engineer investigates new principles and processes which a development engineer can utilize for designing the prototype of a new device. The production engineer can then modify the prototype design so that it is more easily manufactured, while operational and maintenance engineers can use practical experience to shape the design to fit given applications. Throughout all these processes, the central activity is designing, which must take into account production, marketing, maintenance, and use. Designing, in turn, is taken into account by research. Engineering research exists to contribute not to knowledge *per se* but to the design activity, that is, to "the creation of systems, devices, and processes useful to, and sought by, society."[11]

The exact character of design activity is the subject of debate. For present purposes it is not necessary to explore all aspects of these debates, but simply to note that design involves a kind of making, or making in miniature,[12] and as such has immediate impact on the world, however small that impact might be. Unlike science, then, which can plausibly claim that the outcome of its central activity, research, is knowledge—which can only have an indirect or mediated impact on the world—the outcome of *engineering design* is a physical object that perforce becomes part of the physical world. If it succeeds, it may even become a very big part of the physical world.

What is distinctive about *engineering research* as research is what has already been called its pushy character, its determination to discover and apply "new facts, techniques, and natural laws."[13] The application of techniques in engineering is further motivated by a "creative imagination" that "is always dissatisfied with present methods and equipment," and that ever seeks "newer, cheaper, better means of using natural sources of energy and materials to improve the standard of living and diminish toil."[14] The engineer's uneasiness or restlessness imparts to and picks up from research a more profoundly active character—so that engineering research is more active than scientific research, and engineering based on or utilizing research is more active than engineering otherwise. Engineering research, oriented toward providing more effective foundations and support for design, both takes on and transmits the engineer's restlessness into effective and powerful means of transforming projects. Whereas science might be said to take the world into the laboratory, engineering research takes the laboratory into the world. Indeed, it eventually makes of the world a laboratory.

The method of "testing to destruction," in which researchers intentionally load or operate materials or devices until failure, in order to discover their limits, is a particularly revealing form of engineering research. One may instructively compare testing to destruction with the systematic observation of biological field work—and even with the controlled measurement of isolated events under varied conditions in physics. The latter case, however, where scientific experiments constrain nature in order to confirm a hypothesis, as with Galileo's inclined planes, simply involves the altering of a natural motion for effective observation, without any explicit intent to destroy. Testing to destruction is, of course, closely related to traditional "cut and try" methods of construction; the difference is that, with testing to destruction, these methods are developed and pursued systematically. Moreover, with systematic development, testing to destruction readily leaves the engineering laboratory and becomes part of general engineering practice. This is the upshot of civil engineer Henry Petroski's book, *To Engineer Is Human* (1985). According to Petroski, "the concept of failure . . . is central to understanding engineering." Although

> colossal disasters . . . are ultimately failures of design, . . . the lessons learned from those disasters can do more to advance engineering knowledge than all the successful machines and structures in the world. Indeed, failures appear to be inevitable in the wake of prolonged success, which encourages lower margins of safety. Failures in turn lead to greater safety margins and, hence, new periods of success. To understand what engineering is and what engineers do is to understand how failures can happen and how they can contribute more than successes to advance technology.[15]

Because public testing or "using to failure" is a normal part of the engineering-society interaction, the philosopher-engineer team of Mike Martin and Roland Schinzinger argue that engineering is properly described as "social experimentation." According to Martin and Schinzinger, although experimentation is crucial to engineering, what is involved is not . . . an experiment conducted solely in a laboratory under controlled conditions. Rather, it is an experiment on a social scale involving human subjects.[16]

This transformation of the world into a laboratory, in which engineering design research reaches out through engineering practice, is the foundation of the unique ethical challenges numerous authors identify as the special burden of technological society. Because of engineering research, the practice of engineering now has a greater impact across space and through time than any other human action. It also extends more deeply into human nature, both psychologically (behavior modification) and physiologically (genetic engineering). Finally, the opening of such technical possibilities through engineering design research tends to draw human action into its vortex.[17] As the atomic scientist J. Robert Oppenheimer remarked about Edward Teller's design for an H-bomb, the possibility was so "technically sweet" it could not fail to be tried.[18] The wisdom of promoting such restlessness must be an ultimate issue of the ethics of engineering design research.

The external features of engineering design research are complemented by an "internal" trait of modeling. Modeling is not only miniature making but also a simplification with a paradoxical character. On the one side, because simplification is oriented toward making, it is not particularly concerned with truth. Less than fully true models, although conceptually shallow, can be technologically powerful or rich.[19] But engineering modeling, in giving up on explicit concern for truth, unavoidably takes on an ethical dimension. On the other side, precisely because of the simplifications of engineering research modeling, ethical reflection on all aspects of the design research becomes especially difficult. Free body diagrams, for instance, treat an object *as if* all forces were acting directly on its center of gravity, in order to model matter-force interactions. But this "as if" also denotes something that *is not*. The simplified model is not the complex reality. All forces do not act on the center of gravity of some object; many act on its surface which, given certain shapes, may subtly distort the result. To concentrate on gross problems it is not only permissible to ignore complex subtleties, but better to do so. The paradox is that precisely because models do not reflect the complexity of reality, they have the power to change what is. The Euclidean model of the landscape as a flat surface, for example, enables one more easily to divide it. Likewise, the modeling of terrestrial gravity—as independent of the sun, the moon, the planets, and all variations in geology or physical geography—makes possible calculation of the trajectories of military projectiles. The carefully defined boundary conditions within which the mechanical engineer determines efficiency, taking into account only mechanical energy and heat, but not social dislocation, pollution, or biological destruction, makes possible improvements in the strictly mechanical functioning of engines.

More generally, looking at the world as a whole as if it were a clock or the brain as if it were a computer brings with it tremendous power to transform the thing modeled precisely by overlooking the rich complexity of its reality, by abstracting from the life-world within which we actually live. It is thus no accident that engineering design research, given its inner demands for simplification, should sometimes fail to consider one of the most subtle dimensions of the life-world—ethics.

Ethics in Engineering Design Research

When engineers overlook many aspects of reality, an essential inner feature of engineering design research, they not only harness power, but they court the danger of overlooking something important. Indeed, engineering failures typically reveal that something has been overlooked. Such failures are social as well as technical. Because failures, like successes, can be expected outcomes of the simplified modeling inherent in engineering design research, such research has also developed counter or compensatory principles. These principles force engineering projects to develop more complex models. Thus, engineering design research contains not only a movement toward simplification but also a countermovement toward "complexification." Systems engineering, interdisciplinary engineering research, the transformation of civil into environmental engineering, and multifactor technology assessments all illustrate this latter tendency.

In the BART case, for instance, Hjortsvang argued for a more complex testing of the ATC system. He was concerned that the piecemeal testing being done was not able to reveal the full potential for problems, and that isolated problems-solving did not adequately consider the ways various solutions might interact under real world conditions to render the system dysfunctional; to harm users; to cover up real design problems; and to produce bad engineering. Hjortsvang thus argued for establishing an interdisciplinary research team to oversee ATC design and development. The problem Hjortsvang pointed to is a specific instance of a more general difficulty related to "the paradox of information technology." This paradox is grounded in the fact that, beyond a certain point, human beings *"will never be able to model"* (and thereby check) in all relevant ways—particularly speed and complexity—data processing operations. Indeed, "the possibility of controlling information processing systems diminishes in proportion to the introduction of modeling or checking instances" because these actually further complicate a program.[20]

In the early 1990s the National Academy of Engineering held a symposium on "Engineering as a Social Enterprise" that argued for a sociotechnical systems interpretation of the profession. As symposium organizer, aeronautical engineer Walter Vincenti pointed out how engineers regularly have to deal with technical systems and are thus familiar with how such systems must be subdivided for analysis. "In the sociotechnical model, the entire society is visualized," according to Vincenti, "as a vast integrated system, with varied social and technical areas of human activity as major interacting subsystems." And although "this subdivision is made so that each subsystem can be analyzed in quasi isolation," for Vincenti "the crucial point" is that "analysis must be carried out . . . with attention at all times to the interactions between and constraints on the subsystems and to the eventual need to reassemble the system."[21] Only such a complex understanding can address the problems raised by previous failures in engineering simplification.

While implicit in systems and interdisciplinary engineering design research, the principle at issue here is seldom formulated. From the perspective of engineering design research, the fundamental technical obligation in the face of failure amid complexity can be phrased as: "Take more factors into account." The obligation to take more into account also has a moral dimension, not simply because it can on occasion avoid some specific harm. In fact, as in the BART case, an objection against taking more into account by means of more complex testing is almost always that it will cause one type of harm (i.e., greater financial costs) while only possibly avoiding another type of harm. The moral dimension of taking more into account is only realized by linking engineering design research into general reflections on the good. In this sense the duty to take more into account may be termed a duty *plus respicere* (from the Latin *plus*, more + *respicere*, to be concerned about).[22] Indeed, a central feature of deeply ethical behavior is that it is based on as wide a reflective base as possible. One reason why altruism is superior to selfishness is that it takes more into account—others as well as oneself—and considers a broader perspective. In the historico-philosophical development of ethics codes in professional engineering, one way of arguing the superiority of the principle of social responsibility is to maintain that it calls for more generous or inclusive reflection, and that through social responsibility company loyalty and technical efficiency are placed in a more comprehensive framework. Stating the issue even more pointedly: To take more into account in engineering will include taking ethics into account. Thus an imperative to seek to reduce ethical remoteness becomes part of the duty *plus respicere.*

Three Examples

Consider briefly three examples: engineering design research for developing countries, for the military, and for mass consumer products such as toys. Each of these cases shows the importance of considering more factors.

With regard to engineering research for developing countries, E.F. Schumacher's *Small Is Beautiful* (1973) argued that the mere transposition of hardware from a highly technological country to a much less technological country almost certainly does not constitute an effective technology transfer. As Schumacher says,

> To do justice to the real situation it is necessary to consider the reactions and capabilities of people, and not confine oneself to machinery or abstract concepts. [I]t is wrong to assume that the most sophisticated equipment, transplanted into an unsophisticated environment, will be regularly worked at full capacity. . . .[23]

The use of the terms ''sophisticated'' and ''unsophisticated'' here require qualification. Technically unsophisticated societies can be very sophisticated in other ways. But the basic point is that development—even conceived too simply as no more than a move from the use of technically simple (and labor intensive) tools to the technically complex (capital intensive) machines—can only proceed through the use of appropriately ''intermediate'' technologies. Such technologies must be designed by engineers who consider more than strictly technical factors, who make themselves aware of the broader social context of the countries within or for which they are working. For instance, the idea of research for the design of intermediate or appropriate technologies for developing countries, taking into account more than strictly technical factors, has become allied with concerns in developed countries for the design of environmentally sensitive technologies. The design of alternative energy technologies for developed countries, sometimes termed "soft technologies," also must look beyond presently available technical processes and expectations to consider broader issues such as long-term availability of resources, the proper allocation of social capital, and environmental impacts. This is certainly another form of taking more factors into account.[24]

With regard to military weapons in advanced technological societies, considerations of context also readily point beyond the strictly technical. Such considerations can include, for example, questions as diverse as those concerning the effective use of a weapon by a military force of some defined educational level and distinctions between offensive versus defensive capabilities. Of course, to some extent these questions involve military policy and politics, not engineering. But the research that goes into weapons development, even to be effective engineering, cannot wholly ignore such factors. No hard and fast line divides strictly technical issues (associated, for example, with the engineering design research for a wire-guided anti-tank missile) and military tactics and strategy. General design specifications devised by military strategists depend on end-user beliefs about technical capabilities, and attempts to meet such specifications can in turn alter these beliefs. Because of this, the military research design engineer will on occasion be called upon to engage in a dialogue of mutual education with military policy analysts and perhaps even politicians. Such dialogue stretches engineering practice beyond simple laboratory analysis. Indeed, as both a technical professional and a citizen in a democracy, the engineer involved in design research for the military may even have an obligation to help educate the general public about certain technical issues. Engineers have at least sometimes felt this to be the case, as indicated by the healthy debate that arose within the technical engineering community about President Reagan's Strategic Defense Initiative. Electrical engineer Stephen Unger has gone further and argued that engineers should allow an admitted plurality of personal moral values to influence the kinds of research work with which they become involved. If "conscientious objections create serious problems in staffing a project, then there is good reason indeed to pause and reconsider the arguments against that project."[25] (Somewhat ironically, Unger also thinks that the wide diversity of moral viewpoints among engineers probably undermines the possibility of any strong impact on the course of technical change.)

Engineers in one of the most civilian forms of research—high-tech toys—must likewise consider issues much broader than the simple technical functioning and safety of their designs. Such consideration is required because of the pervasive use of toys by children and the deep influence toys can have over many aspects of psychological development. Subliminal influences from ''Barbie Dolls'' (about sex roles), ''Transformers'' (about personal identity), video games (about isolation and the pleasures of violence)—and even from the pervasiveness of plastics (about the independent featurelessness of the materials of the world)—all deserve consideration. The explicit educational and habit-forming implications likewise deserve attention. The simple technical pleasures of designing and playing with toys should not overshadow such potential critical reflection, although reflection itself need not lead to a rejection of all unmediated delight in the technical. Engineers in their choices of research tasks and the kinds of project possibilities they suggest to corporate employers are simply called upon to help companies exercise true discernment in formulating their fundamental policies of producing and marketing products.

Practical Guidelines for Engineering Design Research

Summarizing and going beyond even these three rather expansive examples, civil engineer George Bugliarello has argued that the social responsibility of the engineer should include upholding human dignity, avoiding dangerous or uncontrolled side effects, making provisions for possible technological failures, avoiding the reinforcement of outworn social systems, and participating in discussions about the ''why'' of various technologies. For Bugliarello, ''engineering can best carry out its social purpose when it is involved in the formulation of the response to a social need, rather than just being called to provide a quick technological fix.''[26] However, the duty to take more into account, the duty *plus respicere*, is an admittedly loose and somewhat shapeless obligation, perhaps even describable as a ''soft'' ethics. To take this soft ethics a bit further, the following questions might serve as useful guidelines for self-interrogation by research engineers.

Reviewing the basic argument concerning the limitations of simplification, a research engineer could ask:

- Are the models we use sufficiently complex to include a diversity of non-standard technical factors?

- Does reflective analysis include explicit consideration of ethical issues?

From the perspective of the three examples of development, weapons, and toys, design research engineers could further ask themselves such questions as:

- Have we made an effort to consider the broad social context of the engineering research, including impacts on the environment?

- Have we critically examined end-user assumptions?

- Have we undertaken the research in dialogue with personal moral principles and with the larger non-technical community?

- Have we given more direct consideration to peripheral implications of the research?

In summary, whereas the research scientist might ask: Is this knowledge significant? The research engineer could ask: Is this project worthwhile?

Throughout this chapter there has been an implicit assumption about the ways engineering differs from science. It is not only crucial to recognize the distinctive difference of engineering design research, but also equally important to attend to how this kind of research influences science. As a number of observers have noted, technological means have increasingly influenced contemporary science. From telescopes and microscopes to particle accelerators, computers, and space probes, contemporary science has become progressively dependent on the engineering research design of scientific instrumentation. As a result one can reasonably hypothesize that those duties most characteristic of ethics in engineering research—that is, duties related to participation, public disclosure, and *plus respicere*—may play a role in the ethics of scientific research as well.

10

Public Health Research and Uncertainty[1]

Carl F. Cranor
University of California, Riverside

Toxic substances like carcinogens pose threats to human health and well-being.[2] However, such toxins are invisible, often undetectable intruders whose harm, if it materializes, may have a long latency period.[3] Because we remain ignorant for the most part of the mechanisms by which toxins are transmitted and by which they harm us, their causal path is difficult to trace.[4] Many toxins have the potential for catastrophic consequences, i.e., death and serious disease, yet typically we associate them with modest benefits.[5] The catastrophic injuries, however, are frequently low-probability events.[6] Because of carcinogens' invisibility, long latency, obscure mechanisms, and untraceability to responsible agents, assessing their risks is difficult. We must also try to obtain evidence of the harm they threaten before it materializes.

Several of the scientific fields that might enable us to discover and accurately assess the risks of toxins are either in their infancy (risk assessments based upon animal studies), or are too insensitive to detect hazards of concern (human epidemiological studies). Thus, I argue that in these circumstances scientists and regulatory personnel, using the demanding standards of evidence and requirements for certainty commonly considered a part of research science, often will be frustrated in their efforts to identify, regulate, and control toxic substances for public-health purposes. Further, I suggest that when research is done for public-health purposes, scientists should adopt more health-protective

169

evidentiary standards, even when they are not consistent with the most demanding inferential standards of the field. That is, scientists may be forced to choose between the evidentiary ideals of their fields and the moral value of protecting the public from exposure to toxins; frequently they cannot realize both. Thus, scientists strike an appropriate balance between these goals. In the concluding section I sketch an abstract procedure for finding that balance.

Introduction

Epidemiological studies, discussed in section two, are blunt instruments for detecting many risks. They are frequently insensitive and likely to be plagued by numerous practical problems: either may prevent the detection of risks of concern. Risk estimations based upon animal studies, discussed in section three, likewise contain substantial uncertainties, poorly understood biological processes, and few as well as inconclusive data. Also, present scientific procedures for estimating risks are time-consuming, labor-intensive, and costly, all of which prevent more rapid identification, assessment and, ultimately, regulation of carcinogenic risks.

Risk estimation procedures pose special problems of research ethics where the scientific results will be used in the law or for public health purposes. Inaction in the face of great scientific uncertainty or adherence to demanding standards of evidence in either animal or human epidemiological studies can leave the public at risk; precautionary action risks other mistakes. One kind of mistake (a false positive) can occur when a substance is wrongly thought to cause harm or risks of harm but in fact it does not. In this case, assessment procedures can lead to overregulation—greater regulation of the substance under the applicable law than is warranted by the harm it does. A mistake in the opposite direction (a false negative) results when a substance is wrongly believed to be safe when it is not. The lesser error is underregulation—lesser regulation of the substance under the appropriate law than its potential for harm requires. Such mistakes, if they occur, impose costs on the public: false positives and overregulation affect manufacturers of the substance, their shareholders, and the consumers of their products. These mistakes may misdirect investment (in unneeded control technologies), which in turn may deprive the public of useful products or force them to pay higher prices for them. False negatives and underregulation impose costs on the victims or on those put at risk from the toxicity of the substance and misdirect investment by producing too much of a socially costly product. On whom should the costs of such mistakes fall? Designers of evidentiary standards for research in these areas must acknowledge and take into account this question, although it is ordinarily not considered. On the one hand, the very existence of firms or their product lines or the welfare of the public may be threatened.[7] On the other, human death, disease, and compromised quality of life and their associated economic costs may result.

I argue that the number and kinds of risk-estimation mistakes will depend, among other things, upon how scientific research is used for legal and public health purposes. In many cases, traditional scientific practices in using these tools, practices typical of research science where the discovery of truth for its own sake is the primary aim, will beg or frustrate some of the normative goals of the law or of public health protection. I also argue that we can address many of the shortcomings of traditional risk assessment procedures if we use a different approach—a change in philosophy in the use of science for legal purposes. Failure to modify our approaches in these institutions will likely leave us at greater risk from toxic substances than we otherwise would be. However, such choices can be justified if we appreciate more of the social consequences of using scientific practices in their legal settings, in particular the costs of false negatives and underregulation. Thus, the science for assessing toxic substances must not follow exclusively the goals of research science, where the pursuit of truth is the main or sole aim, but also other standards, including the norms of the institutions in which the information will be used.

Problems with Human Epidemiological Studies

Epidemiological studies and animal studies used to identify risks to human beings from carcinogens illustrate some of the generic problems of research ethics. One class of problems is conceptual. For research that rests upon statistical studies using hypothesis acceptance and rejection procedures with small samples, a *conceptual* problem arises between adherence to doing the best scientific research as judged by the standards of the profession and adherence to pursuing sensitive studies designed to detect health risks to persons. That is, a conceptual tension can arise between the evidentiary standards of good research science and the evidentiary standards used for good public health protections. Scientists and the public assume these evidentiary norms are or should be the same, but often they cannot be; it is logically impossible to maximize both research reliability and protection of public health. To see this point, consider hypothesis acceptance and rejection for a cohort epidemiological study.

In trying to determine whether, for example, a substance such as benzene is a human carcinogen, a scientist considers two hypotheses. The first (the null, H_0) hypothesis is that exposure to benzene *is not* associated with greater incidence of a certain disease (e.g., leukemia or aplastic anemia) than that found in a nonexposed population. The second (the alternative hypothesis H_1) predicts that exposure to benzene *is* associated with a greater incidence of such diseases. Because epidemiologists use *samples* of both exposed and unexposed populations, by chance alone they risk inferential errors from studying a sample instead of the whole population in question. They risk false positives [the study shows that the null hypothesis should be rejected (and the alternative hypothesis accepted), even though the null hypothesis is true]. Likewise they risk false negatives [when the study shows that the null hypothesis should be accepted when in fact the null hypothesis is false (and the alternative hypothesis is true)]. A false positive is designated a *type-I error*, and a false negative is called a *type-II error* (summarized in Table 1). Statistical theory provides estimates of the probability of committing such errors by chance alone. The probability of a type-I error is normally designated α and the probability of a type-II error is designated β. Conventionally, α is set at .05 so that there is only a 1 in 20 chance of rejecting the null hypothesis when it is true;[8] researchers want to be 95 percent certain that when new knowledge is gained and the null hypothesis is rejected, it is correctly rejected. These relationships are summarized in Table 1.

Epidemiologists aspire to have studies with low β values (e.g., between .05 and .20 when α is .05), although this is not always possible. When β is .20, one takes 1 chance in 5 of accepting the null hypothesis as true when it is false; for example, the chance of saying benzene is not associated with leukemia when in fact it is.[10] When $\beta = .20$, the *power* (or sensitivity) $(1 - \beta)$ of one's statistical test is .80, which means scientists have an 80 percent chance of rejecting the null hypothesis as false when it is false.

The desire to have a low value for α probably reflects a philosophy about scientific progress that may constitute part of its justification.[11] When the chances of false positives are kept low, a positive result can be added to scientific knowledge with the confidence that only 1 time out of 20 will the result be mistaken as a matter of random chance.[12]

Table 1: False Positives and False Negatives in Epidemiology[9]

Possible Test Results	Possibilities in the Real World of Causal Relationships	
	Null hypothesis is true: Benzene *is not* positively associated with leukemia	Null hypothesis is false: Benzene exposure *is* positively associated with leukemia
Test does not show that benzene exposure is associated with leukemia	No error	Type II error False negative β
Test shows that benzene exposure *is* associated with leukemia	Type I error False positive α	No error

Were one to tolerate higher risks of false positives, take greater chances of new information being false by chance alone, the knowledge edifice of science would be much less secure. A secure edifice of science, however, is not the only important social value at stake. This concern with avoiding false positives illustrates a cautious scientific attitude that protects the field and the researchers from mistakenly adding to the stock of scientific knowledge and from chasing research chimeras.

One can think of α, β and 1-β as measures of the "risk of error" or "standards of proof." What *chance of error* is a researcher willing to take that the results may be mistaken? When employees or the general public may be contracting cancer (unbeknownst to all), even though a study (with high probability) shows they are not, is a risk to their good health worth a 20 percent gamble? The following examples illustrate these risks of error and conceptual problems of interpreting studies. Consider first an ideal research study. Suppose we want to discover whether a suspected carcinogen C is associated with a particular cancer L. Suppose the incidence of L in the general population is 8/10,000, and suppose we want to be 95 percent sure that when no association exists between C and L, our study shows that none does; that is, that there are no false positives. Thus we are committed to α = .05. Suppose we also wish to have low odds of false negatives; thus, we want a study large enough so that β = .05. The chances, then, of false positives and false negatives are *equal* and *low*. Suppose further that we regard a relative risk of 3 as a "serious" risk worth investigating for public health purposes.[13] In order to achieve these antecedent desiderata we would have to study at least 13,495 people exposed to *C*, and (I assume for the sake of simplicity) an equal number who are not exposed (or 26,990 people total) to obtain statistically significant results and have a sufficiently sensitive study to detect a relative risk of 3 with 95 percent confidence.[14,15] That very likely would be prohibitively expensive (because of the large numbers) and it would be practically very difficult to follow participants. Thus, in the *design* of a study, moral considerations can enter—considerations of scientific respectability, study sensitivity, and the cost of achieving these results versus the consequences of not investing in sensitive studies. If, in the absence of ideal circumstances, one is forced to use smaller samples, for example, then it is logically impossible to achieve the same false positive and false negative rates, if one wants to be able to detect a relative risk of 3 with a high degree of confidence. Something must give. That is, as a matter of the mathematics involved, one must accept a higher false positive rate (thus sacrificing ideal scientific respectability) or accept a higher false negative rate (thus failing to have as sensitive a public health study). Or, finally, if one uses smaller samples and tries to maintain equal and low false positive and false negative rates, then one will be unable to detect a relative risk as low as 3, even if one exists. But by hypothesis this was the relative risk of concern.

This tradeoff between adhering to the demanding standards of scientific evidence versus having sensitive studies (protective of public health) must be faced as a matter of the *design* and *funding* of the research. How much are researchers willing to invest for fully accurate studies and is a large enough study even feasible as a matter of design? Once a study is completed, the tradeoff must also be addressed in the *interpretation* of it. Does one permit type I errors to be greater than .05 in order to have a more sensitive study?[16] The conceptual problems of epidemiological studies (design, funding, interpretation) also plague the statistics of animal bioassays, the foundation of much knowledge about the effects of toxic substances. However, animal bioassays tend to have smaller sample sizes.[17]

Not all ethical issues associated with human epidemiological research, however, result from *conceptual* tensions. Some result from *research practices* that in science are features of good scientific work and matters of professional pride, but in other contexts may frustrate public health protections. For example, even if one has established a statistical association between exposure to a substance such as cigarette smoke and contraction of a disease such as lung cancer, one wants to be sure that there are no confounding factors, that is, no mixing of ''the effect of the exposure of interest [cigarette smoke] with the effect of an extraneous factor . . ." [personality type].[18] If researchers have some evidence that a substance causes harm to health, e.g., cigarette smoke or asbestos, but continue to search for possible confounders to explain away observed associations between exposure to the substance and contraction of the disease, this can delay action and frustrate health protections. It is certainly *possible* that confounding factors account for the statistical associations, and these are sometimes found, but one needs to be careful about the extent of the skepticism. As Sander Greenland notes, "One can *always* invoke unmeasured confounders to explain away observational associations. Thus, actions should not depend upon the absence of such explanations, for otherwise action would never be taken."[19]

The motivations to search for confounders appear similar to those that require demanding standards of scientific evidence: sufficient proof to justify a *scientific* inference of a causal connection. Advocates of a careful search for confounders, such as H.J. Eysenck, seek to establish causal connections with "proof in the sense usually accepted in science" or possibly "proof beyond a reasonable doubt," because such facts will "slay a beautiful hypothesis."[20] However, such an approach, while important, or even essential for purely research purposes, may frustrate public health protections. In my judgment Greenland's views, rather than Eysenck's, more closely approach the correct procedure, because in applied research greater weight should be given to consequences for the public than typically would be given in pure research. Thus, when doing research for public health purposes, scientists face moral issues in their research practices, issues about how skeptical they are in searching for alternative hypotheses to account for a given effect. While good research practice rules out all alternative hypotheses to account for a disease effect, the unwise search for confounders can frustrate public health protections and prevent the taking of precautionary actions. Researchers need to develop a sense for how much scientific evidence is appropriate for different public health and public policy purposes. This in turn depends on the value of accurate scientific information (e.g., the importance of accurate scientific information and the value of avoiding false positives and false negatives) and the importance of avoiding different kinds of mistakes (i.e., false positives and false negatives). I return to both points later.

Finally, a number of other factors unrelated to the nature and extent of the risks in question may result in negative studies and frustrate discovery of the risks that concern public health, even when such risks exist. Unwisely requiring several positive epidemiological studies, all with low-type I error rates, can prolong decisions and leave innocent people at risk; one test may be sufficient. Moreover, conducting good epidemiological studies with adequate samples to detect the risks of concern, but making the study too short for the latency period of the disease in question, can prevent its detection. Thus, in general we should distinguish between the evidentiary standards and practices appropriate to scientific inquiry—which aims to develop credible research on interesting and confirmable hypotheses for a scientific subfield—and the standards and practices needed to establish early warning of probable hazards from toxic substances in order to take preventive public health actions. Such studies for public health protection need to be *good enough* to establish some evidence of the harm (to find suspect substances) but not so demanding that they frustrate the very purpose of the investigation.

Problems with Risk Assessment
Based Upon Animal Studies

When we turn to the use of animal bioassays to try to predict risks to human beings from carcinogens, somewhat different problems plague scientific efforts. Here costs, fields in their infancy, poorly understood biological mechanisms, information gaps and uncertainties, and slow assessments all plague research and public health efforts.

The primary method for estimating cancer risks to persons in the regulatory setting is to study the carcinogenic effects of substances on animals and then to project risks to human beings based upon this information. For these purposes, three or four small experimental groups of rodents are fed high doses of a substance to see whether the tumor rate in the experimental groups is significantly greater than the cancer rate in a control group.[21] If it is, then scientists extrapolate from response rates to high-dose exposures in rodents to response rates at low-dose exposures in rodents (an exposure rate much closer to the typical human exposure dose). Risk assessors then use low-dose response rates along with principles of biology, toxicology, and pharmacology (if appropriate) to estimate, on the basis of rodent-to-human extrapolation models, a dose-response function for the likely risks that human beings would face at hypothetical levels of exposure. This risk information is then combined with actual exposure information at all doses for the appropriate population at risk in order to estimate the magnitude and extent of the risk to human beings. Finally, the risk information is combined with economic, policy, statutory, and technological feasibility information so that regulatory agencies can decide how best to manage the risks in question.

There are a number of advantages to using animal studies as evidence that a substance causes cancer in human beings. Most substances that induce cancer in one mammalian species also induce cancer in others; the pathology of tumors in various species of animals in most cases is believed to resemble that in humans; and human and animal molecular, cellular, tissue, and organ functions are thought to be similar.[22] Moreover, "in the absence of adequate data on humans, it is reasonable, for practical purposes, to regard chemicals for which there is sufficient evidence of carcinogenicity in animals *as if they presented* a carcinogenic risk to humans."[23] Animal studies also have some advantages over human epidemiological studies. For one thing, few industrial chemicals have been adequately tested by epidemiological studies to discover whether they cause cancer in humans; epidemiological studies can lack the sensitivity to detect relative risks of concern (as we have seen); and long latency periods for carcinogens (up to 40 years) may prevent the discovery of carcinogenic effects of many substances.[24] Even with sufficient latency periods, it can be difficult to trace diseases to particular substances, because almost no toxic substances leave a unique "fingerprint" of their presence.[25] Animal studies are faster and cheaper than human studies. Moral considerations also provide reasons for using animal studies; there is no justification to wait for "evidence of harm in exposed people when risks can be established relatively quickly by animal experimentation."[26]

Animal studies have some limitations, however. Estimating risks from animal studies requires a number of inferences from the established animal data to the projection of end-point risks to human beings. Thus, controversy surrounds their reliability as predictors of human cancer. These inferences are plagued by a number of gaps and uncertainties that arise from the insufficient information (in both theories and data) available to settle the scientific questions at issue. In such cases researchers typically use mathematical models or other generalizations to fill the gaps. However, because more than one model may be plausible, different models might result in substantially different predictions. Thus, the range of possible answers will yield a range of uncertainty. Additional uncertainties stem from the inherent variability in biological responses among individuals.[27] Uncertainties in arriving at dose-response (potency) estimates for substances lead to considerable scientific and political controversy among experts about their use in predicting risks to human beings.[28] Nonetheless, a substantial consensus continues to argue for use of animal studies because of the reasons cited above.[29] In summary, uncertainties come into animal-based estimates of human cancer risks because: the etiology of carcinogenesis is insufficiently understood, the use of different rodent-to-human extrapolation models can produce differences in risk estimates, the relative weighting of positive and negative animal studies for the same substance may differ, benign and malignant tumors can be weighted differently as evidence of carcinogenicity in animals (and thus in humans), and disputes arise about how data from two or more nonhuman species should be combined.[30,31] Finally, although environmental-fate models provide a way of estimating actual exposures of human beings to a substance, substantial uncertainties can exist as to the correct result.[32] Such uncertainties could make substantial differences in the subsequently issued regulations.

Like the problems inherent in human epidemiological studies, uncertainties associated with animal research pose ethical issues for scientists beyond those resulting from conceptual tensions in statistical studies. If researchers adopt typical research practices (e.g., acquiring, among other things, more and better data, better understanding of the biological mechanisms involved, and better exposure data) toward uncertainties and knowledge gaps, scientists may frustrate public health goals; agnosticism and inaction will likely result. Although the typical scientific response is to improve the data, information, and understanding, such improvement takes additional time, money, and human resources, all of which may be in short supply and leave the public at risk in the meantime. Further, even if scientists avoided the uncertainties that exist at present in animal studies, evaluating carcinogens on a detailed, case-by-case basis would still be extremely slow. This slowness has enormous opportunity costs, because other potential toxins would not be evaluated.[33] Moreover, if some, but not the best, evidence supports addressing risks to public health, failure to act may frustrate or beg public health issues, just as an unwise search for confounders can. *Inaction* is a decision and can have as many adverse consequences as hasty action.

Typical scientific practices, then, unwisely adopted in circumstances when one has usable, but not the best, evidence can frustrate public health goals. Such conflicts between public health goals and the ideals of research practices pose ethical dilemmas for research scientists and for agency scientists trained in traditional research disciplines. On the one hand, if research scientists maintain fidelity to the ideals of their discipline when they are asked to contribute to research decisions affecting public health, they may frustrate public health goals. On the other hand, if they extrapolate beyond present data and theories (in ways not licensed by the best inferential procedures of a discipline) out of concern for public health issues, they risk censure by colleagues who remain committed to evidentiary practices of the field, but who do not understand the broader moral and social issues at stake, e.g., preventive public health protection. Thus, tension between the research ideals of the profession and broader moral concerns poses moral issues for scientists and will likely lead to a felt cognitive dissonance, unless scientists resolve the issue to their own satisfaction. In closing I suggest a general solution to this problem.

Ethical Issues Introduced by Inference Guidelines

Apart from the evidentiary, ethical, and cognitive tensions just described, the most common solutions to the presence of uncertainties and scientific ignorance can introduce additional moral issues. In regulatory contexts, the information gaps, uncertainties, and lack of theoretical understanding typically are addressed by the use of policy or inference guidelines.[34] A National Research Council report defines an inference guideline as ''an explicit statement of a predetermined choice among options that arise in inferring human risk from data that are not fully adequate or drawn from human experience.''[35] Inference guidelines constitute assumptions to bridge the gaps in question, e.g., the gaps when mathematical models are used to estimate the effects of exposure at low doses from experimental results based on higher doses.[36] Agencies have adopted four kinds of inference guidelines:

- Assumptions used when data are not available in a particular case
- Assumptions that are potentially testable, but have not yet been tested
- Assumptions that probably cannot be tested because of experimental limitations
- Assumptions that cannot be tested because of ethical considerations.[37]

The assumptions and policies adopted as inference guidelines can lead to considerable controversy, because they can make a difference in the estimation of risks to human beings. Frequently, little in the way of biological evidence determines the choice of guidelines.[38] Nevertheless, in the present state of knowledge I believe that we cannot avoid the use of inference guidelines, because we need to make decisions concerning the effects of toxic substances on human beings, and we should not leave the innocent public at risk while we pursue our research. In carcinogen risk assessment, therefore, some choices between different inference guidelines cannot be avoided, if risk assessors are going to provide timely evidence for the evaluation and regulation of toxic substances. Of course, choices about inference guidelines must be made on the basis of some reason. But because scientific data underdetermine the choice, and perhaps more radically underdetermine this choice than similar choices in any other areas of science, some other consideration(s) must determine it. Some inference guidelines are scientific or empirical generalizations, but ones not necessarily well supported in a particular case. Other guidelines are chosen on the basis of aesthetic criteria, such as *simplicity*, or on the basis of ease of calculation.[39] And sometimes agencies compromise and adopt a guideline simply because it falls midway between alternatives open to them.[40]

More important, however, nearly all regulatory agencies acknowledge that some of the decisions about inference guidelines are chosen on nonscientific policy or moral grounds. Typically they reason that risk-assessment procedures should not underestimate hazards to human beings at the end of the process, or that risk assessors must be prudent in protecting public health. For example, they might choose not to underestimate the risks to human beings by using a health-protective high-dose to low-dose extrapolation model.[41] However, individuals can disagree about the required level of ''prudence'' or protection. Thus, the use of inference guidelines introduces additional ethical issues into the science that is part of carcinogen risk assessment. We might somewhat oversimplify the point by saying that whether research indicates a risk to human beings, and the seriousness of that risk, are in part normative, policy matters. Thus, not only the notion of an *acceptable risk* (an obvious normative concept) but also (in the present state of knowledge of carcinogen risk assessment) the ideas of *a risk* and the *severity of a risk* are partly normative notions, because they are the product of normative judgments.[42]

Given the uncertainties in risk assessment, and given the typical procedures adopted by agencies for coping with such uncertainties (and even the recommendations of the National Academy of Sciences[43]), the ethical neutrality of factual inquiries typical in normal scientific inquiries (in subatomic physics, molecular biology, geology, etc.) does not apply to risk assessment. Risk assessment requires normative choices.

An Ethical Solution: Balancing Research Goals

Up to this point I have focused on some of the evidentiary tensions between the ideals of pure research science and the goals of public health research that can result from conceptual issues or from typical research practices. These tensions pose ethical concerns for scientists doing research on public health problems and for decisionmakers in the public health area. However, I have not suggested, except in passing, how they might address the resulting ethical issues. This I do in closing.

My argument has presupposed that the standards of evidence (or burdens of proof) that apply to various areas of human endeavor in pure research differ from those that guide research for public health protections (exemplified by regulatory efforts to protect the public from exposure to carcinogens). Although it may seem obvious, this claim warrants some discussion. What is the connection between burdens of proof and institutional norms for the practice and use of research?

The burden of proof that research must satisfy, in order to ground a particular institutional decision, will depend at least in large part upon the kinds of mistakes one seeks to avoid. Some institutions will aim to provide greater protections against certain kinds of mistakes; some will protect against other kinds of mistakes. The criminal law, for example, stringently protects against convicting innocent people. To avoid the equivalent of false positives, the state must overcome a high burden of proof to establish its case. By contrast, physicians in screening patients for life-threatening diseases try to avoid missing someone who has the disease, to avoid false negatives. Thus, they want to make it very easy to detect the presence of disease, even if this means in some cases wrongly identifying some as diseased who are not.

Mistakes will impose costs upon someone; thus, in the design of institutions one must consider the larger consequences of adopting different evidentiary procedures. If mistakes will occur, on whom should these costs fall? How should they be distributed? Both the distribution of costs and the kinds of institutional mistakes to be avoided, in turn, depend upon what is at stake—the values the institution or activity seeks to protect. Institutions embody a variety of values that help set the various standards of proof needed to reach a decision. In research, scientists have devised research strategies, inferential standards, the peer review process, and disciplinary practices to prevent accepting false information as true, so that additions to the stock of scientific knowledge are well-founded, and so that scientists do not chase chimeras. In criminal law, we attempt to avoid wrongly punishing innocent people (because of the particular injustice this inflicts upon them). We also attempt to equalize to some extent the competition between the state and defendants; thus criminal law imposes high burdens of proof on the state in order to secure these values and prevent false positives. By contrast, in screening women for antibodies in order to prevent congenital rubella, doctors incur a modest number of false positives in order to be sure to prevent the devastating effect of the disease, because "[t]he inefficiency of vaccinating a number of women who are already immune is a small price to pay."[44] These examples and the preceding argument suggest that institutional norms and goals guide the kinds of mistakes the institution—e.g., the criminal law or environmental health law—seeks to avoid, which in turn determine the burdens of proof that are adopted for decisionmaking within it. Burdens of proof determine how easy or how difficult it will be to make certain kinds of mistakes in decisions.

In the preceding sections, I have suggested that an "appropriate" balance must be struck between false positives and false negatives, and thus some balance between the burdens of proof in legal and public health contexts that differs from that relied upon in scientific research. Several considerations support this point. For one thing, inaction is just as much a decision under uncertainty as a decision to take precautionary action in the meantime. Clinical physicians have long recognized such costs. In assessing potentially toxic substances a decision not to act risks false negatives, whereas a decision for precautionary regulation risks false positives. Since one risks both mistakes, one should acknowledge both and design the decision process to find a balance between them that fits the institutional context. However, neither of the two extremes is appropriate. On the one hand, I do not indicate either that regulatory agencies should always make a precautionary decision to regulate (which would always prevent false negatives at the cost of false positives), or that agencies should never act (which would always prevent false positives at the cost of false negatives). Either strategy would be analogous to Pascal's Wager—that because of the importance of what is at stake one decision alternative should always dominate the other. I have suggested that scientists, because of their training, may be tempted to overemphasize concerns with false positives; instead they should have a substantial concern for false negatives when researching public health issues. Thus, I do not suggest simple decision rules, but call attention to the need for modifications in complex institutional procedures to try to achieve a more appropriate balance of the different mistakes and different burdens of proof. Take this one step further.

One strategy to achieve this balance would be to minimize the social costs of errors, to account for the costs of both false positives and false negatives taken together. The appropriate balance for a given institution, therefore, would be one that minimizes the costs of the two mistakes considered together in that institutional context. False positives will impose dollar costs on manufacturers, their shareholders, and consumers of their products, which will result in misdirected investment and the loss of social utility from not using the substances in question in products. False negatives and underregulation typically will impose dollar costs on the victims or on those put at risk from exposure to toxic substances and will also result in misdirecting investment in socially (public health) costly products. They will also result in the very real, but non-monetary, human costs associated with disease and death. The costs to an institution and to society of mistakes in evaluating potentially harmful substances are a function of four factors:

- the relative costs of false negatives (C_{fn}) and false positives (C_{fp});
- the probability that a substance is a carcinogen (p_c);
- the error rates of the institutional procedures (the chances of false positives [a] and false negatives [b]) for discovering whether a substance is a carcinogen or not;
- the costs of testing a substance (C_T).

This complex relationship is summarized symbolically as follows:

$$\min \left[(C_{fp} \times (1 - p_c) \times a) + (C_{fn} \times p_c \times \beta) + C_T \right][45]$$

Costs here might be dollar costs, social utility losses as valued by the community, or normative (moral) costs of mistakes.

The quantitative formulation of the complex relation just described merely symbolizes succinctly the relationships among the ideas. To actually use the formula, and to have guidance on the appropriate balance between the kinds of mistakes for an institution, one must assign quantitative values for the costs, either in monetary or non-monetary terms (social utility or other moral costs). One must also estimate the chances of false positives and false negatives and the probability that a substance is a carcinogen. None of these evaluations is easy. However, for the crucial variable, the costs of false negatives and false positives, several economists have suggested for conceptual and modeling purposes that the former on average cost 10 times as much as the latter.[46] If they are correct, then everything else being equal, institutions charged with protecting the public health should risk (roughly) 10 times more false positives than false negatives (ignoring the costs of testing). That is, the error rates and burdens of proof should reflect such institutional values. The strategy for a particular institution, therefore, is to have evaluation procedures for assessing toxins and burdens of proof that—given the respective costs of false negatives, false positives, and the procedures themselves—minimize the total costs of evaluating the universe of substances. This will provide an appropriate balance between different kinds of mistakes as a function of the values at stake in the institutional context.[47]

Others using the general formula just described have shown that the use of animal bioassays is not justified when compared with somewhat less "accurate" but much faster carcinogen identification procedures. They argue that animal studies are not cost effective, provide limited and uncertain information, and take up to 10 years to complete. Thus, they conclude that "it is cheaper for society to use a battery of short-term tests, despite resulting false positives and false negatives, rather than to continue tolerating thousands of unregulated carcinogens because there are no animal bioassay results."[48] One can also show that expedited carcinogen potency assessments have far lower social costs than the conventional time-consuming potency assessments ordinarily employed by regulatory agencies.[49] That is, given the typically more serious health costs of false negatives compared with false positives, it is much better to survey a universe of known animal carcinogens and provide estimates of human carcinogenicity than to perform a careful assessment of each one and greatly delay evaluating the remainder.

The procedure just sketched indicates in a general way a solution to some of the ethical issues and evidentiary tensions to which I called attention earlier. I have not resolved them definitively in this chapter, for I have not indicated particular assignments of the values at stake or probabilities that a given substance is a carcinogen.[50] However, as I indicated in the previous paragraph, plausible assignments of values to the variables give content to the abstract relationships, which in turn can provide practical guidance about the appropriateness of using somewhat more, rather than less, public health protective standards of evidence in an institution that aims to protect the public. If this sketch is correct, it shows that the evidentiary standards adopted in the research used for particular purposes are in large part a function of the values at stake either for the institution in question or for the larger community. Thus, the important larger point is that in doing research for public health purposes, the evidentiary standards should be a function not only of the scientific disciplines in question, but also of the larger public health goals (the costs of false negatives to the community). A univocal commitment to the evidentiary standards internal to a branch of research science such as toxicology, biology, pharmacology, or epidemiology appears unwarranted and perhaps misguided in such contexts. We need more complex evidentiary and decision standards for public health research than for analogous research in a basic or pure science. Otherwise we risk imposing the consequences of poor information, uncertainty, small samples, and scientific skepticism on an innocent public.

Notes

Chapter 1

1. R. Jeffrey Smith, ''Scientists Implicated in Atom Test Deception,'' *Science* 218, no. 4572 (5 November 1982): 545–47.

2. International Physicians for the Prevention of Nuclear War and Institute for Energy and Environmental Research, *Radioactive Heaven and Earth: The Health and Environmental Effects of Nuclear Weapons Testing In, On, and Above the Earth* (New York: Apex Press, 1991). See also N. Lenssen, ''Confronting Nuclear Waste,'' in *State of the World 1992*, ed. L. R. Brown *et al.* (New York: Norton, 1992), pp. 46–65; hereafter cited as: Brown *et al.*, SW 1992.

3. See, for example, U.S. Senate, *National Atmospheric Nuclear Testing Compensation Act of 1990*, U.S. Senate, Second Session (Washington, D.C.: U.S. Government Printing Office, 1990).

4. For these statistics, see Lenssen, ''Confronting Nuclear Waste.'' See also K. S. Shrader-Frechette, *Burying Uncertainty: Risk and the Case Against Geological Disposal of Nuclear Waste* (Berkeley: University of California Press, 1993), ch. 9; hereafter cited as: Shrader-Frechette, BU.

5. Robert J. Levine, ''Clarifying the Concepts of Research Ethics,'' *Hastings Center Report* 9 (July 1979): 21–26; hereafter cited as: Levine, ''Clarifying Concepts.''

6. Richard L. Miller, *Under the Cloud: The Decades of Nuclear Testing* (New York: Free Press, 1986), p. 113; hereafter cited as: Miller, UC.

7. Levine, ''Clarifying Concepts,'' p. 21.

8. Philip G. Zimbardo, ''On the Ethics of Intervention in Human Psychological Research,'' *Cognition* 2, no. 2 (1973): 246, 243–56; hereafter cited as: Zimbardo, ''Ethics of Intervention.''

9. For information about all these developments, see Philip Pettit, ''Instituting a Research Ethic,'' *Bioethics* 6, no. 2 (April 1992): 89–112, esp. 95–97; Michael Davis, ''The New World of Research Ethics,'' *International Journal of Applied Ethics* 5, no. 1 (Spring 1990): 1–10; hereafter cited as: Davis, ''New World''; B. Gustafsson and Gunner Tibell, ''Critics of Science and Research

Ethics in Sweden,'' *Philosophy and Social Action* 15, nos. 3–4 (1989): 59–74; Tom L. Beauchamp, ''Ethical Issues in Funding and Monitoring University Research,'' *Business and Professional Ethics Journal* 11, no. 1 (Spring 1992): 5–16; hereafter cited as: Beauchamp, ''Ethical Issues''; Lucas Bergkamp, ''The Rise of Research Ethics Committees in Western Europe, *Bioethics* 3, no. 2 (1989): 122–34; hereafter cited as: Bergkamp, ''Ethics Committees''; Nicholas Steneck, ''Commentary: The University and Research Ethics,'' *Science, Technology and Human Values* 9, no. 4 (Fall 1984): 6–15; hereafter cited as: Steneck, ''Commentary.''

10. Rachelle Hollander and Nicholas Steneck, ''Science- and Engineering-Related Ethics and Values Studies,'' *Science, Technology, and Human Values* 15, no. 1 (Winter 1990): 84–104.

11. Edward R. David and the Panel on Scientific Responsibility and the Conduct of Research, *Responsible Science*, 2 vols. (Washington, D.C.: National Academy Press, 1992, 1993).

12. Herbert C. Kelman, ''Research, Behavioral,'' in *Encyclopedia of Bioethics*, ed. Warren T. Reich (New York: Macmillan, 1978), p. 1470 of pp. 1470–92.

13. See, for example, Howard Ball, *Justice Downwind* (New York: Oxford University Press, 1986); Philip L. Fradkin, *Fallout: An American Nuclear Tragedy* (Tucson: University of Arizona Press, 1989); Miller, UC; U.S. Congress, *Government Liability for Atomic Weapons Testing Program*, Hearings Before the Committee on the Judiciary, U.S. Senate, 99th Congress, Second Session, June 27, 1986 (Washington, D.C.: U.S. Government Printing Office, 1987).

14. Miller, UC, pp. 186–87.

15. Kelman, ''Research, Behavioral,'' p. 1472; Pettit, ''Instituting a Research Ethic,'' p. 97.

16. Davis, ''New World,'' pp. 1–10, esp. p. 5.

17. Steneck, ''Commentary,'' p. 12; see pp. 6–15.

18. Shrader-Frechette, BU, esp. pp. 26, 155.

19. For discussion of ''statistical casualties,'' deaths not traceable individually to particular events, even though the events cause them, see K. S. Shrader-Frechette, *Risk Analysis and Scientific Method* (Boston: Kluwer, 1985), pp. 145ff.

20. For discussion of problems with causality in such cases, see K. S. Shrader-Frechette, *Risk and Rationality* (Berkeley: University of California Press, 1991), pp. 60–63, 200–205.

21. See notes 1–4, 6, 13, and 14 in this chapter.

22. See Shrader-Frechette, BU, esp. pp. 139–41, 195ff.

23. See, for example, Y. Brackbill and A. Hellegers, ''Ethics and Editors,'' *Hastings Center Report* 10 (April 1980): 20–22.

24. See Zimbardo, ''Ethics of Intervention,'' pp. 243–56 for discussion of the Stanford research. The Stanford research was published in C. Haney, C. Banks, and P. Zimbardo, ''Interpersonal Dynamics in a Simulated Prison,'' *International Journal of Criminology and Penology* 1 (1973): 69–97.

25. See S. Milgram, *Obedience to Authority* (New York: Harper and Row, 1974).

26. See, for example, R. Faden and T. Beauchamp, *A History and Theory of Informed Consent* (New York: Oxford, 1986); hereafter cited as: Faden and Beauchamp, HTIC; T. Beauchamp and J. Childress, *Principles of Biomedical Ethics* (New York: Oxford, 1989); hereafter cited as: Beauchamp and Childress, PBE; Bergkamp, ''Ethics Committees,'' pp. 122–34; R. T. Bower and P. de Gasparis, *Ethics in Social Research* (New York: Praeger, 1978); J. S. Habgood *et al.*, ''Ethical Problems of Repetitive Research,'' *Journal of Medical Ethics* 3 (1977): 14–17. C. B. Klockars and F. W. O'Connor, *Deviance and Decency* (London: Sage, 1979); hereafter cited as: Klockars and O'Connor, DD. See also Levine, ''Clarifying Concepts,'' pp. 21–26; O. Osborne, ''Cross-Cultural Social Science Research and Questions of Scientific Medical Imperialism,'' *Bioethics Quarterly* 2, no. 3 (Fall 1980); E. L. Pattullo, ''Who Risks What in Social Research?'' *Hastings Center Report* 10 (April 1980): 15–18.

27. One of the best accounts of consent in medical ethics, and the account followed here, is that of Beauchamp and Childress, PBE, pp. 74ff. See also M. Curry and L. May, *Professional Responsibility for Harmful Actions* (Dubuque: Kendall/Hunt, 1984); hereafter cited as: Curry and May, PR; and Faden and Beauchamp, HTIC.

28. Albert R. Jonsen and Michael Yesley, ''Rhetoric and Research Ethics,'' *Bioethics Quarterly* 2, no. 4 (Winter 1980): 212–25, esp. p. 215.

29. Murray L. Wax, ''Fieldworkers and Research Subjects: Who Needs Protection?'' *Hastings Center Report* 7 (August 1977): 29–32; hereafter cited as: Wax, ''Fieldworkers.''

30. A. Soble, ''Deception in Social Science Research: Is Informed Consent Possible?'' *Hastings Center Report* 8 (October 1978): 40–46; hereafter cited as: Soble, ''Deception.''

31. See, for example, C. B. Klockars, ''Dirty Hands and Deviant Subjects,'' in Klockars and O'Connor, DD, pp. 261–282.

32. Soble, ''Deception,'' pp. 40–46; see also Wax, ''Fieldworkers,'' pp. 29–32.

33. Kelman, ''Research, Behavioral,'' p. 1473.

34. Kelman, ''Research, Behavioral,'' pp. 1473–74.

35. See Faden and Beauchamp, HTIC; and Beauchamp and Childress, PBE. For a discussion of biomedical research and ethics, see Kathi E. Hanna (ed.) and Carl W. Gottschalk *et al.*, Committee to Study Biomedical Decision Making, *Biomedical Politics* (Washington, D.C.: National Academy Press, 1991).

36. Beauchamp, ''Ethical Issues,'' p. 6.

37. See Diether H. Haenicke, *Ethics in Academia* (Kalamazoo: Western Michigan University, 1988), pp. 10–15; hereafter cited as: Haenicke, EA; Mitchell Silverman, William Blount, and Marson Johnson, ''Teaching and Demonstrating Ethics in the Classroom,'' *International Journal of Offender Therapy and Comparative Criminology* 36, no. 3 (1992): 169–72, esp. pp. 170–71.

38. See Melville Cottrill, ''Academic Ethics Revisited,'' *Business and Professional Ethics Journal* 8, no. 1 (Spring 1989): 57–64; S. L. Payne and B. H. Charnov (eds.), *Ethical Dilemmas for Academic Professionals* (Springfield, Illinois: Thomas, 1987).

39. See, for example, D. E. Blevins and S. R. Ewer, ''University Research and Development Activities,'' *Journal of Business Ethics* 7 (1988): 645–56; hereafter cited as: Blevins and Ewer, ''University Research.''

40. M. Kenney, ''The Ethical Dilemmas of University-Industry Collaborations,'' *Journal of Business Ethics* 6 (1987): 127–35; hereafter cited as: Kenney, ''Ethical Dilemmas.'' I. Stark, ''The University Goes to Market,'' *Thought and Action: NEA Higher Education Journal* 1, no. 1 (Fall 1984): 9–21.

41. Stark, ''The University Goes to Market,'' pp. 9–21; T. Tolbert, ''The Monsanto Experience,'' *Thought and Action: NEA Higher Education Journal* 1, no. 1 (Fall 1984): 65–78; hereafter cited as: Tolbert, ''Monsanto Experience.''

42. W. Lepkowski, ''Academic Values Tested by MIT's New Center,'' *Chemical and Engineering News* (March 1982): 7–12; hereafter cited as: Lepkowski, ''Academic Values.''

43. T. Zasloff, ''The University, by Definition, May Be the Wrong Place for Military Research,'' *The Chronicle of Higher Education* (April 20, 1988): A52; hereafter cited as: Zasloff, ''University.''

44. E. H. Berman, ''Foundations, United States Foreign Policy, and African Education, 1945–1975,'' *Harvard Educational Review* 49, no. 2 (May 1979): 145–79.

45. Tolbert, ''Monsanto Experience,'' pp. 65–78.

46. Michael Gold, *A Conspiracy of Cells* (Albany: SUNY Press, 1986); Wayne Leibel, ''When Scientists Are Wrong,'' *Journal of Business Ethics* 10 (1991): 601–4.

47. L. Minsky, ''Greed in the Groves: Part Two,'' *Thought and Action: NEA Higher Education Journal* 1, no. 1 (Fall 1984): 43–49; hereafter cited as: Minsky, ''Greed.'' See Haenicke, EA, pp. 7–8; and Beauchamp, ''Ethical Issues in Funding,'' pp. 7–8.

48. Minsky, ''Greed,'' pp. 43–49.

49. R. Nader, ''Greed in the Groves: Part I,'' *Thought and Action: NEA Higher Education Journal* 1, no. 1 (Fall 1984): 41–42.

50. Kenney, ''Ethical Dilemmas,'' pp. 127–35; Lepkowski, ''Academic Values,'' pp. 7–12.

51. See, for example, A. H. Goldman, ''Ethical Issues in Proprietary Restriction on Research Results,'' *Science, Technology, and Human Values* 12, no. 1 (Winter 1987): 22–30; hereafter cited as: Goldman, ''Ethical Issues.''

52. Kenney, ''Ethical Dilemmas,'' pp. 127–35; H. Ehrlich, ''The University–Military Research Connection,'' *Thought and Action: NEA Higher Education Journal* 1, no. 1 (Fall 1984): 117–24.

53. Lawson Crowe, ''The Federal Government, University Science, and the

Social Contract," *From the Center* (University of Colorado) 9, no. 1 (Spring 1990): 1–2.

54. I. Winn, "The University and the Strategic Defense Initiative," *Thought and Action: NEA Higher Education Journal* 1, no. 1 (Fall 1984): 19–32; hereafter cited as: Winn, "University."

55. Winn, "University," p. 23.

56. J. T. Edsall and the AAAS (American Association for the Advancement of Science) Committee on Scientific Freedom and Responsibility, *Freedom and Responsibility* (Washington, D.C.: AAAS, 1975); R. Merton, *The Sociology of Science* (Chicago: University of Chicago Press, 1973), pp. 9, 318, 456; M. Bayles, *Professional Ethics* (Belmont, Calif.: Wadsworth, 1981); A. Cournand and H. Zuckerman, *The Code of Science: Analysis and Reflections on its Future* (New York: Columbia University Institute for the Study of Science in Human Affairs, 1970), p. 14 for confirmation of this point.

57. Stark, "The University Goes to Market," pp. 9–21.

58. Stark, "The University Goes to Market," p. 16.

59. Blevins and Ewer, "University Research," pp. 645–56.

60. Stark, "The University Goes to Market," p. 18.

61. Leonard Minsky, quoted in K. Mangan, "Institutions and Scholars Face Ethical Dilemmas Over Pursuit of Research with Commercial Values," *The Chronicle of Higher Education* (29 July 1987): 12.

62. Zasloff, "University," p. A52.

63. Stark, "The University Goes to Market," p. 17; Winn, "University," p. 28; and Blevins and Ewer, "University Research," p. 651.

64. Quoted in Stark, "The University Goes to Market," p. 18.

65. Blevins and Ewer, "University Research," p. 648.

66. Blevins and Ewer, "University Research," p. 650.

67. Tolbert, "Monsanto Experience," p. 70.

68. Beauchamp, "Ethical Issues," pp. 9–11.

69. For this definition and a discussion of sustainability, see L. R. Brown, C. Flavin, and S. Postel, "Picturing a Sustainable Society," in *State of the World 1990*, ed. L. R. Brown *et al.* (New York: Norton, 1990), pp. 173–90.

70. R. Goldburg, J. Rissler, H. Shand, and C. Hassebrook, *Biotechnology's Bitter Harvest* (Washington, D.C.: National Wildlife Federation, 1990), esp. pp. 5–6; hereafter cited as: Goldburg *et al.*, BBT.

71. Goldburg *et al.*, BBT, p. 54.

72. R. Monastersky, "Science on Ice," *Science News* 143, no. 15 (10 April 1993): 232–35.

73. Monastersky, "Science on Ice," p. 233.

74. Monastersky, "Science on Ice," p. 234. See also N. H. Watson, "Antarctic Incinerator Lawsuit Yields Landmark Ruling," *Environmental Defense Fund Letter* XXIX, no. 3 (May 1993): 1, 5.

75. For discussion of this example, from government document WASH 1224, see K. S. Shrader-Frechette, *Nuclear Power and Public Policy: Social*

and Ethical Problems with Fission Technology (Boston: Reidel, 1983), pp. 57ff.; hereafter cited as: Shrader-Frechette, NPPP.

76. Shrader-Frechette, NPPP, p. 58.

77. Most of this discussion of smoking is based on W. U. Chandler, "Banishing Tobacco," in *State of the World 1986*, ed. L. R. Brown *et al.*, (New York: Norton, 1993), pp. 139–58.

78. For a discussion of the Dow, Monsanto, and Agent Orange studies, see H. Leung and D. Paustenbach, "Assessing Health Risks in the Workplace," in *The Risk Assessment of Environmental and Human Health Hazards*, ed. D. Paustenbach (New York: Wiley, 1989), pp. 699–705. For discussion of weapons tests involving people in the U.S. military service, see the section headed "Are Environmentalists Distrustful?" in chapter two. See also Shrader-Frechette, NPPP, pp. 99–100, and V. P. Bond, "Causality of a Given Cancer after Known Radiation Exposure," in *Hazards: Technology and Fairness*, ed. R. W. Kates *et al.* (Washington, D.C.: National Academy Press, 1986), pp. 24–43. See the last two chapters of this volume for proposed reforms.

79. H. Inhaber, "Risk with Energy from Conventional and Nonconventional Sources," *Science* 203, no. 4382 (23 February 1979): 718–23; hereafter cited as: Inhaber, "Risk with Energy." See also H. Inhaber, *Risk of Energy Production*, Report no. AECB-1119 (Ottawa: Atomic Energy Control Board, 1978).

80. Inhaber, "Risk with Energy," p. 718. For an excellent methodological critique of Inhaber's energy studies, see P. Gleick and J. Holdren, "Assessing Environmental Risks of Energy," *American Journal of Public Health* 71, no. 9 (September 1981): 1046–50; hereafter cited as: Gleick and Holdren, "Assessing."

81. According to L. S. Johns and associates, of the OTA Solar Energy Staff (in *Application of Solar Technology to Today's Energy Needs*, 2 vols. [Washington, D.C.: U.S. Office of Technology Assessment, 1987], vol. 1, p. 3), "Onsite solar devices could be made competitive in markets representing over 40 percent of U.S. energy demand by the mid-1980's." The OTA staff goes on to say that low-temperature uses, which comprise 40 percent of the total U.S. energy needs, are currently competitive economically with existing alternatives (pp. 13–14), even in cities such as Boston, Albuquerque, and Omaha, where heating needs are often significant (pp. 31ff.).

82. Inhaber, "Risk with Energy," p. 721. See Gleick and Holdren, "Assessing."

83. Inhaber, "Risk with Energy," p. 721. See Gleick and Holdren, "Assessing."

84. Inhaber, "Risk with Energy," pp. 721–22. See Gleick and Holdren, "Assessing."

85. Inhaber, "Risk with Energy," pp. 721–22. For further criticism of the Inhaber report, see J. Herbert, C. Swanson, and P. Reddy, "A Risky Business," *Environment* 21, no. 6 (July/August 1979): 28–33; and J. Holdren, K. Smith,

and G. Morris, "Energy: Calculating the Risks," *Science* 204, no. 4393 (11 May 1979): 564–68; and Gleick and Holdren, "Assessing."

86. One drawback associated with emphasizing research ethics is that institutions might create "research ethics" committees to oversee projects, and these committees might cause individual researchers to abdicate their ethical responsibilities and to turn them over to the committees. Some scholars (see, for example, P. J. Lewis, "The Drawbacks of Research Ethics Committees," *Journal of Medical Ethics* 8 (1982): 61–64) have argued that this abdication occurred, that it is undesirable, and that it encourages individual researchers to be less responsible.

87. For a discussion of these various prejudices, see John Searle, "The Storm Over the University," *The New York Review of Books* 19, no. 37 (6 December 1990): 34. See also R. Kimball, *Tenured Radicals: How Politics Has Corrupted Our Higher Education* (New York: Harper and Row, 1990).

88. J. Raloff, "Exxon's *Valdez* Studies Ignite Controversy," *Science News* 143, no. 19 (8 May 1993): 294–95.

89. Rebecca Dresser, "Wanted: Single White Male for Medical Research," *Hastings Center Report* 22, no. 1 (January–February 1992): 24–29; hereafter cited as: Dresser, "Wanted."

90. For discussion of this point, see Sigma Xi, The Scientific Research Society, *Honor in Science* (New Haven, Conn.: Sigma Xi, 1986), pp. 11ff.

91. In this regard see, for example, John M. Braxton (ed.), "Perspectives on Research Misconduct," *The Journal of Higher Education* (May/June 1994): entire issue.

Chapter 2

1. G. B. Harrison (ed.), *Shakespeare: The Complete Works* (New York: Harcourt, Brace, and World, 1952), "Hamlet," Act 1, ll. 189–90, p. 896.

2. Eugene Wigner, "The Scope and Promise of Science," in *The Ethics of Teaching and Scientific Research*, ed. Sidney Hook, Paul Kurtz, and Miro Todorovich (Buffalo: Prometheus, 1977), pp. 131–33.

3. For a discussion of the trusteeship model, see William B. Griffith, "Ethics and the Academic Professional: Some Open Problems and a New Approach," *Business and Professional Ethics Journal* 1 (Spring 1982): 75–95.

4. Quoted in S. M. Cahn, *Saints and Scamps: Ethics in Academia* (Totowa, NJ: Rowman and Littlefield, 1986), p. 44; hereafter cited as: Cahn, SS.

5. Much of this discussion follows Michael Bayles, *Professional Ethics* (Belmont, Calif.: Wadsworth, 1981), pp. 109–10; hereafter cited as: Bayles, PE.

6. Bayles, PE, p. 111.

7. Cahn, SS, pp. 42–43.

8. U.S. National Research Council/National Academy of Sciences, *Pesticides in the Diets of Infants and Children* (Washington, D.C.: National Academy Press, 1993).

9. Kelman, "Research, Behavioral," p. 1478.

10. The 80-percent figure comes from P. Slovic, J. Flynn, and M. Layman, "Perceived Risk, Trust, and the Politics of Nuclear Waste," *Science* 254 (13 December 1991): 1604.

11. See K. S. Shrader-Frechette, *Burying Uncertainty: Risk and the Case Against Geological Disposal of Nuclear Waste* (Berkeley: University of California Press, 1993), pp. 202–5; hereafter cited as: Shrader-Frechette, BU.

12. G. E. Pence, *Classic Cases in Medical Ethics* (New York: McGraw-Hill, 1990), pp. 185–88; hereafter cited as: Pence, CC.

13. Pence, CC, p. 188; Pettit, "Instituting a Research Ethic," pp. 94–95.

14. See, for example, Alexander M. Capron, "Medical Research in Prisons," *Hastings Center Report* 3 (1973): 4–6; see also Beauchamp and Childress, PBE; Curry and May, PR; Faden and Beauchamp, HTIC.

15. Richard M. Ratgan, "Being Old Makes You Different," *Hastings Center Report* 10 (October 1980): 32–42.

16. Pence, CC, pp. 251–62.

17. See previous note; see also Terrence F. Ackermann, "Moral Duties of Parents and Nontherapeutic Clinical Research Procedures Involving Children," *Bioethics Quarterly* 2, no. 2 (Summer 1980): 94–111; James J. McCartney, "Research on Children," *Hastings Center Report* 8 (October 1978): 26–31.

18. See, for example, Peter Singer and Karen Dawson, "IVF Technology and the Argument from Potential," *Philosophy and Public Affairs* 17, no. 2 (Spring 1988): 87–104; Russell Scott, "Experimenting and the New Biology," *Law, Medicine, and Health Care* 14, nos. 3–4 (September 1986): 123–128; Peter Singer and Helga Kuhse, "The Ethics of Embryo Research," *Law, Medicine, and Health Care* 14, nos. 3–4 (September 1986): 133–37; H. J. J. Leenen, "The Legal Status of the Embryo *in Vivo* and *in Vitro*," *Law, Medicine, and Health Care* 14, nos. 3–4 (September 1986): 129–32; George J. Annas, "The Ethics of Embryo Research: Not As Easy As It Sounds," *Law, Medicine, and Health Care* 14, nos. 3–4 (September 1986): 138–40, 148; Peter Singer, Helga Kuhse, Stephen Buckle, Karen Dawson, and Pascal Kasimba (eds.), *Embryo Experimentation* (Cambridge: Cambridge University Press, 1990). See also Steve Olson, *Shaping the Future: Biology and Human Values* (Washington, D.C.: National Academy Press, 1989).

19. See, for example, James Ogloff and Randy Ott, "Are Research Participants Truly Informed?" *Ethics and Behavior* 1, no. 4 (1991): 239–52, and, more generally, Mary Gibson (ed.), *To Breathe Freely: Risk, Consent, and Air* (Totowa, NJ: Rowman and Littlefield, 1985), and Robert E. Goodin, *Protecting the Vulnerable* (Chicago: University of Chicago Press, 1985).

20. A. M. Brandt, "Racism and Research: The Case of the Tuskegee Syphilis Study," *Hastings Center Report* 8 (December 1978): 21–29; Pence, CC, pp. 184–205.

21. See for example, J. Feinberg, "The Rights of Animals and Unborn Generations," in *Philosophy and Environmental Crisis*, ed. W. T. Blackston (Ath-

ens, Georgia: University of Georgia Press, 1974), pp. 43–68; M. A. Fox, "Animal Suffering and Rights: A Reply to Singer and Regan," *Ethics* 88 (January): 134–38; B. G. Norton (ed.), *The Preservation of Species: The Value of Biological Diversity* (Princeton: University Press, 1986); T. Regan, "The Moral Basis of Vegetarianism," *Canadian Journal of Philosophy* 5 (October): 181–214; T. Regan and P. Singer, (eds.), *Animal Rights and Human Obligations* (Englewood Cliffs, NJ: Prentice-Hall, 1976), pp. 205–19. See also Birgitta Forsman, *Research Ethics in Practice: The Animal Ethics Committees* (Göteborg, Sweden: Center for Research Ethics, 1993).

22. Pence, CC, pp. 167–83.

23. See, for example, Tom Regan, *The Case for Animal Rights* (Berkeley: University of California Press, 1983); Peter Singer, *Animal Liberation* (New York: Anon Books, 1977).

24. See, for example, Carl Cohen, "The Case for Use of Animals in Biomedical Research," *New England Journal of Medicine* 315, no. 14 (October 1986): 865–69; Dennis Feeney, "Human Rights and Animal Welfare," *American Psychologist* (June 1987): 593–97; Neal Miller, "The Value of Behavioral Research on Animals," *American Psychologist* 40, no. 4 (April 1985): 423–40; Herbert Pardes, Anne West, and Harold Pincus, "Physicians and the Animal-Rights Movement," *New England Journal of Medicine* 324, no. 4 (6 June 1991): 1640–43; see also Robert Baird and S. E. Rosenbaum (eds.), *Animal Experimentation* (Buffalo: Prometheus Books, 1991).

25. David De Grazia, "The Moral Status of Animals and Their Use in Research," *Kennedy Institute of Ethics Journal* 1 (March 1991): 48–70; John Gluck and Steven Kubacki, "Animals in Biomedical Research," *Ethics and Behavior* 1, no. 3 (1991): 157–73; Rebecca Dresser, "Measuring Merit in Animal Research," *Theoretical Medicine* 10 (1989): 21–34; Ray Mosely, "Ethical Problems with the Use of Animals in Medical Research and Education," *Theoretical Medicine* 10 (March 1989): 1–8.

26. See J. H. Reiman, "Research Subjects, Political Subjects, and Human Subjects," in Klockars and O'Connor, DD, pp. 35–57.

27. Winn, "University," pp. 27–29, and A. Einstein, *Ideas and Opinions*, trans. by S. Bergman (New York: Crown, 1954).

28. Minsky, "Greed," Blevins and Ewer, "University Research," p. 655; see Nicholas Ashford, "A Framework for Examining the Effects of Industrial Funding on the Integrity of the University," *Science, Technology, and Human Values* 8, no. 2 (Spring 1983): 16–23.

29. See, for example, Sissela Bok, *Secrets* (New York: Pantheon Books, 1982).

30. See C. Weiner, "Patenting and Academic Research: Historical Case Studies," *Science, Technology, and Human Values* 12, no. 1 (Winter 1987): 50–62; Goldman, "Ethical Issues," pp. 22–30.

31. Zasloff, "University," p. A52.

32. Margaret Schabas, "The Permissibility of Classified Research in University Science," *Public Affairs Quarterly* 2, no. 4 (October 1988): 47–64.

33. Union of Concerned Scientists and Nuclear Energy Policy Study Group.

34. D. Noble, "Science for Sale," *Thought and Action: NEA Higher Education Journal* 1, no. 1 (Fall 1984): 25–39.

35. Michael Davis, "University Research and the Wages of Commerce," *The Journal of College and University Law* 18, no. 1 (Summer 1991): 29–38, esp. pp. 37–38.

36. S. Postel, "Facing Water Scarcity," in *State of the World 1993*, ed. L. R. Brown *et al.* (New York: Norton, 1993), pp. 22–41, esp. p. 24; hereafter cited as: Brown *et al.*, SW 1993.

37. See K. S. Shrader-Frechette, *Nuclear Power and Public Policy* (Boston: Kluwer, 1983); hereafter cited as: Shrader-Frechette, NPPP; and Shrader-Frechette, BU. See also Lenssen, "Confronting Nuclear Waste," pp. 46–65.

38. See, for example, C. Flavin, "Building a Bridge to Sustainable Energy," in Brown *et al.*, SW 1992, pp. 27–45.

39. For discussion of some of the flaws associated with using economic methods in environment-related research, see K. S. Shrader-Frechette, *Science Policy, Ethics, and Economic Methodology* (Boston: Kluwer, 1985), esp. pp. 121–51. See also Mark Sagoff, *The Economy of the Earth* (New York: Cambridge University Press, 1991).

40. See, for example, Derek Parfit, "Energy Policy and the Further Future: the Social Discount Rate," in *Energy and the Future*, ed. D. MacLean and P. Brown (Totowa: Rowman and Littlefield, 1983), pp. 31–37.

41. L. R. Brown, "A New Era Unfolds," in Brown *et al.*, SW 1993, pp. 4–6; see also pp. 3–21.

42. Sue V. Rosser, "Revisioning Clinical Research: Gender and the Ethics of Experimental Design," *Hypatia* 4, no. 2 (Summer 1989): 125–39.

43. Dresser, "Wanted," p. 24.

44. Dresser, "Wanted," p. 24.

45. Dresser, "Wanted," pp. 24–29.

46. L. Gromova, "Professional Ethics in the USSR," *Ethical and Policy Issues Perspectives on the Professions* 10, no. 1 (August 1990): 5–6.

47. See, for example, T. R. Ireland, "The Relevance of Race Research," *Ethics* 84 (January 1974): 140–45.

48. See, for example, Ralph Keeney, "Mortality Risks Induced by Economic Expenditures," *Risk Analysis* 10, no. 1 (1990): 147–59.

49. See Ruth Macklin, "On the Ethics of *Not* Doing Scientific Research," *The Hastings Center Report* 7 (December 1977): 11–13.

50. See W. Cheston and P. McFate, "Ethics and Laboratory Safety," *Hastings Center Report* 10 (August 1980): 7–8.

51. In this regard, see Peter J. Lewis, "The Drawbacks of Research Ethic Committees," *Journal of Medical Ethics* 8 (1982): 61–64; E. L. Pattulo, "Who Risks What in Social Research?" *Hastings Center Report* 10 (April 1980): 15–18; Philip Pettit, "Instituting a Research Ethic," *Bioethics* 6, no. 2 (1992): 89–112. For discussion of the use of placebos in terminal cases, see Ruth Macklin and Gerald Friedland, "AIDS Research," *Law, Medicine and Health*

Care 14, nos. 5–6 (December 1986): 273–81. For criticisms of worries about overregulation of researchers, see Judith P. Swazey, "Professional Protectionism Rides Again," *Hastings Center Report* 10 (April 1980): 18–19.

52. Oliver H. Osbourne, "Cross-Cultural Social Science Research and Questions of Scientific Medical Imperialism," *Bioethics Quarterly* 2, no. 3 (Fall 1980): 159–63.

53. Henry Grabowski, "The Changing Economics of Pharmaceutical Research and Development," in *The Changing Economics of Medical Technology* vol. II, ed. Annetine Gelijns and Ethan Halm (Washington D.C.: National Academy Press, 1991), pp. 35–52, esp. pp. 37, 40, 47, 49; hereafter cited as: Gelijns and Halm, CE; Peter Hutt, "The Impact of Regulation and Reimbursement on Pharmaceutical Innovation," in Gelijns and Halm, CE, pp. 169–80, esp. p. 170.

54. Ruth Macklin, "On the Ethics of *Not* Doing Scientific Research," *Hastings Center Report* 7 (December 1977): 11–13; Piotr Chwalisz, Piotr Kowalik, *et al.*, "Peculiarities of Practical Research," *Poznan Studies in the Philosophy of the Sciences and the Humanities* 2 (1976): 81–100.

55. G. E. Pence, *Classic Cases in Medical Ethics* (New York: McGraw-Hill, 1990): 206–24, esp. pp. 215–18; hereafter cited as: Pence, CC.

56. Pence, CC, pp. 225–50, esp. pp. 227–35.

57. Bengt Gustafsson and Gunner Tibell, "Critics of Science and Research Ethics in Sweden," *Philosophy and Social Action* 15, nos. 3–4 (July–December 1989): 59–74, esp. p. 68.

58. See, for example, Darryl Macer, Roger A. Balk, Benjamin Freedman, and Marie-Claude Goulet, "Commentary," *Hastings Center Report* 21, no. 1 (January–February 1991): 32–35; Thomas Ireland, "The Relevance of Race Research," *Ethics* 84, no. 2 (January 1974): 140–45.

59. Leonard Berry and the Committee on International Soil and Water Research and Development, *Toward Sustainability* (Washington, D.C.: National Academy Press, 1991), pp. 2–3, 5–6, 23–24, 55; Theodore Hullar and the Board on Agriculture (eds.), *Sustainable Agriculture Research and Education in the Field* (Washington, D.C.: National Academy Press, 1991); see also C. A. Bowers, "The Conservative Misinterpretation of the Educational Ecological Crisis," *Environmental Ethics* 14, no. 2 (Summer 1992): 101–28.

60. Michael E. Frisina, "The Offensive–Defensive Distinction in Military Biological Research," *Hastings Center Report* 20, no. 3 (May/June 1990): 19–22.

61. Rachelle D. Hollander, "Values and Making Decisions about Agricultural Research," *Agriculture and Human Values* 3, no. 3 (Summer 1986): 33–40.

62. J. M. Ziman, "The Problem of Problem Choice," *Minerva* 25 (1987): 92–106.

63. Bayles, PE, p. 109.

64. American Association for the Advancement of Science (AAAS), *Principles of Scientific Freedom and Responsibility*, Revised Draft (Washington, D.C.: AAAS, 1980), p. 2; hereafter cited as: AAAS, PSFR.

65. Albert R. Jonsen and Lewis H. Butler, "Public Ethics and Policy Making," *Hastings Center Report* 5 (August 1975): 19–31, esp. p. 23.

66. J. Ladd, "The Quest for a Code of Professional Ethics: An Intellectual and Moral Confusion," in *AAAS Professional Ethics Project: Professional and Ethics Activities in the Scientific and Engineering Societies*, ed. R. Chalk, M. Frankel, and S. Chafer (Washington, D.C.: AAAS, 1980), p. 154; hereafter cited as: Ladd, "Quest."

67. Ladd, "Quest," p. 154. See also P. Alger, N. Christensen, and S. Olmsted, "Ethical Problems of the Engineer in Industry and Government," in *Ethical Problems in Engineering*, vol. 1, ed. A. Flores (Troy, NY: Center for the Studies in Human Dimensions of Science and Technology, 1980), p. 145; hereafter cited as: Alger *et al.*, "Ethical Problems," p. 145.

68. Ladd, "Quest," pp. 157–58.

69. Ladd, "Quest," pp. 157–58.

70. Ladd, "Quest," p. 154. See also Alger *et al.*, "Ethical Problems," p. 145.

71. Michael Davis, "Codes of Ethics, Professions, and Conflict of Interest," *Professional Ethics* 1, nos. 1 and 2 (1992): 190; hereafter cited as: Davis, "Codes of Ethics."

72. Davis, "Codes of Ethics," p. 189.

73. Davis, "Codes of Ethics," p. 183.

74. John Kultgen, *Ethics and Professions* (Philadelphia: University of Pennsylvania Press, 1988), for example, urges that we adapt a code of professional ethics while we follow it.

75. Indeed there appears to be a lack of significant differences in research ethics attitudes among some professionals in a variety of countries. Ishmael P. Akaah, "Attitudes of Marketing Professionals Toward Ethics in Marketing Research," *Journal of Business Ethics* 9 (1990): 45–53.

76. R. Chalk, M. Frankel, and S. Chafer (eds.), *AAAS Professional Ethics Project: Professional Ethics Activities in the Scientific and Engineering Societies* (Washington, D.C.: AAAS, 1980), pp. 154–59; hereafter cited as: Chalk *et al.*, AAAS PEP.

77. C. I. Jackson, *Honor in Science* (New Haven, Connecticut: Sigma Xi, The Scientific Research Society, 1986), pp. 1–2.

78. Chalk *et al.*, AAAS PEP, p. 102.

79. Chalk *et al.*, AAAS PEP, p. 127.

80. ESA, CE.

81. ESA, CE.

82. Michael Seng, "Responsibilities of Academics for Unethical Conduct of Colleagues or Students," *Perspectives on the Professions* 9, no. 1 (August 1989): 6–7.

83. ESA, CE.

84. ESA, CE.

85. EntSA n.d.

86. EntSA n.d.

87. EntSA n.d.

88. EntSA n.d.

89. American Fisheries Society (AFS), *Code of Practices* (Bethesda, Maryland: American Fisheries Society, 1966); hereafter cited as: AFS, CP.

90. AFS, CP.

91. AFS, CP.

92. Society for Range Management, *Code of Ethics* (Society for Range Management, 1989).

93. A. Chase, *Playing God in Yellowstone* (New York: Atlantic Monthly Press, 1986).

94. AAAS, PSFR, p. 2.

Chapter 3

1. Warren Cheston and Patricia McFate, ''Ethics and Laboratory Safety,'' *The Hastings Center Report* 10 (August 1980): 7–8.

2. For a discussion of utilitarian and deontological or contractarian theories, see, for example, A. K. Sen, ''Rawls Versus Bentham: An Axiomatic Examination of the Pure Distribution Problem,'' in *Reading Rawls*, ed. Norman Daniels (New York: Basic Books, 1981), pp. 283–92; hereafter cited as: Sen, ''Rawls Versus Bentham.'' See also J. J. C. Smart and B. Williams (eds.), *Utilitarianism: For and Against* (Cambridge: Cambridge University Press, 1973). For a discussion of act and rule utilitarianism see, for example, K. S. Shrader-Frechette, *Science Policy, Ethics, and Scientific Methodology* (Boston: Kluwer, 1985), pp. 223–25.

3. Sen, ''Rawls Versus Bentham,'' pp. 283–92. As Amartya Sen argues, the general principles used in deontological or contractarian analysis are necessary in order to evaluate persons' different levels of welfare, whereas the particular consequences discussed in utilitarian analysis are necessary in order to evaluate gains and losses in welfare.

4. R. M. Hare, *Moral Thinking: Its Levels, Methods, & Point* (New York: Oxford University Press, 1981); hereafter cited as: Hare, MT. Hare uses a two-stage method of ethics similar to ours, except that his first stage is deontological and his second stage is utilitarian. In our analysis, the first stage is deontological and the second stage is both deontological and utilitarian. Our reason for using both utilitarian and deontological analyses at the second stage is that utilitarian considerations alone often fail to resolve ethical disputes, or point to alleged resolutions that neglect to take account (adequately) of duties and obligations, as Michael Davis (''The Moral Legislature,'' *Ethics* 102 (January 1992): 312–13; see also pp. 303–18) notes.

5. See Hare, MT, p. 43. Hare also says that ''rule utilitarians perform this type of reasoning. Rule utilitarians hold that we ought to behave in accord with

rules that promote the greatest good consequences for everyone, and hence rule utilitarians subscribe to principles or rules, as do deontologists." W. Frankena, *Ethics* (Englewood Cliffs, NJ: Prentice-Hall, 1963), pp. 30ff.

6. See Hare, MT, p. 38.

7. D. Ross, *The Right and the Good* (Oxford: Clarendon Press, 1930), pp. 18, 33, 41ff.

8. J. Rawls, *A Theory of Justice* (Cambridge, Mass.: Harvard University Press, 1971), pp. 34–341; hereafter cited as: Rawls, TJ.

9. See Hare, MT, p. 40.

10. R. Ladenson, "The Social Responsibilities of Engineers and Scientists," in *Ethical Problems in Engineering*, vol. 1, ed. A. Flores (Troy, New York: Center for the Studies in the Human Dimensions of Science and Technology, 1980) pp. 238–40. See also Rawls, TJ, pp. 136–37.

11. W. Lowrance, *Modern Science and Human Values* (New York: Oxford University Press, 1985), p. 189.

12. G. E. Moore, *Principia Ethica* (Cambridge: University Press, 1951), pp. 39–60. See also W. Frankena, "The Naturalistic Fallacy," *Mind* 48, no. 192 (1939): 467.

13. Michael Bayles, *Professional Ethics* (Belmont, Calif.: Wadsworth, 1991), pp. 60–125; hereafter cited as: Bayles PE.

14. Bayles, PE, pp. 70–86.

15. Bayles, PE, pp. 92–104.

16. Bayles, PE, pp. 109–22.

17. Bayles, PE, p. 24.

18. Bayles, PE, pp. 5–7.

19. J. Ladd, "The Quest for a Code of Professional Ethics: An Intellectual and Moral Confusion," in *AAAS Professional Ethics Project: Professional and Ethics Activities in the Scientific and Engineering Societies,* ed. R. Chalk, M. Frankel, and S. Chafer (Washington, D.C.: AAAS, 1980), p. 158. See also Bayles, PE, pp. 5–7, 19–20; See also A. Cournand, "The Code of the Scientist and its Relationship to Ethics," *Science* 198, no. 4318 (November, 1977): 699–705; hereafter cited as: Cournand, "Code."

20. Ecological Society of America, *Code of Ethics* (Ithaca, New York: Ecological Society of America, 1977); hereafter cited as: ESA, CE.

21. Cournand, "Code," p. 703. See also, J. Monod, *Chance and Necessity* (New York: Knopf, 1971), p. 21; hereafter cited as: Monod, CN.

22. Cournand, "Code," pp. 703–4.

23. Cournand, "Code," p. 703; See also, Monod, CN, p. 21.

24. H. Salwasser, "Conserving a Regional Spotted Owl Population," in *The Preservation and Valuation of Biological Resources*, ed. G. H. Orians, G. M. Brown, Jr., W. E. Kunin, and J. E. Swierzbinski (Seattle and London: University of Washington Press, 1990), pp. 227–47.

25. S. Krimsky, "Emerging Issues in Scientific Freedom and Responsibility," in *Science, Engineering, and Ethics: Report on an AAAS Workshop and Symposium*, ed. M. Frankel (Washington, D.C.: AAAS, 1988), p. 18.

26. C. I. Jackson, *Honor in Science* (New Haven, Connecticut: Sigma Xi, The Scientific Research Society, 1986), pp. 1–2.

27. Bayles, PE, pp. 111ff.

28. American Association for the Advancement of Science (AAAS), *Principles of Scientific Freedom and Responsibility*, Revised Draft (Washington, D.C.: AAAS, 1980), p. 2; hereafter cited as: AAAS, PSFR.

29. AAAS, PSFR, p. 3.

30. ESA, CE.

31. See, for example, R. Hall and the Working Group in Current Medical/ Ethical Problems, ''Ethical Problems of Repetitive Research,'' *Journal of Medical Ethics* 3 (1977): 14–17; Donald Coffey, ''When is Repetitive Publication Justified?'' in *Ethics and Policy in Scientific Publication*, ed. John C. Bailar *et al.* (Bethesda: Council of Biology Editors, 1990), pp. 219–24; hereafter cited as: Bailar, EPSP.

32. See, for example, Steven M. Cahn, *Saints and Scamps: Ethics in Academia* (Totowa, NJ: Rowman and Littlefield, 1986), esp. pp. 42–67; James W. Nickel, *So Professors Need Professional Ethics as Much as Doctors and Lawyers?* (Kalamazoo, Mich.: Center for the Study of Ethics in Society, Western Michigan University, 1989), pp. 23–25. See also K. R. St. Onge, ''The Threshold of Plagiarism''; Linda Bergmann, ''Plagiarism and the Composition Classroom''; Richard A. Matasar, ''Plagiarism in the Law''; and Donald E. Bazzelli, ''Plagiarism in Science,'' respectively, in *Perspectives on the Professions* 13, no. 1 (July 1993): 2–3, 3–5, 5–6, 6–7, respectively. See, finally, Stephen Payne and Bruce Charnov (eds.), *Ethical Dilemmas for Academic Professionals* (Springfield, Ill.: Charles C. Thomas, 1987); Daryl Chubin, ''Research Malpractice,'' *Bioscience* 35 (February 1985): 80–89; Francis Dane, *Research Methods* (Belmont, Calif.: Brooks Cole, 1990); Eugene Garfield, ''What Do We Know About Fraud?'' *Current Contents* 15 (April 13, 1987): 3–10; National Academy of Sciences, *On Being a Scientist* (Washington, D.C.: National Academy Press, 1989); Sigma Xi, *Honor in Science* (New Haven, Conn: Scientific Research Society, 1986); U.S. House of Representatives, Subcommittee on Investigations and Oversight, Committee on Science, Space, and Technology, *Maintaining the Integrity of Scientific Research* (Washington, D.C.: U.S. Government Printing Office, 1990); Bernard Barber, ''Trust in Science,'' *Minerva* 25 (Spring/Summer 1987): 123–34; Robert Bergman, ''Irreproducibility in the Scientific Literature,'' *Perspectives on the Professions* 8 (1989): 2–3; Nicholas Steneck, ''Commentary: The University and Research Ethics,'' *Science, Technology, and Human Values* 9 (Fall 1984): 6–15; hereafter cited as: Steneck, ''Commentary''; Tom L. Beauchamp, ''Ethical Issues in Funding and Monitoring University Research,'' *Business and Professional Ethics Journal* 11, no. 1 (1992): 5–16; Stephen P. Lock, ''Medical Misconduct,'' in Bailar *et al.*, EPSP, pp. 147–54.

33. See, for example, Patricia K. Woolf, ''Accountability and Responsibility in Research,'' *Journal of Business Ethics* 10 (1991): 595–600.

34. For a discussion of value judgments in research, especially scientific research, see Helen Longino, *Science as Social Knowledge* (Princeton: Princeton University Press, 1990), and K. S. Shrader-Frechette, *Risk and Rationality: Philosophical Foundations for Populist Reforms* (Berkeley: University of California Press, 1991), esp. pp. 27–65. For an example of how a particular conceptual frameworks involve one in value judgments, see Joy Penticuff, ''Conceptual Issues in Nursing Ethics Research,'' *The Journal of Medicine and Philosophy* 16 (1991): 235–58.

35. Saul Kripke, ''Wittgenstein on Rules and Private Language,'' in *Perspectives on the Philosophy of Wittgenstein*, ed. I. Black (Oxford: Blackwell, 1982), pp. 239–96.

36. See K. S. Shrader-Frechette, *Burying Uncertainty: Risk and the Case Against Geological Disposal of Nuclear Waste* (Berkeley: University of California Press, 1993).

37. John T. Sanders and Wade L. Robison, ''Research Funding and the Value-Dependence of Science,'' *Business and Professional Ethics Journal* 11, no. 1 (1992): 33–50.

38. Martha Crouch, ''The Very Structure of Scientific Research Militates Against Developing Products to Help the Environment, the Poor, and the Hungry,'' *Journal of Agricultural and Environmental Ethics* 4, no. 2 (1991): 151–58.

39. See, for example, Lowell Hardin and the Panel for Collaborative Research Support for AID's Sustainable Agriculture and Natural Resource Management Program, *Toward Sustainability* (Washington, D.C.: National Academy Press, 1991), pp. viii, 4, 17ff., 47–65.

40. Bayles, PE, pp. 109ff.

41. J. T. Edsall and the AAAS Committee on Scientific Freedom and Responsibility, *Scientific Freedom and Responsibility* (Washington, D.C.: Unpublished manuscript, 1975), p. 16.

42. F. Von Hippel and J. Primack, ''Public Interest Science,'' *Science* 177, no. 4055 (September 20, 1972): 1166–71.

43. Bayles, PE, pp. 111ff.

44. W. P. Metzger, ''Academic Freedom and Scientific Freedom,'' *Daedalus* 107, no. 2 (Spring 1978): 93–114.

45. Von Hippel and Primack, ''Public Interest Science,'' p. 1167.

46. Jack Douglas, ''Living Morality Versus Bureaucratic Fiat,'' in *Deviance and Decency: The Ethics of Research with Human Subjects*, ed. Carl Klockars and Finbarr O'Connor (London: Sage, 1979), pp. 13–33, esp. pp. 23–24.

47. Drummond Rennie, ''The Editor: Mark, Dupe, Patsy, Accessory, Weasel, and Flatfoot,'' in Bailar *et al.*, EPSP, pp. 155–67; hereafter cited as: Rennie, ''Editor.''

48. Rennie, ''Editor,'' pp. 158–60; see also Lawrence Altman, ''The Myth of 'Passing Peer Review,' '' in Bailar *et al.*, EPSP, pp. 257–68; Thomas Stossel,

''Beyond Rejection,'' in Bailar *et al.*, EPSP, pp. 268–72; and Arnold Relman, ''The Value of Peer Review,'' in Bailar *et al.*, EPSP, pp. 272–77; Steneck, ''Commentary,'' pp. 13–14.

49. See, for example, James Lloyd, ''On Watersheds and Peers, Publication, Pimps and Panache,'' *Florida Entomologist* 68 (March 1985): 134–39.

50. See for example, C. Starr, R. Rudman, and C. Whipple (eds.), ''Philosophical Basis for Risk Analysis,'' *Annual Review of Energy* 1 (1976): 638. See also Bayles, PE, p. 116.

51. W. K. Clifford, *Lectures and Essays* (London: Macmillan, 1886).

52. W. Alston, ''Concepts of Epistemic Justification,'' in *Empirical Knowledge*, ed. P. Moser (Totowa, NJ: Rowman and Littlefield, 1986), pp. 30–31. For a defense of the ethics of belief, see K. S. Shrader-Frechette, ''Science Pure and Applied as Essentially Involved with Ethics,'' in *Ethical Issues Associated with Scientific and Technological Research for the Military*, ed. C. Mitcham and P. Siekevitz, Annals of the New York Academy of Sciences, vol. 577 (New York: New York Academy of Sciences, 1989), pp. 86–93. See also Stephen Toulmin, ''Can Science and Ethics Be Reconnected?'' *Hastings Center Report* 9 (1979): 27–34.

53. L. Laudan, *Science and Values* (Berkeley: University of California Press, 1984), pp. 47–49.

54. See, for example, W. James, *The Will to Believe and Other Essays in Popular Philosophy* (New York: Dover, 1956), pp. 17–30.

55. N. Rescher, ''The Ethical Dimension of Scientific Research,'' in *Introductory Readings in the Philosophy of Science*, ed. E. D. Klemke, R. Hollinger, and A. Kline (Buffalo, NY: Prometheus Books, 1980), pp. 338–44.

56. See, for example, H. G. Burström, ''Ethics of Experimental Research,'' *Dialectica* 29, no. 4 (1975): 237–47.

Chapter 4

1. George Robinson and Janice Moulton, *Ethical Problems in Higher Education* (Englewood Cliffs, NJ: Prentice-Hall, 1985), p. 68; see also Louis G. Lombardi, ''Character vs. Codes: Models for Research Ethics,'' *International Journal of Applied Philosophy* 5, no. 1 (Spring 1990): 21–28.

2. Michael Davis, ''The New World of Research Ethics,'' *International Journal of Applied Philosophy* 5, no. 1 (Spring 1990): 1–10, esp. p. 10.

3. *Chicago Tribune*, Sunday, March 19, 1989, Section 4. Cited by Davis, ''The New World of Research Ethics,'' p. 1.

4. American Association for the Advancement of Science (AAAS), *Principles of Scientific Freedom and Responsibility*, Revised Draft (Washington, D.C.: AAAS, 1980), p. 1; hereafter cited as: AAAS, PSFR.

5. R. Baum (ed.), ''Introduction,'' in *Ethical Problems in Engineering*, ed. A. Flores (Troy, NY: Center for the Study of the Human Dimensions of

204   Notes

Science and Technology, 1980), p. 4; hereafter cited as: Flores, EPE. See also J. Ladd, "Philosophical Remarks on Professional Responsibility in Organizations," in Flores, EPE, p. 193–94; hereafter cited as: Ladd, "Philosophical Remarks."

6. Ladd, "Philosophical Remarks," p. 194.

7. See D. Cooper, "Collective Responsibility," *Philosophy* 43 (1968): 258–68. See also D. Cooper, "Collective Responsibility—Again," *Philosophy* 44 (1969): 153–55. See also R. Downie, "Collective Responsibility," *Philosophy* 44 (1969): 67–69. See also J. Feinberg, *Doing and Deserving* (Princeton, NJ: Princeton University Press, 1970). See also A. Flores and D. Johnson, "Collective Responsibility and Professional Roles," *Ethics* 93 (1983): 537–45. See also R. Hardin, *Collective Action* (Baltimore: Johns Hopkins Press, 1982). See also M. Olson, *The Logic of Collective Actions* (Cambridge, Mass.: Harvard University Press, 1971).

8. AAAS, PSFR, p. 6.

9. AAAS, PSFR, p. 1.

10. S. Bok, "Whistleblowing and Professional Responsibilities," in *Engineering Professionalism and Ethics*, ed. J. Schaub, K. Pavlovic, and M. Morris (New York: John Wiley, 1983), p. 413.

11. Michael Bayles, *Professional Ethics* (Belmont, Calif.: Wadsworth, 1981), p. 4; hereafter cited as: Bayles, PE.

12. J. T. Edsall and the AAAS Committee on Scientific Freedom and Responsibility, *Scientific Freedom and Responsibility* (Washington, D.C.: Unpublished manuscript, 1975), p. 45; hereafter cited as: Edsall, SFR.

13. C. I. Jackson, *Honor in Science* (New Haven, Connecticut: Sigma Xi, The Scientific Research Society, 1986), p. 33; hereafter cited as: Jackson, HS.

14. P. Camenisch, "On Being a Professional, Morally Speaking," in *Moral Responsibility and the Professions*, ed. B. Baumrin and B. Freedman (New York: Haven Press, 1982), p. 43; hereafter cited as: Camenisch, "Being a Professional."

15. Elaine Draper, *Risky Business: Genetic Testing and Exclusionary Practices in the Hazardous Workplace* (Cambridge: Cambridge University Press, 1991).

16. Tom L. Beauchamp, "Ethical Issues in Funding and Monitoring University Research," *Business and Professional Ethics Journal* 11, no. 1 (1992), pp. 5–16; see also Bryan Jennett, *High Technology Medicine* (New York: Oxford University Press, 1986), pp. 209, 211.

17. Diether H. Haenicke, *Ethics in Academia* (Kalamazoo, Mich.: Center for the Study of Ethics in Society, Western Michigan University, 1988), p. 9.

18. Richard Taranto, "The Psychiatrist-Patient Privilege and Third-Party Payers," *Law, Medicine, and Health Care* 14, no. 1 (September 1986): 25–29.

19. P. Singer, "Famine, Affluence, and Morality," in *Social Ethics*, ed. T. A. Mappes and J. S. Zembaty (New York: McGraw-Hill, 1977); hereafter cited as: Singer, "Famine." See also H. Shue, "Exporting Hazards," in *Bound-*

aries: National Autonomy and Its Limits, ed. P. Brown and H. Shue (Totowa, NJ: Rowman and Littlefield, 1981), pp. 135ff.; hereafter cited as: Shue, EH.

20. F. Von Hippel and J. Primack, ''Public Interest Science,'' *Science* 177, no. 4055 (September 20, 1972): 1169.

21. R. K. Colwell, ''Natural and Unnatural History: Biological Diversity and Genetic Engineering,'' in *Scientists and Their Responsibility*, ed. W. R. Shea and B. Sitter (Canton, Mass.: Watson, 1989), p. 17.

22. R. Ladenson, ''The Social Responsibilities of Engineers and Scientists,'' in Flores, EPE, pp. 241–42.

23. D. Ross, *The Right and the Good* (Oxford: Clarendon Press, 1930), pp. 18–28. See also Singer, ''Famine.''

24. W. Frankena, *Ethics* (Englewood Cliffs, NJ: Prentice-Hall, 1963), p. 37.

25. David B. Brushwood, ''Riff v. Morgan Pharmacy,'' *Law, Medicine, and Health Care* 14, nos. 3–4 (September 1986): 202–5.

26. Leonard Berry and the Committee on International Soil and Water Research and Development, National Research Council, *Toward Sustainability: Soil and Water Research Priorities for Developing Countries* (Washington, D.C.: National Academy Press, 1991), pp. 2–6, 18, 23–24, 55. Statistics on infant deaths are from Lester R. Brown, ''The Illusion of Progress,'' in *State of the World 1990*, ed. L. R. Brown *et al.* (New York: Norton, 1990), pp. 3–16, esp. p. 11.

27. See, for example, James Childress, ''Fairness in the Allocation and Delivery of Health Care,'' and Robert Veatch, ''Equality, Justice, and Rightness in Allocating Health Care,'' both in *A Time to Be Born and a Time to Die: The Ethics of Choice*, ed. Barry Kogan (New York: Aldine de Gruyter, 1991), pp. 179–204 and pp. 205–18, respectively.

28. Edsall, SFR, p. 33.

29. J. T. Edsall, ''Two Aspects of Scientific Responsibility,'' (Cambridge, Mass.: Unpublished manuscript available from Edsall at the Biological Laboratories of Harvard University, 1980), p. 6; hereafter cited as: Edsall, ''Two Aspects.''

30. D. C. Erman and E. P. Pister, ''Ethics and the Environmental Biologist,'' *Fisheries* 14, no. 2 (March/April 1989): 7.

31. Yvonne Brackbill and Andre Hellegers, ''Ethics and Editors,'' *Hastings Center Report* 10 (April 1980): 20–22.

32. J. Kultgen, ''Professional Ideals and Ideology,'' in Flores, EPE, p. 40.

33. Nicholas H. Steneck, ''Commentary: The University and Research Ethics,'' *Science, Technology, and Human Values* 9, no. 4 (Fall 1984): 6–15, esp. p. 14.

34. E. Layton, ''Engineering Ethics and the Public Interest,'' in Flores, EPE, pp. 27–28; hereafter cited as: Layton, ''Engineering Ethics.''

35. Layton, ''Engineering Ethics,'' p. 27.

36. Layton, ''Engineering Ethics,'' p. 29.

37. Miron L. Straf, ''Who Owns What in Research Data?'' in *Ethics and*

Policy in Scientific Publication, ed. John C. Bailar and the Council of Biology Editors (Bethesda, Maryland: Council of Biology Editors, 1990), pp. 130–35, esp. p. 132.

38. Shue, "Exporting Hazards," p. 136. See also Bayles, PE, p. 7.

39. Bayles, PE, ch. 6, esp. p. 142.

40. Camenisch, "Being a Professional," pp. 44–45.

41. Camenisch, "Being a Professional," p. 55.

42. Camenisch, "Being a Professional," p. 54.

43. AAAS, PSFR, p. 2.

44. Institute of Electrical and Electronics Engineers (IEEE), Committee on the Social Implications of Technology, in *Ethical Problems in Engineering*, ed. R. Baum (Troy, NY: Center for the Study of the Human Dimensions of Science and Technology, 1980), p. 88; hereafter cited as: Baum, EPE. See also G. Friedlander, "The Case of the Three Engineers vs. BART," in Baum, EPE, pp. 80–87. See also J. Otten, "Organizational Disobedience," in Flores, EPE, p. 182.

45. IEEE, Committee on the Social Implications of Technology in Baum, EPE, p. 89.

46. IEEE, Committee on the Social Implications of Technology in Baum, EPE, p. 89.

47. IEEE, Committee on the Social Implications of Technology in Baum, EPE, p. 90.

48. AAAS, PSFR, p. 3. See also, J. T. Edsall, "Scientific Freedom and Responsibility: Report of the AAAS Committee on Scientific Freedom and Responsibility," *Science* 188, no. 4189 (1975): 689; cited hereafter as: Edsall, "Scientific Freedom." See also, W. P. Metzger, "Academic Freedom and Scientific Freedom," *Daedalus* 107, no. 2 (Spring 1978): 93–114.

49. R. Merton, *Social Research and the Practicing Professions* (Cambridge, Mass.: AH Books, 1982), p. 9.

50. See, for example, E. D. McCoy, "Letter to the Editor, 31 July 1987," *Ecological Society of America Bulletin* 68 (1987): 535.

51. AAAS, PSFR, p. 4.

52. See the earlier discussion and H. Salwasser, "Conserving a Regional Spotted Owl Population," in *The Preservation and Valuation of Biological Resources*, ed. G. H. Orians, G. M. Brown, Jr., W. E. Kunin, and J. E. Swierzbinski (Seattle and London: University of Washington Press, 1990), pp. 227–47.

53. A. Cournand, "The Code of the Scientist and its Relationship to Ethics," *Science* 198, no. 4318 (November, 1977): 699–705. See also J. Monod, *Chance and Necessity* (New York: Knopf, 1971), p. 21.

54. Bayles, PE, p. 65.

55. AAAS, PSFR, pp. 1–2. See also J. Ladd, "The Quest for a Code of Professional Ethics: An Intellectual and Moral Confusion," in *AAAS Professional Ethics Project: Professional and Ethics Activities in the Scientific and Engineering Societies*, ed. R. Chalk, M. Frankel, and S. Chafer (Washington,

D.C.: AAAS, 1980), p. 154, who also argues that professionals have no special rights.

56. Kultgen, "Professional Ideals and Ideology," p. 42.

57. Bayles, PE, p. 67.

58. Bayles, PE, p. 67.

59. K. S. Shrader-Frechette, *Science Policy, Ethics, and Economic Methodology* (Boston: Kluwer, 1985), pp. 216ff.

60. Cited in, D. Bazelon, "Risk and Responsibility," *Science* 205, no. 4403 (1979): 277–80.

61. AAAS, PSFR, p. 4.

62. AAAS, PSFR, p. 4.

63. Von Hippel and Primack, "Public Interest Science," p. 1168.

64. Von Hippel and Primack, "Public Interest Science," p. 1168.

65. Von Hippel and Primack, "Public Interest Science," p. 1168.

66. National Academy of Sciences, National Academy of Engineering, Institute of Medicine, and National Research Council, *1992 Report to Congress* (Washington, D.C.: National Academy of Sciences, 1992), p. 1.

67. Bayles, PE, p. 114.

68. Jackson, HS, pp. 34–35.

69. R. Merton, *The Sociology of Science* (Chicago: University of Chicago Press, 1973), pp. 318, 456.

70. K. S. Shrader-Frechette, *Nuclear Power and Public Policy* (Boston: Kluwer, 1983), pp. 78–79. See also U.S. Atomic Energy Commission (USAEC), "Theoretical Possibilities and Consequences of Major Accidents in Large Nuclear Power Plants," USAEC Report WASH-740, (Washington, D.C.: U.S. Government Printing Office, 1957). See also R. J. Mulvihill, D. R. Arnold, C. E. Bloomquist, and B. Epstein, *Analysis of United States Power Reactor Accident Possibility*, PRC-R-695 (Los Angeles: Planning Research Corporation, 1965).

71. Edsall, SFR, p. 21.

72. Jackson, HS, p. 29.

73. Louis Provencher, "Inheriting Ecology from the Ivory Tower, *Ecological Society of America Bulletin* 74 (1993): 182–83.

74. AAAS, PSFR, p. 4.

75. Otten, "Organizational Disobedience," p. 182. See Myron Glazer and Penina Glazer, *The Whistleblowers* (New York: Basic Books, 1989); see also Marcia Miceli and Janet Near, *Blowing the Whistle* (New York: Macmillan, 1992). For a discussion of dangerous research practices that need whistleblowing, see Elaine Draper, *Risky Business: Genetic Testing and Exclusionary Practices in the Hazardous Workplace* (Cambridge: Cambridge University Press, 1991).

76. Otten, "Organizational Disobedience," pp. 183–84.

77. Otten, "Organizational Disobedience," p. 185.

78. Jackson, HS, pp. 29–37.

79. Edsall, SFR, pp. 31–32. See also Edsall, ''Scientific Freedom,'' p. 690.
80. Edsall, ''Scientific Freedom,'' p. 690.
81. M. Dowie, ''Pinto Madness,'' in Baum, EPE, pp. 167–74.
82. Edsall, ''Two Aspects,'' p. 7.
83. Edsall, ''Two Aspects,'' p. 9. See also A. Weinberg, ''The Obligation of Citizenship in the Republic of Science,'' *Minerva* 16 (1976): 1–3.
84. Otten, ''Organizational Disobedience,'' pp. 185ff.

Chapter 5

1. U.S. National Research Council, *Pesticides in the Diets of Infants and Children* (Washington, D.C.: National Academy Press, 1993).
2. ''Groups Brace for Major Scientific Study on Impact of Pesticides on Children,'' *Inside E.P.A.: Weekly Report* 14, no. 23 (June 11, 1993): 1.
3. P. C. Kangas, ''A Method for Predicting Extinction Rates Due to Deforestation in Tropical Life Zones,'' *Abstract, IV International Congress of Ecology* (Meeting Program, 1986), p. 194. For discussion of the Kangas–Noss controversy, on which this account is based, see K. S. Shrader-Frechette and E. D. McCoy, *Method in Ecology* (Cambridge, UK: Cambridge University Press, 1993), chs. 4, 8; hereafter cited as: Shrader-Frechette and McCoy, ME.
4. R. F. Noss, ''Dangerous Simplifications in Conservation Biology,'' *Bulletin of the Ecological Society of America* 67 (1986): 278–79; hereafter cited as: Noss, ''Dangerous Simplifications.''
5. Noss, ''Dangerous Simplifications,'' p. 279.
6. Noss, ''Dangerous Simplifications,'' p. 278.
7. Noss, ''Dangerous Simplifications,'' p. 278.
8. R. B. Waide, ''Letter to the Editor, April 1987,'' *Bulletin of the Ecological Society of America* (1987): 485; hereafter cited as: Waide, ''Letter.''
9. D. Simberloff, ''Simplification, Danger, and Ethics in Conservation Biology,'' *Bulletin of the Ecological Society of America* 68 (1987): 156–57; hereafter cited as: Simberloff, ''Simplification.''
10. Simberloff, ''Simplification,'' p. 156.
11. E. D. McCoy, ''Letter to the Editor, 31 July 1987,'' *Bulletin of the Ecological Society of America* 68 (1987): 535.
12. P. C. Kangas, ''On the Use of Species Area Curves to Predict Extinctions,'' *Bulletin of the Ecological Society of America* 68 (1987): 158–62.
13. R. F. Noss, ''Letter to the Editor, 22 September 1987,'' *Bulletin of the Ecological Society of America* 69 (1988): 4–5; hereafter cited as: Noss, ''Letter.''
14. American Association for the Advancement of Science (AAAS), *Principles of Scientific Freedom and Responsibility*, Revised Draft (Washington, D.C.: AAAS, 1980), pp. 2–4; hereafter cited as: AAAS, PSFR.
15. J. T. Edsall and the AAAS Committee on Scientific Freedom and Re-

sponsibility, *Scientific Freedom and Responsibility* (Washington, D.C.: AAAS, unpublished manuscript, 1975), p. 3.

16. AAAS, PSFR, p. 2.

17. R. Chalk, M. Frankel, and S. Chafer (eds.), *AAAS Professional Ethics Project: Professional Ethics Activities in the Scientific and Engineering Societies* (Washington, D.C.: AAAS, 1980), pp. 111–14.

18. Sissela Bok, "Whistleblowing and Professional Responsibilities," in *Engineering Professionalism and Ethics*, ed. J. Schaub, K. Pavlovic, and M. Morris (New York: John Wiley, 1983), p. 412; see R. Chalk and F. von Hippel, "Blowing the Whistle," *Technology Review* 81, no. 7 (1979): 48–55.

19. Ecological Society of America, *Code of Ethics* (Ithaca, NY: Ecological Society of America, 1977), tenet 14.

20. W. May, "Notes on the Ethics of Doctors and Lawyers," in *Moral Responsibility and the Professions*, ed. B. Baumrin and B. Freedman (New York: Haven Press, 1982), p. 94.

21. T. Beauchamp and J. Childress, *Principles of Biomedical Ethics* (New York: Oxford University Press, 1983), p. 283.

22. A. Gewirth, *Human Rights* (Chicago: University of Chicago, 1982), pp. 218ff.; hereafter cited as: Gewirth, HR.

23. See W. Frankena, *Ethics* (Englewood Cliffs, NJ: Prentice Hall, 1963), pp. 14, 32; hereafter cited as: Frankena, *Ethics*.

24. Cited in D. C. Erman and E. P. Pister, "Ethics and the Environmental Biologist," *Fisheries* 14, no. 2 (March/April 1989): 5.

25. See I. Kant, *Groundwork of the Metaphysics of Morals*, trans. H. J. Paton (New York: Harper and Row, 1956), pp. 95–98.

26. Gewirth, HR, pp. 226ff.; see Frankena, *Ethics*, p. 14.

27. See, for example, R. Baum (ed.), *Ethical Problems in Engineering* (Troy, NY: Center for the Study of the Human Dimensions of Science and Technology, 1980), p. 4.

28. M. Bayles, *Professional Ethics* (Belmont, California: Wadsworth, 1981), p. 2; hereafter cited as: Bayles, PE.

29. Noss, "Dangerous Simplifications," pp. 278–79. See note 3.

30. Noss, "Letter," p. 4.

31. Waide, "Letter," p. 485.

32. R. Dworkin, *Taking Rights Seriously* (Cambridge, Harvard University Press, 1977); hereafter cited as: Dworkin, TRS.

33. Gewirth, HF, pp. 218ff.

34. Bayles, PE, p. 136.

35. Gewirth, HR, p. 227.

36. Bayles, PE.

37. Bayles, PE, pp. 99ff.

38. For arguments here, see Shrader-Frechette and McCoy, ME, chs. 7–10.

39. J. T. Mathews *et al.*, *World Resources 1986* (New York: Basic Books, 1986), pp, 48–49. See also R. Repetto, *Paying the Price: Pesticide Subsidies in*

Developing Countries, Research Report no. 2 (Washington, D.C.: World Resources Institute, 1985), p. 3.

40. For arguments here, see Shrader-Frechette and McCoy, ME, chs. 7–10; see also ch. 7 in this volume.

41. Dworkin, TRS, pp. 267–79.

42. Shrader-Frechette and McCoy, ME, chs. 7–10.

43. Shrader-Frechette and McCoy, ME, chs. 7–10.

44. Bayles, PE, p. 109.

45. Bayles, PE, p. 94.

46. American Society of Biological Chemists (ASBC), *Bylaws* (Bethesda, Md.: American Society of Biological Chemists, 1977).

47. National Society of Professional Engineers (NSPE), "Criticism of Engineering in Products, Board of Ethical Review, Case no. 76.10," in *Ethical Problems in Engineering*, vol. 1, ed. A. Flores (Troy, NY: Center for the Studies in the Human Dimensions of Science and Technology, 1980), p. 206.

48. National Bulletin.

49. See K. S. Shrader-Frechette, *Nuclear Power and Public Policy* (Boston: Reidel, 1983), pp. 74ff.

50. I. Stark, "The University Goes to Market," *Thought and Action: NEA Higher Education Journal* 1, no. 1 (Fall 1984): 9–21; hereafter cited as: Stark, "University."

51. K. S. Shrader-Frechette, *Risk Analysis and Scientific Method* (Dordrecht: Reidel, 1985), p. 4.

52. See D. Noble, "Science for Sale," *Thought and Action: NEA Higher Education Journal* 1, no. 1 (Fall 1984): 39; and L. Minsky, "Greed in the Groves: Part Two," *Thought and Action: NEA Higher Education Journal* 1, no. 1 (Fall 1984): 47; hereafter cited as: Minsky, "Greed."

53. See W. Lepkowski, "Academic Values Tested by MIT's New Center," *Chemical and Engineering News* (March 15, 1982): 12.

54. See Stark, "University," p. 19.

55. Stark, "University," p. 20.

56. Quoted by Minsky, "Greed," p. 49.

57. D. J. Juvenal, *Satires* IV, no. 1.

58. Stark, "University," pp. 12–13.

59. American Civil Liberties Union (ACLU), "Guidelines on University and Contract Research," *Thought and Action: NEA Higher Education Journal* 1, no. 1 (Fall 1984): 22–23. These guidelines prohibit universities from accepting grants/contracts that confer upon an external party the power to censor or delay research contents or dissemination. They also prohibit research that requires a security clearance and any research that interferes with professors' primary teaching, research, and service missions. The guidelines require that faculty evaluation be the exclusive province of the university, that the evaluation be accomplished primarily in terms of criteria of academic merit, and that all research be open to public and professional judgment as to its merit. Finally,

the guidelines require that universities disclose all funding agreements into which they have entered.

60. H. Ehrlich, ''The University–Military Research Connection,'' *Thought and Action: NEA Higher Education Journal* 1, no. 1 (Fall 1984): 119.

61. Another way to promote university autonomy and objectivity is to found a chapter of the Coalition for Universities in the Public Interest. (National Coalition for Universities in the Public Interest, Box 19367, Washington, D.C. 20036) This is a new organization under the leadership of Leonard Minsky and under the sponsorship of Ralph Nader. Its goal is to prevent industry domination of academia.

62. See I. Winn, ''The University and the Strategic Defense Initiative,'' *Thought and Action: NEA Higher Education Journal* 1, no. 1 (Fall 1984): 29–30.

Chapter 6

1. Arthur Caplan, ''The Ethics of Uncertainty,'' *Agriculture and Human Values* 3, nos. 1–2 (Winter–Spring 1986): 180–90, esp. p. 181.

2. For an account of lay versus expert views on technological and research-related risk, especially in situations of uncertainty, see K. S. Shrader-Frechette, *Risk and Rationality: Philosophical Foundations for Populist Reforms* (Berkeley: University of California Press, 1991), on which much of this account is based; hereafter cited as: Shrader-Frechette, RR. For the Weinberg information, see p. 89. For the Samuels' analysis, see p. 90.

3. For discussion of these alternative points of view, see Shrader-Frechette, RR, esp. chapter 7.

4. Caplan, ''The Ethics of Uncertainty,'' p. 182.

5. See Caplan, ''The Ethics of Uncertainty,'' p. 187.

6. For formulation of a similar principle, see Caplan, ''The Ethics of Uncertainty,'' p. 183. For an extended defense of similar principles, see Robert Goodin, *Protecting the Vulnerable* (Chicago: University of Chicago Press, 1985).

7. For these arguments, see Shrader-Frechette, RR, chs. 7, 8, 10 and the previous endnote.

8. Philip Landigran *et al.*, and the National Research Council, *Pesticides in the Diets of Infants and Children* (Washington, D.C.: National Academy Press, 1993).

9. Bernard Wagner *et al.*, and the National Research Council, *Health Effects of Ingested Fluoride* (Washington, D.C.: National Academy Press, 1993).

10. The DOE policy statement is quoted in full and analyzed in K. S. Shrader-Frechette, *Burying Uncertainty: Risk and the Case Against Geological Disposal of Nuclear Waste* (Berkeley: University of California Press, 1993), pp. 105–14, esp. p. 106; hereafter cited as: Shrader-Frechette, BU.

11. For documentation of all these data and discussion of the Yucca Mountain case, see Shrader-Frechette, BU. For the 80 percent figure and psychometric data to support it, see p. 132.

12. R. F. Noss, "Dangerous Simplifications in Conservation Biology," *ESA Bulletin* 67 (1986): 278.

13. D. Simberloff, "Simplification, Danger, and Ethics in Conservation Biology," *Ecological Society of America Bulletin* 68 (1987): 156.

14. H. Otway and M. Peltu, *Regulating Industrial Risks* (London: Butterworth, 1985), p. 12.

15. K. S. Shrader-Frechette, *Nuclear Power and Public Policy*, second edition (Boston: Reidel, 1983), pp. 82–85; hereafter cited as: Shrader-Frechette, NPPP.

16. J. Raloff and J. Silberner, "Chernobyl: Emerging Data on Accident," *Science News* 129, no. 19 (1986): 292.

17. B. W. Lindgren, *Statistical Theory* (New York: Macmillan, 1968), p. 278. Much of this discussion of types I and II risk is based on K. S. Shrader-Frechette and E. D. McCoy, *Method in Ecology* (Cambridge: Cambridge University Press, 1993); Shrader-Frechette, BU; and Shrader-Frechette, RR.

18. C. W. Churchman, *Theory of Experimental Inference* (New York: Macmillan, 1947); hereafter cited as: Churchman, TEI. See S. Axinn, "The Fallacy of the Single Risk," *Philosophy of Science* 33 (1966): 154–62; hereafter cited as: Axinn, "Fallacy."

19. Statistically, however, although minimizing the probability of type-I error increases the probability of type-II error, minimizing the probability of type-II error does not increase the probability of type-I error.

20. Churchman, TEI. See Axinn, "Fallacy."

21. See the previous note.

22. See for example, J. Thomson, *Rights, Restitution, and Risk* (Cambridge, Mass.: Harvard University Press, 1986), p. 158; hereafter cited as: Thomson, RRR.

23. R. M. Cooke, "Risk Assessment and Rational Decision Theory," *Dialectica* 36, no. 4 (1982): 330-351; hereafter cited as: Cooke, "Risk Assessment."

24. J. Harsanyi, "Can the Maximin Principle Serve as a Basis for Morality," *American Political Science Review* 69, no. 2 (1975): 594.

25. Cooke, "Risk Assessment," pp. 341–42.

26. H. Shue, "Exporting Hazards," in *Boundaries: National Autonomy and Its Limits*, ed. P. Brown and H. Shue (Totowa, NJ: Rowman and Littlefield, 1981), pp. 107–45; hereafter cited as: Brown and Shue, *Boundaries*. J. Lichtenberg, "National Boundaries and Moral Boundaries," in Brown and Shue, *Boundaries*, pp. 79-100.

27. J. Bentham, "Principles of the Civil Code," in *The Works of Jeremy Bentham*, vol. 1., ed. J. Bowring (New York: Russell and Russell, 1962), p. 301; hereafter cited as: Bentham, "Principles."

28. L. C. Becker, ''Rights,'' in *Property*, ed. L. C. Becker and K. Kipnis (Englewood Cliffs, NJ: Prentice Hall, 1984), p. 76.

29. Bentham, ''Principles,'' p. 36; J. Feinberg, *Social Philosophy* (Englewood Cliffs, NJ: Prentice-Hall, 1973), pp. 29, 59; A. Gewirth, *Human Rights* (Chicago: University of Chicago, 1982), p. 228; J. Rachels, ''Euthanasia,'' in *Matters of Life and Death*, ed. T. Regan (New York: Random House, 1980), p. 38; K. S. Shrader-Frechette, *Science Policy, Ethics, and Economic Methodology* (Boston: Reidel, 1985), pp. 77–78; hereafter cited as: Shrader-Frechette, SP.

30. W. M. Hoffman and J. V. Fisher, ''Corporate Responsibility: Property and Liability,'' in *Property*, ed. L. C. Becher and K. Kipnis (Englewood Cliffs, NJ: Prentice Hall, 1984), pp. 211-220.

31. I. Kant, *Foundations of the Metaphysics of Morals*, trans. H. J. Paton (New York: Harper and Row, 1956), pp. 95–98; Gewirth, ''Human Rights,'' p. 226; Shrader-Frechette, SP, pp. 71–72; Shrader-Frechette, NPPP, pp. 33–35.

32. W. Frankena, ''The Concept of Social Justice,'' in *Social Justice*, ed. R. Brandt (Englewood Cliffs, NJ: Prentice-Hall, 1962), pp. 10–14; Shue, ''Exporting Hazards,'' pp. 107–45; Lichtenberg, ''National Boundaries and Moral Boundaries,'' pp. 79–100. See Nicholas Ashford, ''Science and Values in the Regulatory Process,'' *Statistical Science* 3, no. 3 (1988): 377–383.

33. M. Peltu, ''The Role of Communications Media,'' in *Regulating Industrial Risks*, ed. H. Otway and M. Peltu (London, Butterworth, 1985), p. 132; hereafter cited as: Peltu, ''Communications Media.''

34. Peltu, ''Communications Media,'' pp. 132–36.

35. A. Leopold, *A Sand County Almanac* (New York: Oxford University Press, 1949), p vii.

36. Thomson, RRR, p. 156.

37. Shrader-Frechette, SP, pp. 107ff.

38. T. Schelling, *Choice and Consequence* (Cambridge, Mass.: Harvard University Press, 1984), pp. 145–46; hereafter cited as: Schelling, CC.

39. Schelling, CC, pp. 145–46.

40. J. S. Mill, *On Liberty* (Buffalo, NY: Prometheus, 1986).

Chapter 7

1. E. O. Wilson, *Biodiversity* (Washington, D.C.: National Academy Press, 1988), p. 13.

2. Geerat J. Vermeij, ''Biology of Human-Caused Extinction,'' in *The Preservation of Species: The Value of Biological Diversity*, ed. Bryan G. Norton (Princeton, NJ: Princeton University Press, 1986), p. 31; hereafter cited as: Norton, PS.

3. E. O. Wilson, *The Diversity of Life* (Cambridge: Harvard University Press, 1992).

4. John C. Ryan, ''Conserving Biological Diversity,'' in *State of the World 1992*, ed. L. R. Brown *et al.* (New York: Norton, 1992), p. 10.

5. Thomas Lovejoy, ''Species Leave the Ark,'' in Norton, PS, p. 15.

6. Ryan, ''Conserving Biological Diversity,'' p. 11.

7. Ryan, ''Conserving Biological Diversity,'' p. 15.

8. Lovejoy, ''Species Leave the Ark,'' p. 17.

9. For a case study of the Florida panther, on which much of this account is based, see K. S. Shrader-Frechette and E. McCoy, *Methods in Ecology* (Cambridge: Cambridge University Press, 1993); hereafter cited as: Shrader-Frechette and McCoy, ME.

10. H. C. Kelman, ''Research, Behavioral,'' in *Encyclopedia of Bioethics*, ed. Warren T. Reich (New York: Macmillan, 1978), p. 1478 in pp. 1470–81.

11. E. R. Hall, *The Mammals of North America* (New York: J. Wiley and Sons, 1981); hereafter cited as: Hall, MNA.

12. E. A. Goldman, ''Classification of the Races of the Puma,'' in *The Puma, Mysterious American Cat*, ed. S. P. Young and E. A. Goldman (Washington, D.C.: National Wildlife Federation, 1946); hereafter cited as: Goldman, ''Classification.''

13. O. Bangs, ''The Land Mammals of Peninsular Florida and the Coast Region of Georgia,'' *Proceedings of the Boston Society of Natural History* 23 (1898): 157–235.

14. R. C. Belden, ''Florida Panther Recovery Plan Implementation—A 1983 Progress Report,'' in *Cats of the World: Biology, Conservation and Management*, ed. S. D. Miller and D. D. Everett (Washington, D.C.: National Wildlife Federation, 1987), pp. 159–72.

15. Goldman, ''Classification.''

16. K. R. Dixon, ''Mountain Lion (*Felis concolor*),'' in *Wild Mammals of North America: Biology, Management, and Economics*, ed. J. A. Chapman and G. A. Feldhamer (Baltimore, Md.: Johns Hopkins University Press, 1982), pp. 711–27; hereafter cited as: Dixon, ''Mountain Lion''; Hall, MNA.

17. Hall, MNA.

18. J. D. Ballou, T. J. Foose, R. C. Lacy, and U. S. Seal, *Florida Panther Population Viability Analysis* (Tallahassee, FL: Florida Game and Freshwater Fish Commission, 1989); hereafter cited as: Ballou *et al.*, FPP.

19. Ballou *et al.*, FPP.

20. See P. A. Colinvaux, *Why Big Fierce Animals are Rare: an Ecologist's Perspective* (Princeton, NJ: Princeton University Press, 1978), pp. 256.

21. See Dixon, ''Mountain Lion''; D. S. Maehr, R. C. Belden, E. D. Land, and L. Wilkins, ''Food Habits of Panthers in Southwest Florida,'' *Journal of Wildlife Management* 54 (1990): 420–23.

22. Ballou *et al.*, FPP.

23. C. Cristoffer and J. Eisenberg, *On the Captive Breeding and Reintroduction of the Florida Panther in Suitable Habitats* (Tallahassee, Fla.: Florida Game and Freshwater Fish Commission, 1985).

24. See U.S. Fish and Wildlife Service, *Florida panther (Felis concolor coryi) Recovery Plan* (Atlanta, Ga.: U.S. Fish and Wildlife Service, 1987); hereafter cited as: U.S. Fish and Wildlife Service, FP.

25. R. McBride, *Population Status of the Florida Panther in the Everglades National Park and Big Cypress National Preserve* (Tallahassee, Fla.: Florida Game and Freshwater Fish Commission, 1985).

26. See Ballou *et al.*, FPP.

27. U.S. Fish and Wildlife Service, FP.

28. U.S. Fish and Wildlife Service, FP.

29. S. J. O'Brien, M. E. Roelke, N. Yuhki, K. W. Richards, W. E. Johnson, W. L. Franklin, A. E. Anderson, O. L. Bass, Jr., R. C. Belden, and J. S. Martenson, "Genetic Introgression within the Florida Panther *Felis concolor coryi*," *National Geographic Research* 6, no. 4 (1990): 485–94; D. E. Wildt, J. G. Howard, L. L. Hall, and M. Bush, "The Reproductive Physiology of the Clouded Leopard," *Biology of Reproduction* 34 (1987): 937–48; L. Laikre and N. Ryman, "Inbreeding Depression in a Captive Wolf (*Canis lupus*) Population," *Conservation Biology* 5 (1991): 33–40; R. K. Wayne *et al.*, "Conservation Genetics of the Endangered Isle Royle Gray Wolf," *Conservation Biology* 5 (1991): 41–51.

30. M. E. Roelke, E. R. Jacobsen, G. V. Kollias, and J. Forrester, *Medical Management and Biomedical Findings on the Florida Panther, Felis concolor coryi* (Tallahassee, Fla.: Florida Game and Freshwater Fish Commission, 1985).

31. U.S. Fish and Wildlife Service, FP.

32. Ballou *et al.*, FPP.

33. See Shrader-Frechette and McCoy, ME.

34. L. D. Harris and P. B. Gallagher, "New Initiatives for Wildlife Conservation: The Need for Movement Corridors," in *Preserving Communities and Corridors*, ed. G. MacKintosh (Washington, D.C.: Defenders of Wildlife, 1989); hereafter cited as: Harris and Gallagher, "New Initiatives."

35. Shrader-Frechette and McCoy, ME, ch. 8; D. S. Maehr, "The Florida Panther and Private Lands," *Conservation Biology* 4 (1990): 167–70; Dixon, "Mountain Lion."

36. See Ballou, FPP.

37. Harris and Gallagher, "New Initiatives"; R. F. Noss, "Corridors in Real Landscapes: A Reply to Simberloff and Cox," *Conservation Biology* 1 (1987): 159–64; R. F. Noss and L. D. Harris, 1986, "Nodes, Networks, and MUMs: Preserving Diversity at All Scales," *Environmental Management* 10 (1986), pp. 299–309.

38. D. Simberloff and J. Cox, "Consequences and Costs of Conservation Corridors," *Conservation Biology* 1, no. 1 (1987): 63–71; hereafter cited as: Simberloff and Cox, "Consequences"; D. Simberloff, J. A. Farr, J. Cox, and D. W. Mehlman, "Movement Corridors: Conservation Bargains or Expensive Snake Oil?" *Conservation Biology* 6, no. 4 (1992): 493–504.

39. Michael A. Stoto, "From Data to Analysis to Conclusions," in *Ethics and Policy in Scientific Publication*, ed. John C. Bailar *et al.*, Editorial Policy Committee, Council of Biology Editors (Bethesda, Md.: Council of Biology Editors, 1990), p. 207 of pp. 207–18.

40. This discussion of the benefits of conservation/preservation is based on Shrader-Frechette and McCoy, ME. See M. Bayles, *Professional Ethics* (Belmont, Calif.: Wadsworth, 1981), p. 117.

41. M. Duda, *Floridians and Wildlife*, Nongame Wildlife Program, Technical Report no. 2 (Tallahassee, Fla.: Florida Game and Freshwater Fish Commission, April 1987), p. 108; hereafter cited as: Duda, FW.

42. See J. Vining (ed.), *Social Science and Natural Resource Recreation Management* (Boulder, Colo.: Westview Press, 1990); hereafter cited as: Vining, SS.

43. See C. Haar and L. Liebman, *Property and Law* (Boston: Little, Brown and Company, 1977), p. 113, pp. 969–79.

44. R. Dworkin, *Taking Rights Seriously* (Cambridge: Harvard University Press, 1977); hereafter cited as: Dworkin, TRS.

45. Dworkin, TRS, pp. 267–79; see K. S. Shrader-Frechette, ''Locke and Limits on Land Ownership,'' *Journal of the History of Ideas* 54, no. 2 (April 1993): 201–19; hereafter cited as Shrader-Frechette, ''Locke and Limits.''

46. Shrader-Frechette and McCoy, ME; and see Shrader-Frechette, ''Locke and Limits.''

47. B. A. Emmett, ''The Distribution of Environmental Quality,'' in *Environmental Assessment*, ed. D. Burkhardt and W. Ittelson (New York: Plenum, 1978), pp. 367–74; J. Egerton, ''Appalachia's Absentee Landlords,'' *The Progressive* 45, no. 6 (1981): 43–45; K. S. Shrader-Frechette, ''Environmental Ethics and Global Imperatives,'' in *The Global Possible: Resources, Development, and the New Century,* ed. R. Repetto (New Haven: Yale University Press, 1985), pp. 97–122.

48. K. S. Shrader-Frechette, *Nuclear Power and Public Policy* (Boston: Reidel, 1983), ch. 1; hereafter cited as: Shrader-Frechette, NPPP; K. S. Shrader-Frechette, *Burying Uncertainty: Risk and the Case Against Geological Disposal of Nuclear Waste* (Berkeley: University of California Press, 1993); hereafter cited as: Shrader-Frechette, BU.

49. Shrader-Frechette, NPPP, ch. 4; K. S. Shrader-Frechette, *Risk and Rationality* (Berkeley: University of California Press, 1991); hereafter cited as: Shrader-Frechette, RR; Shrader-Frechette, BU; Shrader-Frechette and McCoy, ME.

50. K. S. Shrader-Frechette, *Science Policy, Ethics, and Economic Methodology* (Boston: Reidel, 1985), esp. pp. 133–34; hereafter cited as: Shrader-Frechette, SP.

51. L. Wicke, ''Environmental Damage Balance Sheets,'' in *Maintaining a Satisfactory Environment*, ed. N. Akerman (San Francisco: Westview Press, 1990), p. 52; hereafter cited as: Akerman, MSE; see Vining, SS.

52. Wicke, ''Environmental Damage Balance Sheets,'' p. 52.

53. Wicke, ''Environmental Damage Balance Sheets,'' p. 41.

54. J. A. McNeeley *et al.*, *Conserving the World's Biodiversity* (Washington, D.C.: IUCN and WRI, WWF-US, and World Bank, 1990), pp. 12, 19;

hereafter cited as: McNeeley *et al.*, CWB; see also E. Eden, *Ecology and Land Management in Amazonia* (New York: Belhanen, 1990); hereafter cited as: Eden, ELMA; M. Potier, ''Towards Better Integration of Environmental, Economic, and Other Governmental Policies,'' in Akerman, MSE; W. E. Westman, ''How Much Are Nature's Services Worth?'' *Science* 197 (1977): 960–64; hereafter cited as: Westman, ''How Much''; S. H. Pearsall, ''*In Absentia* Benefits of Nature Preserves,'' *Environmental Conservation* 11, no. 1 (Spring 1984): 3–9.

55. Wicke, ''Environmental Damage Balance Sheets,'' p. 47.

56. Duda, FW, p. 108.

57. Westman, ''How Much,'' p. 961; see also McNeeley *et al.*, CWB, pp. 27–28.

58. J. G. Sobetzer, ''American Land and Law,'' in *Land in America*, ed. R. Andrews (Lexington, Mass.: Lexington Books, 1979), p. 214; hereafter cited as: Andrews, LA; for economic methods for assigning value to natural resources, see S. Barrett, ''Economic Guidelines for the Conservation of Biological Diversity,'' (Costa Rica: IUCN General Assembly, paper presented at Workshop on Economics, February 1988); hereafter cited as: Barrett, ''Economic Guidelines''; G. M. Brown, Jr. and J. H. Goldstein, ''A Model for Valuing Endangered Species,'' *Journal of Environmental Economics and Management* 11 (1984): 303–9; C. Cooper, *Economic Evaluation and the Environment* (London: Hodder and Stoughton, 1981); A. C. Fisher, *Resources and Environmental Economics* (Cambridge, UK: Cambridge University Press, 1981), pp. 284; M. M. Hufschmidt *et al.*, *Environment, Natural Systems, and Development: An Economic Valuation Guide* (Baltimore, Md.: Johns Hopkins University Press, 1983), pp. 338; P-O. Johansson, *The Economic Theory and Measurement of Environmental Benefits* (London: Cambridge University Press, 1987), pp. 238; hereafter cited as: Johansson, ETM; J. V. Krutilla and A. C. Fisher, *The Economics of Natural Environments: Studies in the Valuation of Commodity and Amenities Resources* (Baltimore, Md.: Resources for the Future/John Hopkins University Press, 1975), pp. 292; W. D. Pearce, *Environmental Economics* (London: Longmans, 1976); G. L. Peterson and A. Randall, *Valuation of Wildlife Resource Benefits* (Boulder, Colo.: Westview Press, 1984), pp. 258; J. Sinden and A. Worrell, *Unpriced Values: Decisions Without Market Prices* (New York: J. Wiley, 1979); R. Prescott-Allen, *National Conservation Strategies and Biological Diversity* (Gland, Switzerland: Report to IUCN, 1986), pp. 67.

59. Wicke, ''Environmental Damage Balance Sheets,'' p. 37.

60. Westman, ''How Much,'' p. 962; see Wicke, ''Environmental Damage Balance Sheets,'' p. 52.

61. McNeeley *et al.*, CWB, p. 57; see also Eden, ELMA, pp. 171–86; see Shrader-Frechette and McCoy, ME, ch. 7.

62. Barrett, ''Economic Guidelines''; Johansson, ETM; McNeeley *et al.*, CWB, pp. 26ff; Vining, SS.

63. Wicke, "Environmental Damage Balance Sheets," p. 52.

64. Wicke, "Environmental Damage Balance Sheets," p. 52.

65. Potier, "Towards Better Integration of Environmental, Economic, and Other Governmental Policies"; Wicke, "Environmental Damage Balance Sheets"; Eden, ELMA; McNeeley *et al.*, CWB.

66. Forest Service Southern Region, *National Forests in Florida, Facts of FY 1989* (Washington, D.C.: USDA, 1990).

67. Wicke, "Environmental Damage Balance Sheets," p. 52.

68. R. G. Healy, "Land Use and the States," in Andrews, LA, p. 10; hereafter cited as: Healy, "Land Use."

69. C. E. Little, "Preservation Policy and Personal Perception," in Andrews, LA, pp. 83–98; see Wicke, "Environmental Damage Balance Sheets"; Potier, "Towards Better Integration of Integration of Environmental, Economic, and Other Governmental Policies."

70. See Healy, "Land Use," p. 10.

71. I. Kant, *Groundwork of the Metaphysics of Morals*, trans. H. J. Paton (New York: Harper and Row, 1964), pp. 95–98; hereafter cited as: Kant, GMM; see also J. Rawls, *A Theory of Justice* (Cambridge, Mass.: Harvard University Press, 1971), pp. 179–83; hereafter cited as: Rawls, TJ.

72. W. Frankena, "The Concept of Social Justice," in *Social Justice*, ed. R. Brandt (Englewood Cliffs, NJ: Prentice-Hall, 1962), pp. 9–15; see, for example, Kant, GMM, pp. 95–98; A. Gewirth, *Human Rights* (Chicago: University of Chicago, 1982), p 226; Shrader-Frechette, SP, pp. 71–72; Shrader-Frechette, NPPP, pp. 33–35.

73. Shrader-Frechette and McCoy, ME.

74. Ballou *et al.*, FPP, p. 2; see U.S. Fish and Wildlife Service, FP; for discussion of this objection, see Shrader-Frechette and McCoy, ME, ch. 9.

75. D. Simberloff, "Simplification, Danger, and Ethics in Conservation Biology," *Ecological Society of America Bulletin* 68 (1987): 156; hereafter cited as: Simberloff, "Simplification."

76. Simberloff, "Simplification," p. 157.

77. Simberloff, "Simplification," pp. 156–57.

78. Simberloff, "Simplification," p. 157.

79. Shrader-Frechette and McCoy, ME, see ch. 2.

80. See, for example, U.S. Congress, *Congressional Record* Senate, 93rd Congress, First Session 119 (Washington, D.C.: U.S. Government Printing Office, 24 July 1973): 25668; B. Commoner, *The Closing Circle* (New York: Knopf, 1971), p. 38; N. Myers, *A Wealth of Wild Species* (Boulder, Colo.: Westview Press, 1983).

81. R. A. Millikan, "Alleged Sins of Science," *Scribner's Magazine* 87, no. 2 (1930): 119–30.

82. D. Kahneman and A. Tversky, "Availability: A Heuristic for Judging Frequency and Probability," in *Judgment Under Uncertainty: Heuristics and Biases*, ed. D. H. Kahneman *et al.* (Cambridge, UK: Cambridge University

Press, 1982); pp. 63–78; hereafter cited as: Kahneman, JUU; D. Kahneman and A. Tversky, "Judgment Under Uncertainty," in Kahneman, JUU, pp. 4–11.

83. U.S. Nuclear Regulatory Commission, *Reactor Safety Study* (NUREG-75/014) WASH-1400 (Washington, D.C.: U.S. Government Printing Office, 1975).

84. R. M. Cooke, "Problems with Empirical Bayes," *Risk Analysis* 6, no. 3 (1986): 269–72; hereafter cited as: Cooke, "Problems"; see Shrader-Frechette, RR.

85. M. Korchmar, "Radiation Hearings Uncover Dust," *Critical Mass Journal* 3, no. 12 (March 1978): 5; hereafter cited as: Korchmar, "Radiation Hearings."

86. G. Meyer, *Maxey Flats Radioactive Waste Burial Site: Status Report* (Washington, D.C.: Advanced Science and Technology Branch, U.S. Environmental Protection Agency, unpublished report, 1975).

87. H. Kunreuther *et al.*, "A Decision-Process Perspective on Risk and Policy Analysis," in *Resolving Locational Conflict*, ed. R. W. Lake (Rutgers, NJ: Center for Urban Policy Research, 1987), p. 261.

88. N. C. Rasmussen, "Methods of Hazard Analysis and Nuclear Safety Engineering," in *The Three Mile Island Nuclear Accident*, ed. T. Moss and D. Sill (New York: New York Academy of Science, 1981).

89. See Korchmar, "Radiation Hearings."

90. Cooke, "Problems."

91. Simberloff, "Simplification," p. 156.

92. Simberloff and Cox, "Consequences," pp. 68–69; Simberloff, "Simplification," p. 156; see R. E. Grumbine, "Viable Populations, Reserve Size, and Federal Lands Management: A Critique," *Conservation Biology* 4, no. 2 (June 1990): 127–36.

93. Simberloff, "Simplification," p. 156.

94. See, for example, J. Harsanyi, "Advances in Understanding Rational Behavior," in *Rational Choice*, ed. Jon Elster (New York: New York University Press, 1986); J. Harsanyi, "Understanding Rational Behavior," in *Foundational Problems in the Special Sciences*. vol. 2, ed. R. Butts and J. Hintikka (Boston: Reidel, 1977); J. Harsanyi, "Can the Maximin Principle Serve as a Basis for Morality?" *American Political Science Review* 69, no. 2 (1975): 594.

95. Shrader-Frechette, ME, chs. 7–8; Shrader-Frechette, RR, chs. 7–8.

96. Simberloff, "Simplification," p. 157.

97. See Shrader-Frechette and McCoy, ME, chs. 6–9.

98. Shrader-Frechette and McCoy, ME, chs. 6–9.

99. J. Rawls, "Some Reasons for the Maximin Criterion," *American Economic Review* 64 (1974): 141–46; Rawls, TJ, pp. 75–83.

100. See Simberloff, "Simplification"; Simberloff and Cox, "Consequences," pp. 68–69.

101. See Simberloff, "Simplification," p. 156; Shrader-Frechette and McCoy, ME, chs. 6–9.

102. Simberloff, "Simplification"; Simberloff and Cox, "Consequences"; P. C. Kangas, "A Method for Predicting Extinction Rates Due to Deforestation in Tropical Life Zones," *Abstract, IV International Congress of Biology* (Meeting Program, 1986), p. 194; P. C. Kangas, "On the Use of Species Area Curves to Predict Extinctions," *Bulletin of the Ecological Society of America* 68 (1987): 158–62; R. F. Noss, "Dangerous Simplifications in Conservation Ecology," *Bulletin of the Ecological Society of America* 67 (1986): 278–79; R. F. Noss, "Letter to the Editor, 22 September 1987," *Bulletin of the Ecological Society of America* 69 (1988): 4–5.

Chapter 8

1. This essay is an expansion and adaptation of portions of chapters five and six of Helen E. Longino, *Science as Social Knowledge* (Princeton, NJ: Princeton University Press, 1990); hereafter cited as: Longino, SSK. Permission to reprint material from pages 85, 86, 89, 109–11, and 119–21, is gratefully acknowledged.

2. Current debates over the use and treatment of animals in biomedical experimentation are in part debates as to whether and how non-human animals should be considered members of that ethical universe.

3. James Jones, *Bad Blood: The Tuskegee Syphilis Experiment* (New York: The Free Press, 1981).

4. Stanley Milgram, *Obedience to Authority* (New York: Harper and Row, 1974); Sheldon Krimsky, *Genetic Alchemy: The Social History of the Recombinant DNA Controversy* (Cambridge, Mass.: MIT Press, 1982).

5. Margaret Rossiter, *Women Scientists in America: Struggles and Strategies to 1940* (Baltimore, Md.: The Johns Hopkins University Press, 1982); Londa Schiebinger, *The Mind Has No Sex?* (Cambridge, Mass.: Harvard University Press, 1989).

6. Evelyn F. Keller, *Reflections on Gender and Science* (New Haven, Conn.: Yale University Press, 1985); hereafter cited as: Keller, RGS.

7. See also Jane Martin, "Science in a Different Style," *American Philosophical Quarterly* 25 (1988): 129–40, and Ian Hacking, "Philosophers of Experiment," in *PSA 1988*, ed. Arthur Fine and Jarrett Leplin (East Lansing, Mich.: Philosophy of Science Association, 1989), pp. 147–56.

8. Inez Smith Reid, "Science, Politics and Race," in *Sex and Scientific Inquiry*, ed. Sandra Harding and Jean F. O'Barr (Chicago: University of Chicago Press, 1987), pp. 99–124.

9. "House Bill Tells NIH to Stress Women," (News and Comment) *Science* 253 (August 9, 1991): 260. Gina Kolata, "In Medical Research Equal Opportunity Doesn't Always Apply," *New York Times* (March 10, 1991): E16.

10. Carol Korenbrot, "Experiences with Systemic Contraceptives," *Toxic Substances: Decisions and Values, Conference II: Information Flow* (Washington, D.C.: Technical Information Project, 1979).

11. Gregory Pincus, *The Control of Fertility* (New York: Academic Press, 1965).

12. Stephen J. Gould, *The Mismeasure of Man* (New York: W. W. Norton and Co., 1981).

13. For further discussion of both behavioral neuroendocrinology and the human evolution research to be discussed in the next section, see Longino, SSK, chapters six through eight.

14. Ruth Hubbard, ''Have Only Men Evolved?'' in *Women Look at Biology Looking at Women*, ed. Ruth Hubbard, Mary Sue Henifin, and Barbara Fried (Cambridge, Mass.: Schenkman, 1979).

15. See Robert Richardson, ''Biology and Ideology: The Interpenetration of Science and Values,'' *Philosophy of Science* 51, no. 2 (1984): 396–420, for an analysis of these flaws.

16. See Sherwood Washburn and C. S. Lancaster, ''The Evolution of Hunting,'' in *Man the Hunter*, ed. Richard Lee and Irven DeVore (Chicago: Aldine Publishing Co. 1968), pp. 293–303, and Adrienne Zihlman, ''Women as Shapers of the Human Adaptation,'' in *Woman the Gatherer*, ed. Frances Dahlberg (New Haven, Conn.: Yale University Press, 1981), pp. 75–120.

17. For further discussion of these ideas, see Keller, RGS; The Gender and Biology Study Group, ''How Feminist Critique Can Benefit Cellular Biology,'' *Hypatia* 3, no. 1 (Spring 1988), and Elizabeth Potter, ''Modeling the Gender Politics in Science,'' *Hypatia* 3, no. 1 (Spring 1988).

Chapter 9

1. See, e.g., Shakespeare, *Troilus and Cressida* (act 2, scene 3, line 8), where Achilles is termed ''a rare engineer''; and *Hamlet* (act 3, scene 4, line 206), where: '' . . . the engineer / Hoist with his own petard.''

2. The term ''civil engineering'' continues in some European languages to denote all non-military engineering.

3. George S. Morison, ''Address at the Annual Convention at the Hotel Pemberton, Hull, Mass., June 19th, 1895,'' *Transactions of the American Society of Civil Engineers* 33, no. 6 (June 1895): 483. This speech is revised and incorporated as chapter six into Morison's *The New Epoch—As Developed by the Manufacture of Power* (Boston: Houghton Mifflin, 1903).

4. The best single study of this period is Edwin T. Layton, Jr., *The Revolt of the Engineers: Social Responsibility and the American Engineering Profession* (Baltimore: Johns Hopkins University Press, 1986). First published 1971. The focus is on the years 1900–1945.

5. Steven L. Goldman, ''No Innovation Without Representation: Technological Action in a Democratic Society,'' in *New Worlds, New Technologies, New Issues*, ed. Stephen H. Cutcliffe, Steven L. Goldman, Manuel Medina, and José Sanmartín (Bethlehem, PA.: Lehigh University Press, 1992), pp. 148–60.

See also K. S. Shrader-Frechette, *Risk and Rationality: Philosophical Foundations for Populist Reforms* (Berkeley: University of California Press, 1991).

6. For detail on this history see John G. Burke, "Bursting Boilers and the Federal Power," *Technology and Culture* 7, no. 1 (Winter 1966): 1–23. Reprinted in Marcel C. Lafollette and Jeffrey K. Stine, eds., *Technology and Choice: Readings from Technology and Culture* (Chicago: University of Chicago Press, 1991), pp. 43–65.

7. For a good summary of the Hydrolevel case with references to the relevant legal documents and historical studies, see Paula Wells, Hardy Jones, and Michael Davis, *Conflicts of Interest in Engineering* (Dubuque, Iowa: Kendal-Hunt, 1986).

8. For documentation on this case, see Roger Boisjoly, "The Challenger Disaster: Moral Responsibility and the Working Engineer," in *Ethical Issues in Engineering*, ed. Deborah G. Johnson (Englewood Cliffs, NJ: Prentice-Hall, 1991), pp. 6–14.

9. The term "research" is, for instance, conspicuous by its absence in the article on "Engineering Design" (the main entry on engineering) in the *McGraw-Hill Encyclopedia of Science and Technology*, 7th edition (New York: McGraw-Hill, 1992), vol. 6, pp. 392–99, although "research engineering" is often mentioned in standard textbook introductions to the engineering profession.

10. *Oxford English Dictionary*, 2nd edition (1989), vol. 13, p. 692, col. 3, top.

11. "Engineering Design," *McGraw-Hill Encyclopedia of Science and Technology*, 7th edition (New York: McGraw-Hill, 1992), vol. 6, p. 392.

12. For an argument for this thesis plus relevant discussion of the debate concerning design, see Carl Mitcham, "Engineering as Productive Activity: Philosophical Remarks," in *Critical Perspectives on Nonacademic Science and Engineering*, ed. Paul T. Durbin (Bethlehem, PA: Lehigh University Press, 1991), pp. 80–117.

13. "Research," *McGraw-Hill Dictionary of Scientific and Technical Terms*, 3rd edition (New York: McGraw-Hill, 1984), p. 1362.

14. "Engineering," *McGraw-Hill Encyclopedia of Science and Technology*, 7th edition (New York: McGraw-Hill, 1992), vol. 6, p. 387.

15. Henry Petroski, *To Engineer Is Human: The Role of Failure in Successful Design* (New York: St. Martin's Press, 1985), p. xii.

16. Mike Martin and Roland Schinzinger, *Ethics in Engineering*, 2nd edition (New York: McGraw-Hill, 1989), p. 64.

17. For two arguments to this effect, see Hans Jonas, "Technology as a Subject for Ethics," *Social Research* 49, no. 4 (Winter 1982): 891–98; and Hans Lenk, "Notes on Extended Responsibility and Increased Technological Power," in *Philosophy and Technology*, Boston Studies in the Philosophy of Science, vol. 80, ed. Paul T. Durbin and Friedrich Rapp (Boston: D. Reidel, 1983), pp. 196–97.

18. *In the Matter of J. Robert Oppenheimer: Transcript of Hearing before Personnel Security Board*, Washington, D.C., April 12–May 6, 1954 (Washington, D.C.: U.S. Government Printing Office, 1954), p. 251.

19. Cf. Mario Bunge, *Scientific Research II* (New York: Springer, 1967), pp. 123 ff.

20. Walter C. Zimmerli, ''Who Is To Blame for Data Pollution? On Individual Moral Responsibility with Information Technology,'' in *Philosophy and Technology II: Information Technology and Computers in Theory and Practice*, Boston Studies in the Philosophy of Science, vol. 90, ed. Carl Mitcham and Alois Huning (Boston: D. Reidel, 1986), p. 296.

21. Walter G. Vincenti, ''Introduction,'' in *Engineering as a Social Enterprise*, ed. Hedy E. Sladovich (Washington, D.C.: National Academy Press, 1991), p. 2.

22. Note also that *respicere* is composed of *re-*, intensifying prefix + *specere*, to look at or behold, the latter of which is related to the Greek (from whence comes the English ''skepticism''). Indeed, this might also be argued to be the engineering equivalent of René Dubos' motto: ''Think globally, act locally.''

23. E. F. Schumacher, *Small Is Beautiful* (New York: Harper & Row, 1973), p. 182.

24. For a good example of such alternative energy engineering design research, see the work of Amory Lovins, e.g., *Soft Energy Paths: Toward a Durable Peace* (San Francisco: Friends of the Earth; Cambridge, Mass.: Ballinger, 1977).

25. Stephen H. Unger, *Controlling Technology: Ethics and the Responsible Engineer* (New York: Holt, Rinehart and Winston, 1982), p. 38. See also pp. 4–6.

26. George Bugliarello, ''The Social Function of Engineering: A Current Assessment,'' in *Engineering as a Social Enterprise*, ed. Hedy E. Sladovich (Washington, D.C.: National Academy Press, 1991), pp. 77, 81.

Chapter 10

1. Portions of the argument in this chapter are taken from my *Regulating Toxic Substances: A Philosophy of Science and the Law* (New York: Oxford University Press, 1992); hereafter cited as: Cranor, RTS.

2. In discussing research on toxic substances, I focus on carcinogens. There has been more study of and experience with carcinogen risk assessment because carcinogens have been the object of substantial regulatory activity. The debates about the scientific models and information seem more manageable and confined, and the disputes between different scientific strategies more clearly marked out than for other kinds of toxins. Finally, I am more familiar with the numerous scientific and regulatory issues concerning the regulation of carcinogens.

3. Sanford E. Gaines, "A Taxonomy of Toxic Torts," *Toxics Law Reporter* 30 (1988): 831.

4. Talbot Page, "A Generic View of Toxic Chemicals and Similar Risks," *Ecology Law Quarterly* 7 (1978): 208; hereafter cited as: Page, "Generic View."

5. Page, "Generic View," p. 209.

6. Page, "Generic View," pp. 210–11. They have other properties as well. Benefits from using these substances are typically internalized through markets and product prices while nonmarket mechanisms impose the costs on others, thus resulting in externalities. Finally, many impose collective risks that materialize only after a substantial latency period (Page, "Generic View," pp. 212–13).

7. David Rosenberg, "The Dusting of America, A Story of Asbestos—Carnage, Cover-Up and Litigation," *Harvard Law Review* 99 (1986): 1693, 1704, describes the effects of asbestos litigation on the Manville Corporation, which filed for bankruptcy protection because of the potential litigation losses.

8. S. D. Walter, "Determination of Significant Relevant Risks and Optimal Sampling Procedures in Prospective and Retrospective Comparative Studies of Various Sizes," *American Journal of Epidemiology* 105 (1977): 387, 391 (Table 2); hereafter cited as: "Determination."

9. Taken from Cranor, RTS, p. 33.

10. A. R. Feinstein, *Clinical Biostatistics* (St. Louis: C. V. Mosby, 1977), pp. 324–25.

11. The low value for α may also be a mathematical artifice explained historically. As Ronald Giere puts it, "The reason [for the practice of having a 95 percent confidence level to guard against false positives] has something to do with the purely historical fact that the first probability distribution that was studied extensively was the normal distribution." *Understanding Scientific Reasoning* (New York: Holt, Rinehart, and Winston), pp. 212–13.

12. A concern to prevent confounding factors that might lead to false positives may be one of the main reasons for setting *a* so low. Such concerns seem to dominate recent discussion of problems in epidemiology. Alvan R. Feinstein, "Scientific Standards in Epidemiologic Studies of the Menace of Daily Life," *Science* 242 (1988): 1257–63. For a sharp response to some of Feinstein's concerns see Sander Greenland, "Science Versus Advocacy: The Challenge of Dr. Feinstein," *Epidemiology* 2 (1991): 64–72.

13. Relative risk is the ratio of the incidence of disease in an exposed population to the incidence of disease in an unexposed population.

14. From Cranor, RTS, p. 34 and Figure 1–8, p. 37.

15. These numbers are for a cohort study; sample sizes for a case-central study would be much smaller. See Walter, "Determination," pp. 387, 391 (Table II).

16. These points are developed in Cranor, RTS, pp. 35–40.

17. Cranor, RTS, p. 36.

18. Kenneth J. Rothman, *Modern Epidemiology* (Boston: Little, Brown and Company, 1986), p. 89.

19. Sander Greenland, "Invited Commentary: Science Versus Public Health Action: Those Who Were Wrong and Still Wrong," *American Journal of Public Health* 133(5) (1991): 435–36.

20. H. J. Eysenck, "Were We Really Wrong?" *American Journal of Epidemiology* 133, no. 5 (1991): 429, 432.

21. High doses, not typical of human exposure, are used in order to keep costs down and to provide sensitive studies. Larger groups of control and experimental animals could be used, but this increases the costs and length of studies.

22. D. P. Rall, "The Role of Laboratory Animal Studies in Estimating Carcinogenic Risks for Man," *Carcinogenic Risks: Strategies for Intervention* (Lyon, France: International Agency for Research on Cancer, 1979), p. 179.

23. U.S. Interagency Staff Group on Carcinogens, "Chemical Carcinogens: A Review of the Science and its Principles," *Environmental Health Perspectives* 67 (1986): 201–83, quoting the International Agency on Cancer, p. 234; hereafter cited as: U.S. Interagency Staff Group on Carcinogens, "Chemical Carcinogens."

24. L. Tomatis, "Environmental Cancer Risk Factors: A Review," *Acta Oncologica* 27 (1988): 465–72.

25. Asbestos is one substance that leaves a unique trace behind, as often fibers of asbestos can be found in the tissues that are diseased. Other sources of disease may be easily detected because they cause extremely rare diseases, thus raising the odds of detection (as is the case with vinyl chloride causing a very rare form of liver cancer or with diethylstilbestrol, which causes the very rare form of cervical cancer in the daughters of mothers who took DES during pregnancy).

26. Testimony of Dr. David Rall, Director, National Institute of Environmental Health Sciences, U.S. Department of Labor, Occupational Safety and Health Administration, "Identification, Classification, and Regulation of Potential Occupational Carcinogens," *Federal Register* 45 (1980): 5002 at 5061.

27. This point was suggested to me by Lauren Zeise, senior toxicologist and chief of the Reproductive and Cancer Hazard Assessment Section, Office of Environmental Health Hazard Assessment, California Environmental Protection Agency.

28. Office of the President, *Regulatory Program of the United States Government* (Washington, D.C.: GPA, 1990), pp. 13–26. See also *OMB v. the Agencies: The Future of Cancer Risk Assessment* (Cambridge, MA: Harvard School of Public Health, Center for Risk Analysis, 1991), for a survey of some of these issues.

29. U.S. Interagency Staff Group on Carcinogens, "Chemical Carcinogens."

30. For further discussion about some of these issues see National Research Council, *Risk Assessment in the Federal Government* (Washington, D.C.: U.S.

Government Printing Office, 1983), pp. 29–33; hereafter cited as: National Research Council, RA.

31. U.S. Department of Labor, "Identification, Classification and Regulation of Potential Occupational Carcinogens," *Federal Register* 45 (1980): 5190.

32. D. Y. Lee and A. C. Chang, " Evaluating Transport of Organic Chemicals in Soil Resulting from Underground Fuel Tank Leaks," in 46 *Purdue Industrial Waste Conference Proceedings* (Chelsea, Mich.: Lewis Publishers, 1992), pp. 131–40.

33. See Cranor, RTS, pp. 137–47 for an argument.

34. National Research Council, RA, pp. 17–50.

35. National Research Council, RA, p. 51.

36. U.S. Congress, Office of Technology Assessment, *Identifying and Regulating Carcinogens* (Washington, D.C.: U.S. Government Printing Office, 1987), p. 25; hereafter cited as: U.S. Congress, Office of Technology Assessment, IRC.

37. U.S. Congress, Office of Technology Assessment, IRC. For a general discussion of risk assessment policies and some of their history, see pp. 23–74 of the OTA study (U.S. Congress, Office of Technology Assessment, IRC) and chapter four of Cranor, RTS.

38. Risk assessment exhibits *in a much more radical form* a feature of all scientific inferences (all empirical inferences for that matter): the evidence available for the inference *underdetermines* the inference or the theory that aims to explain the evidence. At least since Descartes, philosophers have discussed the possibility of people having mistaken beliefs based upon the evidence before them; thus, the evidence does not *guarantee* the conclusions. Moreover, a paradigm of scientific inference, so-called inference to the best explanation, rests on the possibility that there may well be several plausible alternative explanations to account for the available evidence to an observer. Thus, the fact that the available evidence does not uniquely determine a correct model is not *new*, but the underdetermination of models or theories in carcinogen risk assessment is so much more *radical* in carcinogen risk assessments as to make it substantially different from ordinary scientific inferences.

39. The U.S. Food and Drug Administration chose to use the Gaylor–Kodel high-dose to low-dose extrapolation procedures to ensure the decision procedure was independent of all models (with a claim to scientific accuracy) and easy to use. The Gaylor–Kodel procedure takes the last data point from an animal bioassay arrived at with confidence (or perhaps extrapolates from that with the 95 percent upper confidence linearized multistage model to the 25 percent risk response) and draws a straight line through the origin with a ruler. Personal communication, David Gaylor, U.S. Food and Drug Administration.

40. See Howard Latin, "Good Science, Bad Regulation, and Toxic Risk Assessment," *Yale Law Journal on Regulation* 5 (1988): 89–142, for a summary of the many reasons for choosing particular features of a risk assessment for benzene.

41. Although prudence in protecting public health is a reason for guideline choice, risk assessors and risk managers do not always make health-protective choices. For example, sensitive subpopulations, such as the elderly or nursing infants, are not always considered. Also, in some cases humans are much more sensitive to substances than test animals (e.g., benzidine), and the timing of exposure is frequently not taken into account. See Adam Finkel, "Is Risk Assessment Too Conservative: Revising the Revisionists," *Columbia Journal of Environmental Law* 14 (1989): 427–67; J. C. Bailar, E. A. C. Crouch, R. Shaiklr, and D. Spiegelman, "One-Hit Models of Carcinogenesis: Conservative or Not?" *Risk Analysis* 8 (1988): 485–97; Lauren Zeise, "Issues in Risk Assessment," in *Proceedings: Pesticides and Other Toxics: Assessing their Risks*, ed. Janet White (Riverside, Calif.: College of Natural and Agricultural Sciences, University of California, Riverside, 1990), pp. 135–44; and Leslie Roberts, "Is Risk Assessment Conservative?" *Science* 247 (1989): 1553.

42. Carl Cranor, "Some Public Policy Problems with the Science of Carcinogen Risk Assessment," *Philosophy of Science Association 1988*, ed. A. Fine and J. Leplin (East Lansing, Mich.: Philosophy of Science Association, 1988), pp. 467–88.

43. National Research Council, RA, p. 77.

44. A. E. Ades, "Evaluating Screening Tests and Screening Programs," *Archives of Disease in Childhood* 65 (1990): 793.

45. A more detailed discussion of this point is in Talbot Page, "A Framework for Unreasonable Risk in the Toxic Substances Control Act (TSCA)," in *Annals of the New York Academy of Sciences: Management of Assessed Risk for Carcinogens*, ed. W. J. Nicholson (New York: New York Academy of Science, 1981), pp. 145–66, and in Cranor, RTS, pp. 155–56.

46. Lester B. Lave and Gilbert S. Omenn, "Cost Effectiveness of Short-Term Tests for Carcinogenicity," *Nature* 324 (1986): 29–34; Page, "A Framework for Unreasonable Risk"; Lars J. Olson, "The Search for a Safe Environment," *Journal of Environmental Economics and Management* 19 (1990): 1–18. Some place the value of a human death prevented as high as $10 million (compared to typical cost of false positives at about $1 million). See J. V. Hall, A. M. Winer, M. T. Kleiman, F. T. Lurman, V. Bonjour, and S. D. Colome, "Valuing the Benefits of Clean Air," *Science* 255 (1992): 812–17; and Schulamit Kahn, "Economic Estimates of the Value of Human Life," in *Ethics and Risk Assessment in Engineering*, ed. Albert Flores (New York: University Press of America, 1989), pp. 57–72, for discussions concerning the value of a death prevented.

47. If one regards the costs of mistakes to be incomparable (because a human death should not be compared to mere economic losses), then one might adopt a strategy other than minimizing costs (which assumes comparability).

48. Lave and Omenn, "Cost Effectiveness of Short-Term Tests for Carcinogenicity."

49. Cranor, RTS, pp. 131–41.

50. Elsewhere I have addressed an aspect of this problem, namely, the institutional procedures for evaluating the potency of carcinogens (Cranor, RTS, pp. 137–46).

Name Index

Ackerman, N., 216–17
Ackermann, Terrence F., 194
Ades, A. E., 227
Akaah, Ishmael P., 198
Algar, P., 198
Almendariz, Pedro, 4
Alston, William, 60–61, 203
Altman, Lawrence, 202
Anderson, A. E., 215
Andrews, R., 217
Annas, George J., 194
Arnold, D. R., 207
Ashford, Nicholas, 195, 213
Axinn, S., 212

Babbage, Charles, 2, 19
Bailar, John C., 201–3, 206, 215, 227
Baird, Robert, 195
Balk, Roger A., 197
Ball, Howard, 188
Ballou, J. D., 214–15, 218
Baltimore, David, 10
Bangs, O., 214
Banks, C., 188
Barber, Bernard, 201
Barnard, Christiaan, 38–39
Barrett, S., 217
Bass, O. L., Jr., 215
Baum, R., 203, 206, 208–9
Baumrin, B., 204, 209
Bayles, Michael, 49–50, 88–90, 191,

193, 197, 200–204, 206–7, 209–
10, 216
Bazelon, D., 207
Bazzelli, Donald E., 201
Beauchamp, Tom L., 66, 188–91,
194, 201, 204, 209
Becker, L., 213
Bedson, Henry, 45
Belden, R. C., 214–15
Benet, Stephen Vincent, 87
Bentham, Jeremy, 46, 112, 212–13
Bergkamp, Lucas, 188–89
Bergman, Robert, 201
Bergman, S., 195
Bergmann, Linda, 201
Berman, E. H., 190
Berry, Leonard, 197, 205
Blevins, D. E., 190–91, 195
Black, I., 202
Blackston, William T., 194
Blankenzee, Max, 158
Bloomquist, C. E., 207
Blount, William, 189
Boisjoly, Roger, 158–59, 222
Bok, Sissela, 195, 204, 209
Bonaparte, Napoleon, 153
Bond, V. P., 192
Bonjour, V., 227
Bower, R. T., 189
Bowers, C. A., 197
Bowring, J., 212

Subject Index

academic freedom, 31, 97
acts of commission/omission, 112–13
African Americans, 19, 28, 48, 51, 56, 142, 144–45. *See* racism; bias.
agriculture, 55, 68
American Association for the Advancement of Science (AAAS), 40–42, 52, 64–65, 71–73, 75, 78, 83–84
American Fisheries Society (AFS), 42–43, 84
American Society of Biological Chemists, 96
American Society of Civil Engineers (ASCE), 153
American Society of Mechanical Engineers (ASME), 69, 157
androcentrism, 147–49
animal research. *See* research, animal.
Antarctica, 14–15
antitrust law, 12, 157
asbestos, 97, 114
Ashwater v. Tennessee Valley Authority, 75
Asia, 68
Atomic Energy Commission (AEC), 1, 79. *See* Department of Energy (DOE).

Bay Area Rapid Transit (BART), 71, 157–58, 163–64

Bayesian decision rules, 110, 137. *See* decisionmaking; decision theory.
belief: rationality of, 134; voluntary control of, 60–61. *See* rationality; ethics of belief.
beneficence/benevolence, 86–91, 97–98; obligation to, 67. *See* public good
benefit-cost analysis, 33–34, 126, 128, 134–35, 156. *See* economics
benzene, 172. *See* toxic substances
bias, 80, 85–92, 132; four types of, 35; gender and racial, ch. 8; lying and, ch. 3; results/reports and, 50–53, 55–58; scientific research and, 18–20, 35–36, 47–61. *See* research results; racism; sexism
biomedical ethics, 6
biotechnology, 10, 13–14, 67, 114
Brookhaven Report (Wash-740), 77
burden of proof, ch. 5, 111, 125–26, 130, 134, 181–84

cancer, 1–5, 17, 77, 81, 94, 98, 106, 115, 133, 143–44, 172–84
censorship, 89
Challenger, space shuttle, 158–59
Chernobyl, 1–2, 5
civil engineers, 154
clients: confidentiality of, 66, 73, 87; goals of, 50–51; public welfare

Engineering Council for Professional Development (ECPD), 155

engineering design research, ch. 9; case studies in, 156–59; ethics in, 163–65; examples of, 165–67; perspectives in, 159–63; practical guidelines for, 167–68; public good and, ch. 9

engineering ethics, ch. 9; three ideas of, 153–56

engineers, ch. 9; business interests and, 155; social responsibilities of, 167

Enovid, 143–44

environment: catastrophe of, 75; conservation/preservation of, 14, 82, 86–95, ch. 7; degradation of, 34, 42; duties and, 32–35; protection of, 13, 15, 80; responsibilities to, 14; sustainability and, 13–14, 17, 32–33, 39; welfare of, 12–17, 32–35, 55

Environmental Defense Fund, 14

Environmental Protection Agency (EPA), 105

epidemiological studies, ch. 10; problems with, 171–76

error: types I and II, 106–16, 120–21, 130–38, 170–76, 181–84; minimizing, 109–17; uncertainty and, 106–16

ethical analysis, chs. 3–5; circumstances and consequences in, 84–86; deontological, 46–48, 90–96; specific duties and, 84–86; stage-two, ch. 5; utilitarian, 46–48, 90–96

ethical decisionmaking: deontological accounts of, 46–47; utilitarian accounts of, 46–47. *See* decisionmaking

ethical principles: justification of, 48, 64–72; prima facie, ch. 3, 63, 83–84; priority ranking of, 46, 48,

ch. 5; public risk and, 103–6; three major areas of, 49. *See* research ethics

ethical responsibilities: three major areas of, 49; university-employed research scientists and, 50. *See* duties

ethics of belief, 20, 58, 60–61; second principle of research ethics and, 60–61

ethics of development, 50

Ethiopia, 10

evolution: theory of, 63, 85, 147. *See* Gould, Stephen J.

extinction, 119–20, 123, 126–30, 134, 137. *See* Kangas-Noss controversy

Exxon oil spill, 18–19

fairness, 105, 113, 136, 143

fallout, 1, 4. *See* weapons tests

false positives/negatives. *See* error, types I and II

Florida panther, 108–9, 120–38

fluoride, 105

Food and Drug Administration (FDA), 4, 5

fraud: scientific research and, 1, 51–52, 57, 63

Freedom of Information Act, 77

future generations, 128. *See* discounting future costs

gross national product (GNP), 34, 120, 126. *See* economics

harm: incompensable, 114–15; priority of protecting against, 111–17; public, 5–6, 12, 36, 126, 169–70; research-related, 4–9, 12. *See* public good; Thomson, Judith Jarvis

Harvard University, 1, 3, 9, 12, 31

hazardous waste, 133. *See* nuclear waste

About the Author

Kristin Shrader-Frechette is currently Distinguished Research Professor at the University of South Florida in the Program in Environmental Sciences and Policy and the Department of Philosophy. She has held professorships at the University of Florida and the University of California. Shrader-Frechette has undergraduate degrees *(summa cum laude)* in mathematics and physics from Xavier University in Cincinnati and a doctorate in philosophy of science from the University of Notre Dame. She has done NSF-funded post-doctoral work in ecology, economics, and hydrogeology. With her research funded continuously by NSF since 1981, she specializes in analysis of ecological methods, environmental ethics/policy and quantitative risk assessment.

Shrader-Frechette is author of 185 refereed articles and twelve books, including *Method in Ecology* (Cambridge University Press, 1993) and *Burying Uncertainty: Risk and the Case Against Geological Disposal of Nuclear Waste* (University of California Press, 1993). She is on the boards of 15 professional journals and is Associate Editor of *BioScience* and Editor-in-Chief of the Oxford University Press Monograph Series on ''Environmental Ethics and Science Policy.'' Shrader-Frechette is a member of the U.S. National Research Council/National Academy of Sciences Board on Environmental Studies and Toxicology and the NRC Committee on Risk Characterization.